CW00685944

APPROACHING

THE

BIBLE

Quotations from the Bible have been taken from the *New International Version* unless otherwise stated. Other translations are indicated in the usual way: e.g. *KJV = King James Version*; *RAV = Revised Authorised Version*; *RV = Revised Version*; *GNB = Good News Bible*; *Youngs = Young's Literal Translation*.

GB ISBN 0 947778 50 0
US ISBN 1 880573 03 2

Library of Congress Catalog Card Number 92-70157

Library of Congress Cataloging-in-Publications Data

Penny, Michael, 1943-
Approaching the Bible / by Michael Penny
p. cm.
Includes bibliographical references and index
ISBN 0-947778-50-0 (GB), ISBN 1-880573-03-2 (US:pbk): $15.00
1. Biblical - Criticism, interpretation, etc.
2. Dispensationalism.
I. Title
BS511.2.p455 1992
220.6'01-dc20 92-70157
CIP

First published in 1992
Printed in the USA by Bookcrafters, Cheslea, MI.
Typeset in the USA by Martens Graphics, Pewaukee, WI.

Publications of the Open Bible Trust and Grace Publications Inc. must be in accordance with their evangelical, fundamental and dispensational basis. However, beyond this minimum, writers are free to express whatever beliefs they may have as their own personal understanding, provided their aim in so doing is to further the aims of the Open Bible Trust Trust and Grace Publications Inc. A copy of the doctrinal basis is available from:

THE OPEN BIBLE TRUST
36 St Laurence Avenue, Brundall,
Norwich, Norfolk, NR13 5QH, U.K.

GRACE PUBLICATIONS INC.
4800 South Calhoun Road
New Berlin, WI 53151, USA

APPROACHING

THE BIBLE

by

Michael Penny

Author of

Isaiah Six - its Old and New Testament Fulfilments

The Use and Abuse of Joel's Prophecy; Saturday, Sunday and the Sabbath

The Manual on the Gospel of John; The Bible - Myth or Message?

Signs of the Second Coming; Paul's Three Ministries

Studies in Colossians; The Dream - Daniel 2

Gifts and Rewards from God

Editor of

Studies in Philippians; Studies in John's Epistles

Israel in the New Testament

and

Search magazine

Dedicated to the memory and work of

Keith Sherwood McDonald
Toronto, Canada

1930 - 1988

Throughout his ministry Keith McDonald's emphasis was that believers are complete in Christ (Colossians 2:9, *KJV*) and that they need to rightly divide the word of truth if they are to fully understand this completeness and the accompanying blessings (2 Timothy 2:15).

CONTENTS

Preface

Some time ago the Trustees of the Open Bible Trust asked me to write a book outlining the approach to the Bible advocated by the Trust. The task has involved reading widely, more widely than I would otherwise have done. I have found the labours of this research most stimulating and pray that I have managed to convey some of what I discovered interestingly enough to enthuse and motivate the reader.

The first draft of this booklet was read by a number of people. However, I am most grateful to Lloyd Allen, Bryan and Elizabeth Conway, Elizabeth McDermott, Charles Ozanne and Roland Priddle, who made detailed comments and criticisms of the text. Roger Barnett and Elizabeth Conway helped with the proof reading.

I would also like to express my deep thanks to the Canadian Bible Fellowship and their supporters, as well as others in Britain, who have underwritten the cost of publishing this book. This has, indeed, been a joint labour of love. However, the views and opinions are my own and I do not wish to implicate anyone else in any errors there may be.

I am sure that we would all agree that the most important Christian message is the gospel, summarised by Paul in 1 Corinthians 15:3-4.

> For what I received I passed on to you as of *first importance*: that Christ died for our sins according to the Scriptures, that he was buried, that he was raised on the third day according to the Scriptures.

However, once someone has come to believe that Christ died for his sins and was raised on the third day, he will naturally want to learn more about the whole plan of salvation and the God who wrought it. The most natural place to turn is the Bible for without it we would know so little of God and His Son. Although some parts of the Bible are easy to understand, others may appear confusing unless we adopt a systematic approach. It is my prayer that this book will be a help in enabling us to obtain a greater understanding and appreciation of all that God has done for us.

Soli Deo gloria

Michael Penny
March 1992

Part I

Approaching the Bible

On one occasion an expert in the law stood up to test the Lord Jesus Christ. "Teacher," he asked, "What must I do to inherit eternal life?" (Luke 10:25-26). There was no direct reply from the Saviour. "What is written in the Law?" was His reply, but He did not stop there. He went on and asked, "How do you read it?" (*NIV*); "What is your reading of it?" (*NEB*, *RAV*); "How do you interpret it?" (*GNB*).

The Lord Jesus not only wanted to know if the man knew the Law; He was interested in finding out if the man understood it, how he read it, how he interpreted it.

All Christians have the same Bible, yet their understanding of certain parts may differ greatly. Why is this? Can it be avoided? Is there a way in which the followers of Christ can approach the Bible to promote convergent understandings rather than divergent divisions? The answer is "Possibly!", but first we must acknowledge that there are different approaches to the Scriptures and we must do so with neither a spirit of criticism nor an attitude of judgment towards those who uphold them.

1. What is your approach?

To illustrate some of the alternative approaches adopted by Christians in gaining an understanding of the Word of God, consider the words of one of the best known and loved choruses.

> Seek ye first the kingdom of God
> and his righteousness;
> And all these things will be added unto you:
> Allelu, Alleluia.

These words come from Matthew 6:33. What is their context? What are "all these things" which are to be added to those who seek first the kingdom of God and His righteousness? Before we can answer these questions, we need to read the whole passage.

> Therefore I tell you, do not worry about your life, what you will eat or drink; or about your body, what you will wear. Is not life more important than food, and the body more important than clothes? ... So do not worry, saying, "What shall we eat?" or "What shall we drink?" or "What shall we wear?" For the pagans run after all these things, and your heavenly Father knows that you need them. But seek first his kingdom and his righteousness, and all these things will be given to you as well. Therefore do not worry about tomorrow, for tomorrow will worry about itself. Each day has enough trouble of its own. (Matthew 6:25,31-34)

Approach A

The first approach that might be taken towards this passage suggests that each and every follower of the Lord Jesus Christ, whenever or wherever they live, will be physically cared for by God if they have their priorities right. He will provide them with food, drink, and clothing if they seek first His kingdom and His righteousness. If any Christian is deprived of food, drink, and clothing then it is because that person has not put God, His kingdom, and His righteousness first.

Approach B

The second approach suggests that although the Lord Jesus was talking about food, drink, and clothing, these were just physical illustrations of the deeper, spiritual truths that He was really promising. He was trying to teach the people that if they had their priorities right, then they would be cared for *spiritually*. If they put God, His kingdom, and His righteousness first, then their faith would increase and He would provide them with grace, love, and peace. Such spiritual qualities are far more important than physical entities such as food, drink, and clothes. God may or may not provide these, but He will equip all Christians spiritually, provided they put first things first.

Approach C

A third approach to this passage suggests that it may have been added by over-zealous followers some time after Christ's death and resurrection. Such people wanted to build up a picture of the Lord Jesus as the supplier of all needs, physical as well as spiritual, and so attributed to Him various words and actions which He never said or did. Clearly there have been many Christians throughout the ages, and even some in certain countries of the world today, who have put God, His kingdom, and His righteousness first, yet they have little or no food, drink, or clothing. Thus Christ could not have given such a categorical promise as to provide for the physical needs of His followers. Such words must, therefore, have been added. To interpret the physical necessities of food, drink, and clothing as symbolic of such spiritual needs as faith, grace, love, and peace, as suggested by the previous approach, is really untenable.

Approach D

This last approach suggests that the words apply only to those to whom they were spoken, namely the disciples. Thus, as the words of Matthew 6:33 were addressed to the disciples, the *only* people to whom Christ promised food, drink, and clothing for putting God, His kingdom and His righteousness first were the disciples. This approach states that this passage cannot be used to claim that God equips faithful Christians throughout the ages either physically with food, drink, and clothing or spiritually with faith, grace, love, and peace. He may or may not do either or both of these, but justification for His doing so cannot come from this passage.

Comment

We have purposely avoided using labels to describe the above-mentioned approaches because names and descriptions can be emotive and stimulate unchristian criticism and judgment. However, the above four do illustrate the point we wish to make, that although Christians have the same Bible, their understanding of parts of it can vary greatly. That being the case, we shall have to consider in some detail the advantages and disadvantages of each approach.

Approach A

Undoubtedly the appeal of this approach is its simplicity. It encourages people to approach the Bible and take the words read as being true of every faithful follower of the Lord Jesus Christ, wherever and whenever they live. Thus they are true for present-day readers. Provided they put God's kingdom and righteousness first, they will have food, drink, and clothing.

Because it is straightforward and direct many are attracted to this approach, which steers readers towards taking every word of the Bible as a message to themselves. Without dispute, there is something in every book of the Word of God that can be taken directly by Christians today, but can every word of it be applied? Some would say "Yes!"

> Every promise in the Book is mine;
> Every chapter, every verse, every line.

These are the words of a chorus taught to children to give them confidence in the Scriptures, but is every promise in the book mine? As I turn the pages of one of my Bibles, I read the following at the tops of the pages of Isaiah, the Old Testament prophet.

> A prophecy against Israel and Judah.
>   The church's joy.
> The deep hypocrisy of the Jews.
>   God's mercies to his church.
> Israel is reproved.
>   The church is comforted.
> The woes of Jerusalem.
>   The church's safety.
> The sins of the Jews.
>   The church's blessing.

It is evident that the writer of these added headings has taken the promises of blessing which had been given to the Jews and is teaching that they are true of the Christian Gentile church today. However, the promises of judgment have been left with Jerusalem, Judea, and the Jews! Is such an approach to Isaiah consistent? Clearly not! It would be consistent either to take all the promises, both judgments and blessings, or to leave them all - unless, of course, from other parts of Scripture certain of the promises made to the Christian church of today are the same as those given to Israel in Isaiah.

Thus the greatest advantage of this approach to the Bible - its simplicity and directness - is also its greatest disadvantage, for it is simply impossible to take every chapter, every verse, and every line as being true of all believers in every age. Clearly, every promise in the book is not mine - and I am glad that some are not.

> "... if you resist and rebel, you will be devoured by the sword." (Isaiah 1:20).

> If you do not obey the Lord your God and do not carefully follow all his commands and decrees I am giving you today, all these curses will come upon you ... (Deuteronomy 28:15; see verses 16-68 for the list of curses.)

Other disadvantages of this approach can be best illustrated by returning to the discussion of Matthew 6:33. Those who put God's kingdom and righteousness first were promised food, drink, and clothing. It requires little knowledge of church history to know that there have been many saints who have not enjoyed the basic necessities of life. It takes even less knowledge of the world situation in recent years to appreciate that there have been, and still are, people in certain countries who have been taken from their families, put in prison, and given no food and clothing for one simple reason: they have preached forgiveness of sins through faith in the Lord Jesus Christ. They have had their priorities right, yet they did not receive the promises made in Matthew 6:33.

Christians living in the industrialised, westernised, tolerant and affluent countries of this world may sing the words of this chorus with great gusto. We may enjoy applying them to ourselves. We may give God the glory, offer Him our thanks, and praise His name for all that we have, which is right and proper. However, if we deduce that we have plenty to eat, much to drink, and a wardrobe of clothes because we have our spiritual priorities right and have put God's kingdom and His righteousness first, we may be making a gross error. We are in danger of patting ourselves on our spiritual backs and of elevating Christians in the West above those in the East. Yet how many of us would testify openly of Christ in a Communist or Islamic country? Do we even do so in our own?

Another problem of this approach can be illustrated by considering some other words uttered by the Lord Jesus Christ. He sent out the twelve and told them "Take nothing for the journey - no staff, no bag, no bread, no money, no extra tunic" (Luke 9:3). Should Christians today follow this command, especially those going to the missionfield? Some who adopt this approach to the Scriptures would say "Yes!" However, towards the end of Christ's time on earth, He gave His disciples other, and different, instructions.

> Then Jesus asked them, "When I sent you without purse, bag or sandals, did you lack anything?" "Nothing," they answered. He said to them, "But now if you have a purse, take it, and also a bag; and if you don't have a sword, sell your cloak and buy one." (Luke 22:35-36)

A comparison of Luke 22:35-36 with Luke 9:3 illustrates that the Lord's commands can change, even to the same group of people. To read any part of the Bible in isolation and apply it to all Christians of all times can be the cause of serious error; Luke 9:3 is a case in point.

Lastly, we must mention a different type of problem which can arise from this approach. It may lead readers to place themselves in the centre of the Scriptures. We may see the Bible as a book for *us* and about *us*. As we read we want to find out only what God wants *us* to do, only what He wants to teach *us*, only what He has done for *us* and will do for *us*. However, we must never forget that the person in the centre of the Scriptures is the *Lord*: *He* is on every page, *not us*. The Bible is a book about *Him*, what *He* has done, is doing and will do. It contains what *He* wants to teach people and from it we can learn of *Him*, *His* character, *His* plans and *His* purposes, including *His* will for the world today - which *includes us*. That is where *we* come in.

To sum up: the major advantage of this first approach to the Bible is its simplicity and directness, yet this leads to its greatest disadvantages.

(a) It is impossible to take any part of the Bible in isolation from the rest, especially from what comes later.
(b) It is impossible to apply every part of the Bible to all believers of all ages.
(c) In attempting to use this method there is a danger that we will rejoice in, concentrate upon, and apply to ourselves any promises of

blessings, but will turn a blind eye to promises threatening judgment. This can lead to picking and choosing; that is, we pick those parts we like but leave those we do not. This destroys all attempts at a systematic approach to the Bible.

(d) It can lead to serious misunderstanding when we try to take for Christians today something which has been changed in the later parts of Scripture: for example, the Lord's words in Luke 22:35-36 over-ruling his earlier ones in Luke 9:3. Or the law of "an eye for an eye", etc., being changed by the injuction to "turn the other cheek". (Cf. Exodus 21:24; Matthew 5:39.)

(e) We could forget that it is the Lord, Himself, and not we ourselves, Who is the centre and subject of the Scriptures. The Bible is a book about Him.

There are other disadvantages which relate directly to the passage under consideration. With respect to Matthew 6:33 these are:

(f) Clearly the promise of Matthew 6:33 has not been true of many worthy Christians of the past and is not true of some today.

(g) It may encourage us to have an exalted opinion of ourselves by thinking that the reason we have much food, drink, and clothing is because we have our spiritual priorities right, rather than because we live in an affluent part of the world.

Approach B

Recognising many of the problems mentioned above, the second approach suggests that although the Lord Jesus Christ spoke of food, drink, and clothing, He did not mean these. This second approach suggests that He used the physical necessities of life to illustrate deeper, spiritual truths. If any put God's kingdom and righteousness first, their faith will increase, they will receive greater grace from God, know His love more deeply, and have a deeper experience of His peace.

One merit of this approach is that it removes many of the objections and difficulties of the previous approach for, clearly, many devoted Christians have not enjoyed the physical necessities of life. However, have all Christian worthies grown in faith and known more of God's grace, love, and peace? The answer may well be "Yes!", but it would be impossible to verify. One can see clearly whether people have food, drink, and clothing, but growth in faith and an inner increase in grace, love, and peace are not as easily seen and cannot be measured. That being the case, who can say whether this approach to Matthew 6:33 is correct?

Not only that, even if people do increase in such spiritual qualities, does that justify a spiritual interpretation of Matthew 6:33? There could be other reasons for the growth. For instance:

(a) In Romans 10:17 Paul wrote that "faith comes from hearing the message, and the message is heard through the word of Christ".
(b) Then, in 2 Corinthians 12:9, Paul's prayer for the removal of his thorn in the flesh was answered with the words, "My grace is sufficient for you".
(c) For the Ephesians Paul prayed that they might "grasp how wide and long and high and deep is the love of Christ". He wanted them to "know this love that surpasses knowledge". (Ephesians 3:18-19)
(d) Finally, in Philippians, he wrote, "Do not be anxious about anything, but in everything, by prayer and petition, with thanksgiving, present your requests to God. And the peace of God, which transcends all understanding, will guard your hearts and your minds in Christ Jesus" (Philippians 4:6-7).

Other parts of the Bible speak of promises of grace and we learn that faith comes from hearing the word of Christ. People offer prayers for love and make petitions for peace. Thus growth in these spiritual qualities may be the result of a personal study of the Scriptures or of prayer. To state that Christians grow in faith and have a greater experience of God's grace, love, and peace when they have their priorities right may not be wrong, but were these what Christ meant in the passage under consideration, when He spoke of food, drink, and clothing? It would appear not, for when He wanted to speak of such spiritual qualities He did so. For example:

(a) Faith - He spoke of little faith in Matthew 6:30; 8:26; 14:31 and 16:8. He spoke of great faith in Matthew 8:10 and 15:28, and there are many other references to faith.
(b) Grace - John uses the word grace four times in his opening chapter (1:14,16 [twice], 17) and the New Testament is full of the word.
(c) Love - Christ talked of love three times in Matthew 5:43,44,46. Three times He dealt with loving your neighbour as yourself (Matthew 5:43; 19:19 and 22:39). There are other references to love in Matthew and they abound throughout the Bible.
(d) Peace - Four times the Lord spoke of peace in Matthew 10, verses 13 (twice) and 34 (twice).

If Christ wished to inform people that they would be equipped with such spiritual qualities as faith, grace, love, and peace for putting God's kingdom and righteousness first, why didn't He plainly say so? They would certainly have understood Him, for these subjects were spoken of frequently.

There can be little doubt that when the Lord Jesus spoke of food, drink, and clothing, He meant just that: food, drink, and clothing. When He spoke of faith, grace, love, and peace, He meant just that: faith, grace, love, and peace. To reinterpret Christ's words must be suspect. To reinterpret some like food, drink, and clothing, but not others - like God's kingdom and righteousness, will not help build a consistent approach to the Scriptures. If Christ had wanted to promise His followers spiritual qualities for having their priorities correct then He would have said so, as is evident from other parts of the Gospels.

To sum up: the advantages of this approach are that it removes many of the objections raised by the first approach and that what it teaches on a particular passage can be justified from other parts of the Bible. However, there are a number of disadvantages.

(a) It asserts that Christ did not really mean what He said: that is, He said one thing but meant another. It is suggested that He did this because the people would not have fully understood Him had He spoken of the spiritual qualities, but this cannot be correct as He spoke plainly of such matters on other occasions. Thus there was no need for Him to veil His meaning.
(b) It is very difficult to verify whether such a view is correct, for such spiritual qualities are not as measurable and verifiable as the necessities of life. Also, the teaching that faithful Christians will grow in faith, grace, love, and peace is clearly supported from other parts of the Bible, but that does not prove that the spiritual understanding of Matthew 6:33 is the correct one.
(c) Certain words of Christ, but not all, are reinterpreted to mean something different. This is inconsistent and is open to a variety of opinions over which words should be reinterpreted and what that reinterpretation should be. This can only hinder attempts to encourage convergent views and will not assist a systematic approach to the Bible.

Approach C

A third approach acknowledges the problems caused by the previous two methods. Clearly, not all who have put God, His kingdom, and His righteousness first have been blessed with food, drink, and clothing. However, it is equally clear that when speaking of these the Lord Jesus was not referring to spiritual qualities such as faith, love, and peace. What, then, did He mean?

This third approach suggests that passages such as Matthew 6:33 are not authentic. It argues that in the years following Christ's ministry, His followers exaggerated both His words and His actions. They did so for the best of motives, to give Him greater glory and to win others to the cause of Christianity.

The appeal of such an approach is that it does remove from the mouth of the Saviour various statements which seem untrue, incorrect, or impossible. We are then left with teachings which are obviously true and clearly correct. These we can accept and put into practice. The others we can ignore.

However, if we follow this approach, where do we stop? What may appear impossible to one person may not appear so to another. What is outside one person's experience may well be within another's. What seems incorrect to you may seem perfectly right to me.

There is also a danger that our own opinions will change. When we have little faith in God and an inadequate knowledge of His word, there may be much that we do not understand and many things which appear impossible, even wrong. However, when we know more about the Bible and have a fuller picture of God's purposes and His power, we may have a greater understanding. Things which once appeared impossible and incorrect become necessary and right.

Certainly this third approach will not foster convergent views nor can it be a basis for a systematic study of the Bible unless it can clearly demonstrate which parts of the Bible, in general, and the Gospels, in particular, are additions and interpolations. There is no consensus of opinion on this matter amongst those who follow this approach to the Scriptures.

To sum up: the advantages of this third approach are that it removes the objections to the two previous approaches and takes from the mouth of Christ various statements which seem untrue and impossible. However, there are disadvantages.

(a) There is no consensus as to which words were originally spoken by the Lord Jesus and which ones have been put into His mouth by over-zealous followers.
(b) If the criteria for deciding which words and actions of Christ have been added is what appears impossible and incorrect, not only will that vary from person to person, but it will change for each person as greater knowledge and insight is gained.

Approach D

It is impossible to decide which parts of the Bible, if any, are not authentic. No one can say which words and actions, if any, have been attributed to Christ after His time on earth. This last approach accepts, as a presupposition, the reliability and integrity of *all* the Scriptures.

Consistent with this premise, it takes the statements in the Bible at face value, and does not reinterpret them. In other words, they mean what they say and must be understood in the way the original hearers or readers would have understood them. Thus in the passage in Matthew 6, food means food, drink means drink, and clothing means clothing.

This approach also notes that, although a promise may be made to one group of people at a particular time, it should not be assumed that it is necessarily operative for any other group, or even for the same group at a later time.

As a result, this fourth approach accepts that the Lord Jesus Christ did utter the words recorded in Matthew 6:33, but it rejects the notion that instead of food, drink, and clothing He meant spiritual graces like faith, love, and peace.

It also rejects the idea that the promise of Matthew 6:33 was for all Christians at all times. In searching the context it notes that, "His *disiciples* came to him, and he began to teach *them*" (Matthew 5:1- 2). Certainly, some of what He taught them will be relevant to Christians today. If so, such teaching will be seen to occur throughout the Bible, indicating that it is truth for all people of all times. However, some of what He promised to the disciples was peculiar to them, and even parts of that were for a limited time period.

Here, in Matthew 6:33, He promised them food, drink, and clothing if they put God's kingdom and righteousness first. In Luke 9:3 he sent the same disciples out to preach the kingdom, but they took nothing for the journey - no staff, no bread, no money, no extra clothes. Yet when asked by the Saviour if they had lacked anything, they said, "Nothing!" (Luke 22:35).

In the Bible we read of the mighty miracles when the Lord Jesus fed thousands. How many times did He feed His disciples? We are not told, yet we read that they lacked nothing. He even paid Peter's tax for him (Matthew 17:24-27). However, Luke 22:36, as we saw earlier, heralded a change for them. There they were told to take their purse and bag, even a sword. The time of special divine provision and protection was soon to be over.

When we enter the Acts of the Apostles we find the rich providing for the poor (Acts 2:45; 4:34-37). When famine struck the land, the concern of the Christians in other countries, who were unaffected by it, was to make a collection for those Christians who were (Acts 11:28-30; Galatians 2:10; 1 Corinthians 16:2-3; Romans 15:25-26).

When we come to the letters, which deal with events after Christ's time on earth, the man who did not work was not to eat (2 Thessalonians 3:10). The Christian who did not provide for his family and immediate relatives was considered worse than an unbeliever (1 Timothy 5:8). From these, alone, it can be seen that it was no longer the case that the person who put God's kingdom and righteousness first was to be provided with food, drink, and clothing. Matthew 6:33 was promised to the disciples, but only for a limited period of time. Others may also have benefited during that time, but the original promise was made only to them.

The advantages of this fourth approach are that it upholds the reliability and accuracy of the Scriptures and, at the same time, allows believers today to maintain their honesty and integrity. The words are left in the mouth of the Lord Jesus and are taken to mean what they actually say. However, the promise is left in its historical context so there is no need to remove the words or reinterpret their meaning. Neither is there a need to alter the situation of Christians today, or throughout history, in an attempt to match their circumstances with the words.

However, the potential disadvantage of this approach is that it requires an overall knowledge of the Bible. One needs to trace the teaching on any particular subject through the Bible, which is not easy. In trying to find the correct time context of Matthew 6:33 we have had to quote Luke, Acts, 1 Corinthians, Galatians, 2 Thessalonians and 1 Timothy. Possibly, many other parts of the Old and New Testaments should have been brought in to deal adequately with the issue as to if and when the physical necessities of life are divinely supplied to faithful believers.

This fourth approach recognises not only that different promises are made to different people, but that the promises made to one group can be changed at a later stage. That being the case, the reader of the Bible has to have some idea of the progress of God's revelation to mankind.

Some knowledge of the chronological order of the books of the Bible is essential. The exact date when each was written may not be necessary, or even possible, but unless one is aware of when different parts of the New Testament were written, misunderstandings may arise through failure to appreciate the latest teaching on a particular subject.

A second disadvantage is that, clearly, none of the Bible has been addressed directly to anyone living today. That being the case, there may be a temptation to dismiss much, if not all, of it as having no relevance to life in this century. However, such an extreme position may be a theoretical possibility, but it should not happen in practice. If certain teachings occur throughout the Bible, they will be accepted as being truth for all people of all times, including Christians today. However, if the teaching changes it is right to give the greatest emphasis to the later revelations from God.

Examples of the former, the unchanging teachings, are the sinfulness of man and his need for faith in God. Sin came on the scene with Adam and was still there with Cain. It is evident before the flood and at the tower of Babel. We see it in the lives of Abraham, Isaac, Jacob, Joseph, Joshua, David, Peter, and Paul, and it is there in you and me. Many parts of the Bible comment upon sin and deal with the problems caused by it and their solution. With respect to faith we read of Abel, Enoch, Noah, Abraham, Isaac, Jacob, Joseph, Moses, Joshua, David, Peter, and Paul. All of them pleased God because of their faith. Faith and its outworking occupy large parts of Scripture and without faith it is impossible for anyone at anytime, including you or me, to please God.

To sum up: the advantages of this fourth approach are that it upholds the authenticity of the Bible whilst allowing Christians to maintain their integrity. It allows us to be honest about what we read in the Bible and what we see happening to ourselves and to others in the world today: for example, to those who are suffering because of their faith in Christ. It allows us to accept that the words in the Bible are correct and easily understandable as it recognises that what was promised was fulfilled in the lives of the people to whom it was promised. However, this approach poses some challenges for the Christian.

(a) To be sure that we have the correct understanding of a passage we need an overall view of the Bible and a reasonable knowledge of what it teaches.
(b) As some promises change with time, we need to have some idea as to when the books of the Bible were written and to have some chronological understanding of the Scriptures. We need to appreciate that revelation from God was progressive.

(c) As none of the Bible is directly addressed to anyone living today, there is a danger that some of its teaching may be dismissed as having no direct relevance to Christians today when, in fact, it does.

2. Which approach should we use?

Which of the four approaches to the Bible should we follow? Does it really matter?

If we are dealing with the very foundations of the Christian faith then it is true that followers of the four different approaches can come to the same conclusions. The Bible consistently teaches that man is a sinner in a sinful society where the wages of sin is death. However, God is a God of grace Who can forgive man and give him the free gift of eternal life. This is open to all who put their faith and trust in Jesus Christ and accept His sacrifice on Calvary's Cross as the offering for the sin of the world. Similarly there is Scriptural harmony on moral issues for these are consistently the same in the Law, the Prophets, the Psalms, the Gospels, and the Letters.

The message of salvation from sin and death through faith in Christ and the exhortation to live a new and upright life are the starting blocks of the Christian life: its primary teaching. However, there is more revealed in the pages of the Bible. The approach we follow becomes important when we want to know and understand more about God's ways and purposes, when we want to consider some of the secondary teaching, and when we want to know more about what God has for us and what He requires of us today.

Paul wrote to the Corinthians instructing them that "everything should be done in a fitting and orderly way", informing them that this was right for "God is not a God of disorder" (1 Corinthians 14:40,33). It would seem fitting, then, if Christians could establish an ordered approach to the Bible which would encourage views to converge rather than diverge. Is this possible? Do any of the four approaches we have mentioned help in this? The answer must be "Yes!" It is the fourth approach.

The first two challenges to this fourth approach say similar things, namely that a certain amount of knowledge of the Bible is needed before this approach can be put into practice. However, this should not deter us from adopting it. In Acts we read of the Ethiopian who had gone to Jerusalem to worship. On his way home he was reading the book of Isaiah. Philip asked him if he understood what he was reading and his reply was, "How can I, unless someone explains it to me?" (Acts 8:27-31). Here we see the need of a person to have a teacher, and the words "teacher", "teach", and "teaching" occur frequently throughout the Bible.

There is an old adage which states that good teachers make themselves redundant for they not only teach their students the facts, they also show them how to discover more information for themselves. This, in a measure, is what the fourth approach does. If we follow it, then we accept all that the Bible states as reliable and authentic. We accept the words of the Bible at their face value, understanding them as the people to whom they were addressed would have understood them. Also, as the Bible covers thousands of years and deals with a variety of people in a variety of situations, we accept that different promises and instructions may have been given at different times, either to the same or different people.

If we follow this fourth approach, we may be able to make some headway in coming to an agreed understanding of each part of the Bible. We shall look at the Bible and accept what is there. We shall read the words and establish what they meant. We shall note the people to whom they were addressed and be aware of their circumstances. We shall follow any particular subject under consideration through the Scriptures and note if there are any changes in the way it is treated.

This approach to the Bible may involve us in quite a lot of work and study, but that should not deter us if we really do want to know what God has said on a certain issue. At first sight, this approach may appear somewhat cold and clinical, but it is not. It is the *natural* way of reading a book and as God has chosen to reveal His will for mankind in a book then, presumably, He wants us to read it as a book. He wants us to accept all that is there and to read it as if it means what it says. Naturally, as different people are dealt with, we need to distinguish what God has said to each group or type. As time passes and situations alter, we need to look out for changes in His ways of dealing with people and His instructions for them. This way of approaching God's word is called by some the *normal reading* of the Bible, by others the *plain reading* of Scripture. We have termed it the *natural* way.

This approach recognises that revelation from God is progressive. Not all of God's plans and purposes were revealed to the whole of mankind at one instant in time. It was the same for the disciples. The Lord Jesus told them, "I have much more to say to you, more then you can now bear. But when he, the Spirit of truth, comes, he will guide you into all truth" (John 16:12-13). It is significant that the opening words of the Acts of the Apostles refer to our Lord's ministry on earth as "all that Jesus *began* to do and teach" (Acts 1:1), implying that more was to come from the resurrected and ascended Christ.

There are some who refer to this approach as a *literal* reading of the Bible, but such a description is open to misunderstanding. On the pages of Scripture are many figures of speech and, in prophecy, for example, there is much allegory. These are not meant to be taken literally.

However, every figure and each allegory does have a literal meaning, although it may not be easy to ascertain what that is. Thus, to avoid such misconceptions it is best to talk about a normal, natural or plain reading of the Bible.

Objectivity

If we want to encourage a convergence of views, we must try to avoid subjectivity. This allows our own ideas, opinions, thoughts, and feelings to become part of our interpretation of the Bible. Although these may be of interest, and may have some value, they are bound to increase diversity of understanding. What is needed is an approach which will take us out of ourselves and away from our preconceived notions. We need to be objective in our approach, relating to what is external to our minds, dealing with facts which are unclouded by our feelings, thoughts, and opinions. One way of avoiding subjectivity is to draw up a list of objective instructions as to how to approach a passage.

One of the first people to do this was Bishop Miles Coverdale, who lived over 400 years ago. John Wycliffe had produced the first Bible in English in 1384, but it was not widely available as the printing press had not been invented. It was not until 1526 that William Tyndale brought out the first printed New Testament followed, nine years later, by Miles Coverdale's first printed Bible. This formed the basis for *The Great Bible* of 1539, revised by Cranmer in 1540.

The Scriptures were now available to many more people and Coverdale may have been aware of the danger of an increasing diversity of views and of readers having difficulty in establishing a correct understanding of any passage. He wrote the following words of advice:

> It shall greatly help you to understand Scripture,
> if you mark
> not only what is spoken, or written,
> but of whom,
> and to whom,
> with what words,
> at what time,
> where,
> to what intent,
> with what circumstance,
> considering what goes before,
> and what follows.

Not only must each part of the Bible be taken in its context, the reader must also find out to whom it was addressed and of whom it speaks, where it is about and when it was given, what were the current circumstances when it was given and what were the reasons for the revelation.

Interpretation and application

If we adopt this fourth approach to the Bible, or follow the advice of Miles Coverdale, then we shall be trying to establish the interpretation of the passage. We shall be finding out what it meant to the people to whom it was given, at the time it was given. This is known as the historical-grammatical interpretation: historical, meaning that we have gone back in time to find out what it meant originally; grammatical, indicating that the words and the grammar of the passage have been understood in the normal or natural way, as the people to whom they were given would have understood them.

This leads us back to the third criticism of this approach, namely that there is a danger that we shall see little of relevance to ourselves and our age in many parts of the Bible. However, this danger can be avoided by recognising that once the historical-grammatical interpretation has been established, then we should seek a valid application of the passage for our lives today. However, if we do not first establish a clear understanding and an unambiguous interpretation of the passage, we are likely to make a wrong application. The interpretation must come first, but an application must follow. All Scripture is needed by us and is of value to us, as Paul wrote:

> Everything that was written in the past was written to teach us, so that through endurance and the encouragement of the Scriptures we might have hope. (Romans 15:4)

> All Scripture is God-breathed and is useful for teaching, rebuking, correcting and training in righteousness, so that the man of God may be thoroughly equipped for every good work. (2 Timothy 3:16-17)

Twice in 1 Corinthians Paul states that past events were examples to people living at that time.

> Now these things occurred as examples to keep us from setting our hearts on evil things as they did ... These things happened to them as

examples and were written down as warnings for us. (1 Corinthians 10:6,11)

The things that Paul was referring to were the wilderness wanderings of the people of Israel. From the books of Moses Paul drew examples relevant to the Christians at Corinth. He warned of idolatry, sexual immorality, and discontent, common to both the Corinthians and the Israelites in the wilderness. He spoke of the judgments which fell upon the Israelites and of those falling upon some of the Christians in Corinth (1 Corinthians 10:7-10; 11:29-32). However, Paul did not say that the Corinthians would be fed with manna from heaven, have water from a rock, or that their clothes would not wear out - all of which happened to the Israelites who came out of Egypt (Deuteronomy 29:3-6). This shows us that all Scripture is useful for teaching, rebuking, correcting and training in righteousness, provided we make valid applications. The greatest help in doing this is to establish first the correct historical-grammatical interpretation.

Problems

We have suggested that one desirable feature of any systematic approach to the Bible should be that it helps to converge the views of Christians. This seems possible only if it encourages objectivity and discourages subjectivity. We shall also want consistency within the explanations that any approach gives and it has been suggested that the fourth approach helps all of these.

However, if we do not follow the historical-grammatical system of interpretation, which is based upon the natural or normal reading of the Bible and which recognises that revelation from God has been progressive, then we may run into a number of problems. Our approach needs to establish order out of apparent disorder and to make sense of seemingly contradictory passages. Yet it must guard against distorting the original meaning of those Scriptures and prevent us from forcing them to fit our circumstances. Peter warned of this when he wrote that Paul's "letters contain some things that are hard to understand, which ignorant and unstable people distort, as they do the other Scriptures" (2 Peter 3:16).

The following are examples of the types of problem which may arise if we do not follow this historical-grammatical approach.

(a) We have to ask why the Saviour of the world sent His disciples out with the express orders, "Do not go among the Gentiles or enter any town of the Samaritans" (Matthew 10:5). Why did He first ignore the Canaanite woman and then tell her, "I was sent only to the lost sheep of Israel" (Matthew 15:24)? And why did Paul describe Jesus as a servant of the Jews (Romans 15:8)? How do we, who are Gentiles, view these statements? What sense can we make of them?
(b) And what sense do we make of Paul's statement that he had to speak the word of God to the Jews first (Acts 13:46)? Although the gospel of salvation was for everyone who believes, it was first to the Jews. Furthermore, trouble and distress were to fall on the Jew first, but so, too, were glory, honour, and peace. Over all, there was much advantage in being a Jew (Romans 1:16; 2:9-10; 3:1- 2; 9:4-5). Yet, elsewhere, we read that there were no such advantages, no such prior position. We read of Jews and Gentiles being made one and of Gentiles being heirs together with Israel, members of one body and partakers in the promise in Christ (Ephesians 2:14-18; 3:6).
(c) It was the Lord Jesus Who said, "Do not think that I have come to abolish the Law or the Prophets; I have not come to abolish them but to fulfil them" (Matthew 5:17). Yet we read that "Christ is the end of the law" (Romans 10:4). That being the case, why were James and thousands of Christian Jews "zealous for the law" (Acts 21:20)? Paul undertook the Nazarite vow of Numbers 6 to show that he walked according to the Law. But he wrote that the Law with its commandments and ordinances had been abolished, that the written code with its regulations had been cancelled (contrast Acts 21:23-26 with Ephesians 2:14-15 and Colossians 2:14). What is going on here?
(d) The disciples were told "if you forgive men when they sin against you, your heavenly father will also forgive you. But if you do not forgive men their sins, your Father will not forgive your sins" (Matthew 6:14-15). This contrasts greatly with the sentiments to "be kind and compassionate to one another, forgiving each other, just as in Christ God forgave you", and "bear with each other and forgive whatever grievances you may have against one another. Forgive as the Lord forgave you" (Ephesians 4:32; Colossians 3:13).
(e) We read that "the meek ... will inherit the earth" and the disciples were told to pray "your kingdom come, your will be done on earth" (Matthew 5:5; 6:10). Yet there were those longing for "a better country - a heavenly one" and for a city God had prepare for them, "the heavenly Jerusalem" (Hebrews 11:16; 12:22). Then there are those who are "blessed ... in the heavenly realms", God having "raised us up with Christ and seated us with him in the heavenly

realms" (Ephesians 1:3; 2:6). Will there be a kingdom upon the earth which the meek will inherit? If so, why didn't they desire a better, heavenly country? And what is the difference between this heavenly country, the heavenly Jerusalem, and the heavenly realms?

(f) Can we see any reason for the change in the following situations? Paul healed everyone on Melita, yet later left his friend Trophimus sick at Miletus (Acts 28:8-9; 2 Timothy 4:20). Handkerchiefs and aprons from Paul healed the sick at Ephesus, yet later all he sent to the frequently ill Timothy was advice (Acts 19:12; 1 Timothy 5:23). Paul wrote about and exhibited the gift of healing, yet later had great sorrow for an ill friend there with him, who nearly died (1 Corinthians 12:9,28-30; Philippians 2:26-27).

(g) Christ said, "I will do whatever you ask in my name" and "my Father will give you whatever you ask in my name" (John 14:13-14; 16:23-24). However, three times Paul pleaded with the Lord to remove the thorn in his flesh, a messenger from Satan. It was not removed. He did not have what he asked for. He was told, "My grace is sufficient for you" (2 Corinthians 12:7-9).

The above are just a few of the problems that any approach to the Bible must face and answer. We shall return to these in later chapters to see if we can give consistent answers to the problems they raise. We are seeking answers which will not distort what the Bible states and which at the same time allow readers to maintain their intellectual integrity.

Part II

Developing the approach

One of the first people to advocate an objective approach to the Bible was Miles Coverdale. His advice was that:

> It shall greatly help you to understand Scripture
> if you mark
> not only what is spoken, or written,
> but of whom,
> and to whom,
> with what words,
> at what time,
> where,
> to what intent,
> with what circumstances,
> considering what goes before,
> and what follows.

In this part of the book we shall spend some time looking at the people in the Old Testament and the people in the New. Then we shall consider the places, the time of writing, what was said, and the reason for saying it. Finally, we shall deal with the problem of making an application from Scripture to Christians today. In this way we shall work through the advice given above and see where it leads us.

3. The People - in the Old Testament

Part of the advice given by Miles Coverdale was that it would greatly help us to understand the various parts of Scripture if we noted to whom and of whom they were written. Starting with the Old Testament we shall consider this advice.

The Old Testament - to whom?

Most Christians appreciate that practically the whole of the Old Testament was written to the descendants of Abraham, namely the nation of Israel. Some parts may have been addressed to the nation as a whole. Others may have been addressed to groups within that nation: e.g. the priests, the kings, or certain tribes. However, from Genesis to Malachi the people to whom the books of the Old Testament were addressed were primarily the nation of Israel.

Not only that, the people who wrote them were also Israelites. Thus, when we approach the Old Testament we need to realise that we are reading books which were written by Israelites *for* Israelites. Israel is at the centre of them all. We may find small exceptions to this in such books as Daniel, for example. The fourth chapter is a letter which Nebuchadnezzar, the Gentile King of Babylon, sent to "the peoples, nations and men of every language, who live in all the world" (Daniel 4:1). However, the contents of that letter were of great interest to the Israelites and this may be the reason why it was included in Daniel. It showed how a Jew was needed to interpret a dream God had given to a Gentile.

The Old Testament - of whom?

The first eleven chapters of Genesis deal with Adam and Eve; Cain and Abel; Noah and the flood; the nations of the world; the tower of Babel, and the scattering of those nations. These opening chapters of the Bible deal with both individuals and nations. They say nothing of any specific nation. However, Genesis 12 opens with words which herald a significant change.

> The Lord had said to Abram, "Leave your country, your people and your father's household and go to the land I will show you. I will make you into a great nation and I will bless you; I will make your name great, and you will be a blessing. I will bless those who bless you, and

> whoever curses you I will curse; and all peoples on earth will be blessed through you." (Genesis 12:1-3)

Here commences the division of humanity into two groups. Such is the importance of this promise that it is repeated in part to Abraham (Genesis 18:18 and 22:18), to his son Isaac (Genesis 26:4), and to his grandson Jacob (Genesis 28:14 - see also Genesis 27:29).

In time Jacob had his name changed to Israel and became the father of twelve sons. Their posterity became the twelve tribes of Israel. The division of humanity into two groups, the nation of Israel and all other nations, commenced at Genesis 12 and before we reach the end of Genesis this separation is well defined.

So, too, is the promise that all other nations were to be blessed through that one special nation. This may be best illustrated by Joseph, one of Israel's sons, who was taken to Egypt. There he interpreted the Pharaoh's dreams, stating that they meant seven good years of harvest followed by seven years of famine. As a result, under Joseph's direction great barns were built in Egypt to store the excess food. This not only provided them with sufficient food for the years of famine, but they were able to feed many refugees from the surrounding nations. Thus Egypt and the nations were blessed through Joseph, a descendant of Abraham.

However, a new Pharaoh arose who knew nothing of Joseph's history and who made slaves of the Israelites. The promise of Genesis 12 is seen in operation once more when he and his army were destroyed in the Red Sea. By this time Israel also had a new leader, Moses. Through him came the Law, a Law which, more than anything else, sharpened the distinction between the nation of Israel and all other nations. However, before commenting upon that, let us recapitulate on Genesis.

The first book of the Bible was written for Israelites. However, its opening eleven chapters say nothing about them for they did not, at that time, exist. In chapter 12 a promise was given to Abraham concerning the nation that would come from him and its relationship to all other nations in the world. From then on, in our reading of the Old Testament, we need to note carefully whether a promise or a prophecy is about the nation of Israel, about some other nation (e.g. Egypt), about a group of nations, or about all other nations. Similarly we need to consider whether an instruction is for the nation of Israel, for some other specific nation, for a group of nations, or for all nations. If we do not do that, then we shall be in danger of misinterpreting Scripture. To illustrate this point consider the following:

> Then God said to Abraham, "As for you, you must keep my convenant, you and your descendants after you for the generations to come. This is my covenant with you and your descendants after you, the covenant you are to keep: Every male among you shall be circumcised. You are to undergo circumcision, and it will be the sign of the covenant between me and you. For the generations to come every male among you who is eight days old must be circumcised, including those born in your household or bought with money from a foreigner - those who are not your offspring. Whether born in your household or bought with your money, they must be circumcised. My covenant in your flesh is to be an everlasting covenant. Any uncircumcised male, who has not been circumcised in the flesh, will be cut off from his people; he has broken my covenant." (Genesis 17:9-14)

The covenant of the eighth-day circumcision was only for the descendants of Abraham plus any slaves they might have purchased from other nations. It was not for anyone else.

To help us see how necessary it is to pay particular attention to which people are the subject of a passage, consider a further example.

> Remember the Sabbath day by keeping it holy. Six days you shall labour and do all your work, but the seventh day is a Sabbath to the Lord your God. On it you shall not do any work, neither you, nor your son or daughter, nor your manservant or maidservant, nor your animals, nor the alien within your gates. (Exodus 20:8-10)

> Six days do your work, but on the seventh day do not work, so that your ox and your donkey may rest and the slave born in your household, and the alien as well, may be refreshed. (Exodus 23:12)

The injunction to do no work on the Sabbath was given to the Israelites. However, it went further. Not only were they and members of their family to do no work, but their servants (slaves) and animals were to rest. So, too, was anyone of any other nation who happened to be living or residing with them.

The people concerned are, again, the descendants of Abraham and also their slaves. However, in this case the work prohibition is extended to include all their animals and anyone from any other nation who may be with them.

Further illustrations could be given to demonstrate the point that we need to take special notice of which people (that is, of whom) a given passage speaks. Is it concerning Israel? Or one other nation? Or a group of other nations? Or all other nations, i.e. the Gentiles? Is it about a certain section of Israel or a specific Gentile nation? Does it concern only those Gentiles who have become slaves to the Israelites or who are living amongst them? These are some of the questions we need to ask.

Faithful and obedient or unfaithful and disobedient?

In the previous section we concentrated on national or group distinctions: i.e. Israelite or Gentile; slave or visitor; king or priest. However, there are other differences between people which need to be noted and which are of a spiritual and moral quality.

We have already quoted Genesis 12:1-3, where there is a very clear division between those who blessed Israel and so were blessed by God, and those who cursed Israel and so were cursed by God. The attitude and response of different nations and individuals towards Israel is therefore an important division in the Old Testament. In different places different things are said of them.

Within Israel itself we find its people can be grouped into, perhaps, three categories. First, those who had great faith in God and who acted upon that and who obeyed God's laws. Second, those who had some faith but who were, for one reason or another, reluctant to act upon it and who were lax in keeping some of the commandments. Third, those who were simply unfaithful, disobedient, and rebellious. We must note what is said of each group. For example, the following would not be true of the third group, the unfaithful.

> For this is what the high and lofty One says - he who lives for ever, whose name is holy: "I live in a high and holy place, but also with him who is contrite and lowly in spirit." (Isaiah 57:15)

> He follows my decrees and faithfully keeps my laws. That man is righteous; he will surely live, declares the Sovereign Lord. (Ezekiel 18:9)

What has been said of individuals within Israel can be said of the whole nation. God's desire was for it, as a whole, to be faithful and obedient. He encouraged this by blessing national faithfulness and obedience and by cursing national unfaithfulness and disobedience.

> If you fully obey the Lord your God and carefully follow all his commands that I give you today, the Lord your God will set you high above all the nations on earth. All these blessings will come upon you and accompany you if you obey the Lord your God ... However, if you

do not obey the Lord your God and do not carefully follow all his commands and decrees I am giving you today, all these curses will come upon you and overtake you ... (Deuteronomy 28:1-2,15)

The blessings, listed in verses 3-13, and the curses, listed in 16-44, were to be a sign for Israel (v 46). When they experienced the difficulties listed in verses 16-44, their leaders should have realised that the nation had strayed far from God. These leaders should have called for repentance and turned the nation back to Him. The blessings would then have followed. However, if they continued in their old ways and did not change, the end result would be the destruction of the nation of Israel and the scattering of its people amongst the Gentile nations (vs 63-64). Sadly this did happen in Old Testament times.

Thus, we need to note if a passage of the Old Testament is talking about individual Israelites who may be (a) faithful, (b) disobedient, or (c) rebellious. Similarly, we need to note whether a passage is about the nation of Israel as a whole being (a) faithful, (b) disobedient, or (c) rebellious. This is usually a reflection of its leadership. If the leaders were faithful and obedient so, too, were most of the people. However, if the leaders were lax or went even further, into open rebellion, so, too, did many of the individuals.

Judges and Kings; Israel and Judah; Prophets.

As we progress through the Old Testament we shall also note the changes in the type of leadership to which Israel was subjected. Initially they were led by Moses, who gave them the Law, and Joshua, who took them into the promised land. Once established there, they were governed by the judges, who administered the Law for them. However, in the course of time the people wanted to be like other nations and have a king. The first was Saul, followed by David and then Solomon.

At the end of Solomon's reign the nation of Israel suffered a civil war, with ten of the tribes rebelling against the king and setting up a temple to rival the one in Jerusalem. Only two tribes, Judah and Benjamin, remained faithful to the king and the Jerusalem temple. The northern kingdom of the ten tribes became known as Israel and the southern kingdom of the two tribes was called Judah. At this point the term Israel ceases to refer to all twelve tribes, as it has done previously. It refers only to the ten northern tribes.

As the kings deteriorated and their faithfulness to God waned, He sent the prophets. They proclaimed God's ways, and encouraged repentance and a return to the Law of Moses. Some of the kings responded; some did not. The northern kingdom of Israel was the first to lapse into open rebellion. As a result they were conquered and scattered by the Assyrians. Then it was the turn of the southern kingdom, Judah. They were taken captive by the Babylonians.

After seventy years the exiles were allowed to return to their own country to rebuild the walls of Jerusalem and to build a new temple. From about that time the term Israel began to be used once again of anyone from any of the twelve tribes and the people started to become known as the Jews, from the word Judah.

Conclusion

While we freely admit that the vast majority of the Old Testament concerns Israel and its people, we must not come away from it with any idea that it was exclusively so.

We read earlier, in Genesis 12, how Gentiles were to be blessed through Israel, and saw how Egypt and other nations benefited from the influence of Joseph. Jonah, a prophet of Israel, was instructed to take a message to Nineveh, the capital of the Assyrian nation. They repented at his preaching and so were saved from judgment - another example of how Gentiles were blessed through Israel. Similarly there were great benefits for both the Babylonian and the Medo-Persian Empires through the services of Daniel and others.

However, if we were to summarise the Gentile position in the Old Testament from Genesis 12 onwards, it would be as follows: they received blessings from God *only* through the people of Israel. We have given some examples, but there are many more. Jerusalem, Judea, and the Jews were seen as the centre of God's working and Gentiles went to them to obtain God's wisdom and will, His blessings and bounty: e.g. the Queen of the Sheba visiting Solomon, Naaman visiting Elijah. We first read about Gentile blessing in association with Israel in Genesis 12. However, it continues throughout the whole of the Old Testament. This is also how the prophets depicted the future. For example:

> In the last days the mountain of the Lord's temple will be established as chief among the mountains; it will be raised above the hills, and all nations will stream to it. Many peoples will come and say, "Come, let us go up to the mountain of the Lord, to the house of the God of Jacob. He will teach us his ways, so that we may walk in his paths." The law will go out from Zion, the word of the Lord from Jerusalem. He will judge between the nations and will settle disputes for many peoples. (Isaiah 2:2-4)

> "Arise, shine, for your light has come, and the glory of the Lord rises upon you. See, darkness covers the earth and thick darkness is over the peoples, but the Lord rises upon you and his glory appears over you. Nations will come to your light, and kings to the brightness of your dawn." (Isaiah 60:1-3)

This is the picture painted by the Old Testament. The glory of the Lord is one day to rise upon the nation of Israel and be focused on Jerusalem. When this happens, all nations and kings will go there to learn God's way, to be taught His Law, and to receive His judgment on disputes. This is the way the Gentiles are to receive God's blessings. They come via Israel.

Summary of Old Testament history

Creation, Adam, Abel, Enoch, Noah, Babel.
Genesis 1-11.

Abraham, Isaac, Jacob, Joseph.
From Ur of the Chaldees into Egypt.
Genesis 12-50.
Also written of this time - Job.

Moses.
Out of Egypt into the wilderness. The giving of the Law.
Exodus, Leviticus, Numbers, Deuteronomy.

Joshua.
Into the promised land
Joshua

The Judges.
Othniel, Ehud, Barak, Gideon, Tola, Jair, Jephthah, Ibzan, Eli, Samuel.
Judges, 1 Samuel 1-8.
Also written during this time - Ruth.

The Kings of Israel.
Saul, David, Solomon.
1 Samuel 9-31, 2 Samuel, 1 Kings 1-11. (1 Chronicles 10-29, 2 Chronicles 1-9 cover much of the same period.)
Also written during this time - many of the Psalms and also Proverbs, Ecclesiates, and Song of Songs.

The Northern Kingdom - Israel, the ten tribes.
Kings: Jeroboam, Nadab, Baasha, Elah, Zimri, Omri, Ahab, Ahaziah Jehoram, Jehu, Jehoahaz, Jehoash, Jeroboam II, Zechariah, Shallum, Menahem, Pekahiah, Pekah.
1 Kings 12-22, 2 Kings 1-18. (2 Chronicles 10-32 covers much of the same period.)
Prophets: Jonah, Amos, Hosea.

Summary of Old Testament history continued

The Southern Kingdom - Judah.

Kings: Rehoboam, Abijam, Asa, Jehoshaphat, Jehoram, Ahaziah, Jehoash, Amaziah, Uzziah, Jotham, Ahaz, Hezekiah, Manasseh, Amon, Josiah, Jehoahaz, Jehoiakim, Jehoiachin Zedekiah.

1 Kings 12-22, 2 Kings 1-25. (2 Chronicles 10-36 covers much of the same period.)

Prophets: Isaiah, Micah, Nahum, Habakkuk, Zephaniah, Jeremiah, Joel, Obadiah.

Also written during this time - Lamentations

Judah in Exile.

Prophets: Ezekiel, Daniel.

Also written at this time - Esther.

Back in Jerusalem

Prophets: Haggai, Zechariah, Malachi.

Also written at this time - Ezra, Nehemiah.

4. The People - in the New Testament

Having briefly considered the books of the Old Testament, for whom they were written and of whom they spoke, we turn to the New Testament. We must now consider to whom its books were written.

The New Testament - to whom?

We noted at the beginning of the previous chapter that most Christians appreciate that practically the whole of the Old Testament was written to the descendants of Abraham. They recognise that from Genesis to Malachi the people to whom the books were sent were the nation of Israel. Not only that, but the people who wrote them were also Israelites.

On the other hand, when we turn to the New Testament many Christians subconsciously think that all of its books are addressed to Christians, and by that they mean Gentiles, not Jews. However, this is not the case. Some sections were written for Jews, trying to convince them that Jesus was the Messiah. In fact, most of the New Testament documents were written by Israelites, and many were written for Israelites, either for those who were already committed to Christ or to try to persuade those who were not that Jesus is the Christ.

Let us first consider the people who wrote the various parts of the New Testament. They were Matthew, Mark, Luke (Gospel and Acts), John (Gospel, three letters and Revelation), Paul (fourteen letters if Hebrews is attributed to him), James (one letter), Peter (two letters) and Jude (one letter). All of them, with the possible exception of Luke, were Jews. Most commentators would view him as a Gentile, but a few deem him to be an Israelite who was living in Macedonia, part of Greece. Even if we accept Luke as a Gentile, we can see that the overwhelming influence of the New Testament writers was Jewish.

The writings of Matthew, John, and Peter - to whom?

First we need to consider the ministry these people had been given by Christ. Matthew, John, and Peter were three of the original twelve disciples. They had been sent out by Christ with the following instructions:

> "Do not go among the Gentiles or enter any town of the Samaritans. Go rather to the lost sheep of Israel." (Matthew 10:5-6)

Later they were told that they were to "sit on twelve thrones, judging the twelve tribes of Israel" (Matthew 19:28). It would appear, then, that the twelve were intimately linked with Israel. It is true that these earlier instructions were subsequently widened by Christ just prior to His ascension.

> "This is what is written: The Christ will suffer and rise from the dead on the third day, and repentance and forgiveness of sins will be preached in his name to all nations, beginning at Jerusalem." (Luke 24:46-47)

> "You will be my witnesses in Jerusalem, and in all Judea and Samaria, and to the ends of the earth." (Acts 1:8)

However, these words seem to have Jerusalem and Judea still at the centre of events. In this respect, they follow what was said by the Old Testament prophets - see for example Isaiah 2:2-3 and 60:1-3 quoted at the end of the previous chapter. If we read the book of Acts and the letters written by Peter and John, there can be little doubt that the disciples saw their first duty as being to their fellow-Israelites. Their first task was to convince them that Jesus was the Messiah (Christ), the son of God. Indeed it was for this very purpose that John wrote his gospel (see John 20:30-31).

If we read the beginning of Acts we see the disciples firmly placed in Jerusalem. Even when severe persecution broke out against the church in Jerusalem, "all *except the apostles* were scattered" (Acts 8:1). They stayed put.

Later, to get Peter to visit a Gentile called Cornelius, God gave him a special vision (Acts 10:9-16). This was followed up by words directly from the Holy Spirit (vs 19-20). Even so, Peter did not seem to know why he was going to Cornelius. He asked both him and his men why he had been sent for (vs 21,29). As far as he was concerned, he was breaking the Law (v 28). This would indicate that Peter and the other disciples had no great plan in their minds of leaving Jerusalem, passing through Judea, moving on to Samaria, and presenting Christ to the Gentile world.

Even though Peter went to Cornelius we have no record in Scripture of his preaching Christ to any other Gentile. In fact he may not have done so. In Galatians we read of a meeting between Paul and Barnabas, on the one hand, and Peter, James, and John, on the other. This James was the Lord's half-brother who had, by this time, become the leader of the church in Jerusalem.

> … they saw that I (Paul) had been entrusted with the task of preaching the gospel to the Gentiles, just as Peter had been to the Jews. For God, who was at work in the ministry of Peter as an apostle to the Jews, was also at work in my ministry as an apostle to the Gentiles. James, Peter and John, those reputed to be pillars, gave me and Barnabas the right hand of fellowship when they recognised the grace given to me. They agreed that we should go to the Gentiles, and they to the Jews. (Galatians 2:7-9)

The writings of James, Peter and John - to whom?

We mentioned earlier how, towards the end of the Old Testament, the people of both the northern kingdom and the southern kingdom had been taken captive and scattered amongst the nations. We mentioned also how, after seventy years, some of Judah returned to Jerusalem and Judea. However, not all did so. Many of them remained in the countries to which they had been scattered. They and their families carried on their lives and work there, obeying the Law of Moses as best they could. They visited the temple in Jerusalem as often as possible. They became known as the dispersion of Israel, the scattered ones, the *diaspora*. Peter and James wrote their letters for these people and it would seem that John wrote both his gospel and his letters for their benefit.

From the Scriptures themselves, therefore, it would seem that the ministries of Peter, James, and John were to the people of Israel. James addresses his letter "To the twelve tribes scattered among the nations" (James 1:1). And Peter likewise, "To God's elect, strangers in the world, scattered throughout Pontus, Galatia, Cappadocia, Asia and Bithynia" (1 Peter 1:1). His second letter was to the same group of people (2 Peter 3:1). The Greek word for "scattered" in these verses is *diaspora*, a technical term referring to those Israelites who had been scattered amongst the Gentile nations by the Assyrians and Babylonians. They continued to live amongst these nations and, as far as possible, to follow the Law of Moses. The only other writer to use this term (*diaspora*) is John in his gospel (7:35).

With respect to John's letters we read that Christ "is the atoning sacrifice for our (Israelites) sins, and not only for ours but also for the sins of the whole world (Gentiles)" (1 John 2:2). In this, John not only indicates that he is writing for Israelites, but that he sees them as still being first in terms of the offer of the gospel.

As for Revelation, it was written for the seven churches of Asia. However, from some of the comments made to those churches (e.g. some who are not Jews, but who claim to be, are described as the *synagogue* of Satan, 3:9) and from the contents of the remainder of the book, it seems it was written for Christian Jews. Revelation can be understood only by those who have a thorough understanding of the Old Testament prophets. It would seem, then, that in the seven churches of Asia there were a number of Jewish Christians. They would have been part of the dispersion of Israel. With their knowledge of the Old Testament, they would have had a good understanding of Revelation and could explain it to the Gentile Christians in their church.

The writings of Mark and Jude - to whom?

John's writings, like those of Peter and James, were for Israelites. This is also true of Matthew's Gospel and the letter of Jude, who was James' brother and, hence, a half-brother to Christ. This little letter not only makes several references to the Old Testament, it also alludes to Jewish apocryphal writings, *The Book of Enoch* and the *Assumption of Moses*. The Gospel of Mark is brief and leaves much unsaid, assuming an informed, and therefore Jewish, readership.

All these writings seem to have been for the benefit of Israelites, either those in Jerusalem and Judea, or those scattered throughout the nations. This leaves the writings of Luke and Paul.

The writings of Luke - to whom?

Luke addresses both his Gospel and his Acts of the Apostles to his friend Theophilus (Luke 1:3; Acts 1:1). Whether Luke, himself, was an Israelite or not is, perhaps, a moot point. Theophilus is a Greek name meaning lover of God. From this Greek name, and the use of the title "most excellent" in Luke 1:3, it would appear that in Luke's Gospel we have the only account of Christ's life which was written specifically for the benefit of a Gentile. This may explain why many Christians today find it easier to understand than any of the others. That does not mean that some parts of Matthew, Mark, and John are not easy. However, as a whole, Luke's Gospel is by far the most straightforward for anyone who has little or no knowledge of the Old Testament.

Then, in the Acts of the Apostles, we have an account of what the apostles did in the years following Christ's ascension. Initially, it concentrates on Peter and John. Then James is brought in. Barnabas is introduced. But the dominant character in the second half of Acts is Paul. Why did Luke place so much emphasis on Paul? Why did he think his

Gentile friend, Theophilus, would be so interested in, and want to know so much about, Paul?

The writings of Paul - to whom?

Earlier, on page 47, we quoted Galatians 2:7-9, where we read that Paul was an apostle to the Gentiles. We read also of the agreement that Peter, James, and John were to go to the Jews, and Paul and Barnabas to the Gentiles. This, naturally enough, would have been of interest to the gentile Theophilus. He would have wanted to know more about the activities of Paul than he would of Peter, James, and John. However, before continuing, we need to spend some time on one point which may have already caused confusion. It is the statement that Paul and Barnabas were to go to the Gentiles. If we read through Acts we find that Paul did indeed travel to many nations. The Greek word translated "Gentiles" in Galatians, and in most other places in the New Testament, is *ethne*, which literally means nations or peoples. Thus we may be more correct in our understanding of the Galatians agreement as being Peter, James, and John staying in Jerusalem and Judea and ministering to the Jews there while Paul and Barnabas travelled throughout the nations and ministered to the peoples there: i.e. both Jews and Gentiles. This would appear to be a better interpretation of Galatians 2:7-9 for this is precisely what Acts records.

Following the conversion of Paul, Ananias was told by the Lord that Paul was "my chosen instrument to carry my name before the Gentiles and their kings and before the people of Israel" (Acts 9:15). This would imply that Paul was to have a two-fold ministry. This he had.

When he travelled to the various nations, indeed when he came to any new town, the first place he looked for was the Jewish synagogue. The first people he ministered to were Jews. The only Gentiles who heard him were those who were termed God-fearers and who sat at the backs of the synagogues. For instance:

> From Perga they went on to Pisidian Antioch. On the Sabbath they entered the synagogue and sat down. After the reading from the Law and the Prophets, the synagogue rulers sent word to them, saying, "Brothers, if you have a message of encouragement for the people, please speak." Standing up, Paul motioned with his hand and said: "Men of Israel and you Gentiles who worship God, listen to me!" (Acts 13:14-16)

Paul's speech is summarised in verses 17 to 41. After it the people invited Paul and Barnabas "to speak further about these things on the next Sabbath" (v 42). However, "on the next Sabbath almost the whole city gathered to hear the word of the Lord. When the Jews saw the crowds, they were filled with jealousy and talked abusively against what Paul was saying" (vs 44-45). Paul's reaction to these Jews can be seen from his words to them.

> "We had to speak the word of God to you first. Since you reject it and do not consider yourselves worthy of eternal life, we now turn to the Gentiles." (Acts 13:46)

What happened there, at Pisidian Antioch, happened on many occasions throughout the second half of Acts. That is, Paul arrived at a new town and went first to the Jewish synagogue. There he spoke to the Jews and God-fearing Gentiles. Some believed and some did not. Those who believed brought others to hear Paul. Those Jews who did not believe became jealous of the Jews and, especially, of the Gentiles who did believe that Jesus was the Christ. These unbelieving Jews attempted to cause trouble for Paul and tried to upset those Jews and Gentiles who believed. This pattern, with minor modifications, occurs many times in the remaining chapters of Acts. For example:

> At Iconium Paul and Barnabas went as usual into the Jewish synagogue. There they spoke so effectively that a great number of Jews and Gentiles believed. But the Jews who refused to believe stirred up the Gentiles and poisoned their minds against the brothers. (Acts 14:1-2)

> But when the Jews opposed Paul and became abusive, he shook out his clothes in protest and said to them, "Your blood be on your own heads! I am clear of my responsibility. From now on I will go to the Gentiles." (Acts 18:6)

Acts closes with Paul under house arrest in Rome. When he arrived there "he called together the leaders of the Jews" (Acts 28:17).

> They arranged to meet Paul on a certain day, and came in even larger numbers to the place where he was staying. From morning till evening he explained and declared to them the kingdom of God and tried to convince them about Jesus from the Law of Moses and from the Prophets. Some were convinced by what he said, but others would not believe. They disagreed among themselves and began to leave. (Acts 28:23-25)

When we consider Paul's ministry during Acts, we see that it had two aspects: one to the Jews and one to the Gentiles. The Jews occupied the first place and everywhere Paul went it was to them he spoke first.

During this time Paul wrote seven letters, if we accept his authorship of Hebrews. However, whether he was the author or not matters little for the point we wish to make. As its name suggests, Hebrews is clearly a letter addressed to Hebrews, i.e. Israelites. The remaining six letters which Paul wrote during the second half of the Acts are Galatians, 1 & 2 Thessalonians, 1 & 2 Corinthians, and Romans.

These six letters were written during the Acts period to various churches which Paul either had visited or hoped to visit. These churches were made up of a mixture of Jewish and Gentile Christians, with the Jews often in leadership positions or more numerous. The majority of the Gentile Christians would have been those who had previously been God-fearers, Gentiles who had sat at the back of the synagogues. However, a few had been pagans or idol-worshippers.

> Paul devoted himself exclusively to preaching, testifying to the Jews that Jesus was the Christ. But when the Jews opposed Paul and became abusive, he shook out his clothes in protest and said to them, "Your blood be on your own heads! I am clear of my responsibility. From now on I will go to the Gentiles." Then Paul left the synagogue and went next door to the house of Titius Justus, a worshipper of God. Crispus, the synagogue ruler, and his entire household believed in the Lord; and many of the Corinthians who heard him believed and were baptised. (Acts 18:5-8)

Thus the church at Corinth, like those in Galatia, Thessalonica and Rome, was made up of both Jewish and Gentile Christians. The letters written to them were written to a mixed gathering of Jews, God-fearing Gentiles, and ex-pagan Gentiles. The Christian Jews knew and had a good understanding of the Law of Moses. The God-fearing Gentiles had some knowledge of that Law, while those who had previously been pagans had no knowledge of it at all. It is because these earlier letters of Paul were aimed at this mixed readership that they are so hard to understand. Some parts of the letters are addressed to all in the church. Some parts deal with problems peculiar to the Jewish section of the church. Other parts deal with problems peculiar to Gentiles. For example, in 1 Corinthians there is a section primarily for the Jewish Christians which commences at 10:1 with the words:

> For I do not want you to be ignorant of the fact, brothers, that our forefathers were all under the cloud and that they all passed through the

sea. They were all baptised into Moses in the cloud and in the sea. (1 Corinthians 10:1-2)

Then there is a section for the Gentiles who were previously pagan commencing at 12:1-2.

> Now about spiritual gifts, brothers, I do not want you to be ignorant. You know that when you were pagans, somehow or other you were influenced and led astray to mute idols.

Such subdivisions within Paul's letters are not always so easy to recognise. However, we should be aware of the background of those who orginally read his letters. They were a mixture of Israelites and Gentiles. We need to realise that some of the issues he dealt with related specifically to Jewish Christians whereas other parts concerned those who were Gentiles.

To summarise

It would seem, then, that the Gospels of Matthew, Mark, and John, the letters of Peter, James, John and Jude and the letter to the Hebrews, as well as Revelation, were written primarily for a Jewish readership. Luke's Gospel and his Acts of the Apostles were written for a Gentile. However, Paul's letters to the Galatians, Thessalonians, Corinthians, and Romans were for a mixed readership: some Jews and some Gentiles. And we have to admit it is not always easy to say which parts were written for which group, or for both.

This leaves us with Paul's last seven letters: Ephesians, Philippians, Colossians, 1 & 2 Timothy, Titus, and Philemon.

The later writings of Paul - to whom?

Earlier we quoted from Acts the account of Paul's arrival at Rome. There he was under house-arrest. The first thing he did was call together the leaders of the Jews. Some believed and some did not.

> They disagreed among themselves and began to leave after Paul had made this final statement: "The Holy Spirit spoke the truth to your forefathers when he said through Isaiah the prophet: 'Go to this people and say, "You will be ever hearing but never understanding; you will be ever seeing but never perceiving." For this people's heart has become calloused; they hardly hear with their ears, and they have closed their

eyes. Otherwise they might see with their eyes, hear with their ears, understand with their hearts and turn and I would heal them.' Therefore I want you to know that God's salvation has been sent to the Gentiles, and they will listen!" (Acts 28:25-28)

How final is this *final* statement of Paul's? In other parts of Acts he made similar statements to the Jews, for example at Psidian Antioch in Acts 13:46 and at Corinth in Acts 18:6. However, when he arrived at the next place he went straight to the synagogue and preached to them. One way of reading this passsage is to see it as the dismissal of those unbelieving Jews in Rome. However, why has Paul chosen to quote this judgmental prophecy from Isaiah 6? (A prophecy which has national, not local, implications.) It would seem from what he subsequently wrote that, although this final statement was made to the Jews in Rome, its consequences were nationwide.

The Jews in Judea had rejected Christ. They had crucified him. Some did repent, but not all, and especially not the leadership. The message of the Messiah was proclaimed to the scattered Israelites, but the majority of those rejected the message and became hostile towards Paul and his helpers. He had visited all the regions where there were Israelites, yet the majority had rejected Jesus as their Messiah. What now? It would appear that, because of their hardened hearts, they were blind and deaf to the message that Jesus was the Messiah. They were unusable. If the message of Christ was to go further, something different had to happen, and it did. God's salvation was to be sent direct to the Gentiles. No longer were Gentiles to receive God's blessing only through Israel.

We can learn of this through the books Paul wrote just after he spoke the words recorded in Acts 28:25-28. In verse 30 we read that he spent two whole years in Rome. It was possibly during that time that he wrote Ephesians, Colossians, and Philemon, and, towards the end of the two years, Philippians. It is now recognised that Ephesians was a circular letter sent to many churches. Some of what Ephesians states is in direct contrast to what Paul wrote in Romans, his previous letter and the last one he wrote before Acts 28:25-28.

In Romans he made it clear that the Jews were first and had various advantages. For example:

I am not ashamed of the gospel, because it is the power of God for the salvation of everyone who believes: first for the Jew, then for the Gentile. (Romans 1:16)

This reflects his policy during Acts when, wherever he went, he spoke first to the Jews. It also throws light on his words in Acts 13:46 when he told the Jews, "We had to speak the word of God to you first."

However, Paul has more to say in Romans about the priority and advantages of the Jews.

> There will be trouble and distress for every human being who does evil: first for the Jew, then for the Gentile; but glory, honour and peace for everyone who does good: first for the Jew, then for the Gentile. (Romans 2:9-10)

> What advantage, then, is there in being a Jew, or what value is there in circumcision? Much in every way! First of all, they have been entrusted with the very words of God. (Romans 3:1-2)

> ... the people of Israel. Theirs is the adoption as sons; theirs the divine glory, the covenants, the receiving of the law, the temple worship and the promises. (Romans 9:4)

But today, is there an advantage in being a Jew? In being circumcised? In having temple worship? All Christians say "No!", but when did that change? It was not until the end of Acts. Not until the revelation given to Paul at the end of Acts and which is recorded in such books as Ephesians and Colossians. There he wrote for the first time of the complete equality between Jews and Gentiles.

> This mystery is that through the gospel the Gentiles are heirs together with Israel, members together of one body, and sharers together in the promise in Christ Jesus. (Ephesians 3:6)

The Greek of this verse emphasises the complete unity and equality between the two. It is not easy to translate, but the teaching is that all nations now, including Israel, are on a complete equality. They are *equal* heirs, *equal* members and *equal* sharers. Or, as *The Englishman's Greek New Testament* puts it, "the nations to be joint-heirs and a joint-body and joint-partakers of his promise in the Christ". This is because the Jewish Christians and the Gentile Christians have been made one.

> For he himself is our peace, who has made the two (Jew and Gentile Christians) one and has destroyed the barrier, the dividing wall of hostility, by abolishing in his flesh the law with its commandments and regulations. His purpose was to create in himself one new man out of the two (Jew and Gentile Christians), thus making peace, and in this one

> body to reconcile both of them to God through the cross, by which he put to death their hostility. He came and preached peace to you who were far away and peace to those who were near. For through him we both have access to the Father by one Spirit. (Ephesians 2:14-18)

This teaching of Jew and Gentile believers being made one, being made equal, stands in complete contrast to the promise made to Abraham that Gentiles would be blessed through Israel. That promise was given in Genesis 12, is built upon as we go through the Old Testament, is seen in the Gospels, and is still in operation during the Acts of the Apostles and in the letters written during that time. What Paul announces in Ephesians is described as a mystery, a secret (3:3-9), something never heard of before, and first made known at that time. All differences between Jewish and Gentile believers were abolished. Both were now one. They were on an equality with no special privileges for anyone whose ancestry could be traced back to Abraham, through Isaac and Jacob. Hence Paul's desire:

> To preach to the Gentiles the unsearchable riches of Christ, and to make plain to everyone the administration of this mystery. (Ephesians 3:8-9)

Paul wanted everyone to know the change in God's dealings with mankind. Thus Ephesians, and his later letters - Colossians, Philemon, Philippians, Titus, 1 & 2 Timothy - are addressed to people who are simply Christians. They are not addressed to Jewish Christians or Gentile Christians. They are addressed simply to Christians. This, in many ways, makes them some of the easiest letters in the New Testament to read and understand.

Summary of the New Testament - for whom?

The Gospels

For Jews - Matthew, Mark and John

For Gentiles - Luke

The Acts of the Apostles

For Gentiles

Letters written during Acts

For Jews - Hebrews, James, 1 & 2 Peter, 1 & 2 & 3 John, Jude, Revelation

For a mixture of Jews and Gentiles, with Jews being first - Romans, 1 & 2 Corinthians, Galatians, 1 & 2 Thessalonians

Letters written after Acts 28:25-28

For Christians, where being a Jew or a Gentile is irrelevant - Ephesians, Philippians, Colossians, 1 & 2 Timothy, Titus, Philemon.

The following diagram summarises some aspects of the above in a clearer fashion.

The Gospel Period	*The Acts Period*		*The Post Acts Period*
	The Acts of the Apostles		
	Letters to Jews	Letters to Jews and Gentiles	
Matthew Mark Luke John	Hebrews James 1&2 Peter 1,2,3 John Jude Revelation	Galatians 1 & 2 Thessalonians 1 & 2 Corinthians Romans	Ephesians Colossians Philemon Philippians Titus 1&2 Timothy

Conclusion

When we take a close look at the New Testament we may be surprised to find the majority of it is addressed to Israelites. These were living either in Judea or among the nations of the eastern half of the Roman Empire.

We may also be surprised to see that the special role given to the descendants of Abraham in Genesis 12 (that all other nations would be blessed through them) continues throughout the Gospels. It is still present in the Acts of the Apostles and it is reflected in the letters written during that time. It is not until we get to the last letters of Paul, written after the judgmental prophecy of Acts 28:25-27 and the announcement of Acts 28:28, that Gentile Christians fully come into their own. As Luke wrote Acts for his Gentile friend, Theophilus, we may now have some understanding as to why he concentrated on the actions of Paul in the second half of Acts. We may also better appreciate why he ends Acts with the words, "Therefore I want you to know that God's salvation has been sent to the Gentiles, and they will listen!" (Acts 28:28).

5. The People - in the New Testament (continued)

In the previous chapter we dealt with each of the books of the New Testament, considering the people to whom they were written. We noted that all the writers, with the possible exception of Luke, were Israelites. We saw that many of the books were written for the people of Israel, either those living in the land of Judea or those living amongst the nations.

We need now to turn our attention to the contents of those books. One may have been written for a Jew, another to a church containing both Jews and Gentiles, a third to a church where any distinction between Jew and Gentile was irrelevant. But who is the subject of these books? Which people, or peoples, are featured in these writings? That is our quest.

The Gospels - of whom?

The central person in all four Gospels is our Lord and Saviour, Jesus Christ. However, which of His actions do the Gospels record? Which of His sayings? With whom was He dealing? Of whom did He speak? Before quoting any particular passage it may be interesting to consider the following table. It gives the frequency in each of the gospels, and Acts, of the occurrence of certain words: words which indicate the flavour of a book.

	Matthew	Mark	Luke	John	Acts
Words having to do with Israel					
Israel/Israelite(s)	12	2	12	5	21
Jew(s)(ess)(ish)(ry)	5	6	6	72	81
Circumcis(e)(ed)(ion)(ing)			2	3	9
Hebrew(s)			1	4	4
Abraham, Isaac, Jacob	15	3	22	14	19
Total	32	11	33	98	134
Words having to do with Gentiles					
Gentile(s), Greek(s)	8	3	6	4	42

From the above table it would appear that each of the Gospels, and Acts, is mainly about the people of Israel, although there are some references to Gentiles. Luke may have written his gospel for his Gentile friend, Theophilus, and would have been selective in some of the material he included. Nevertheless, it seems that the picture he painted in his Gospel is not significantly different from that of the others. He shows the dominance of Israel.

However, word frequency tables can be misleading. To get an accurate picture we need to look up each reference and see what it says. For example, in Matthew the frequency of Gentiles/Greeks is one quarter that of the Jewish terms. But when we look up the references to Gentiles what do we find?

The first, in Matthew 4:15, is a quotation from the Old Testament, Isaiah 9:1-2. It simply describes Galilee as "Galilee of the Gentiles".

The second, in Matthew 6:31-32, is translated "pagans".

> "So do not worry, saying, 'What shall we eat?' or 'What shall we drink?' or 'What shall we wear?' For the pagans (Gentiles) run after all these things, and your heavenly Father knows that you need them."

The third, in Matthew 10:5-6, is found in Christ's instructions to the twelve when He sent them out.

> "Do not go among the Gentiles or enter any town of the Samaritans. Go rather to the lost sheep of Israel."

The fourth, in Matthew 10:17-18, also comes in Christ's instruction to the twelve. He warned them:

> "Be on your guard against men; they will hand you over to the local councils and flog you in their synagogues. On my account you will be brought before governors and kings as witnesses to them and to the Gentiles."

The fifth and sixth, in Matthew 12:18-21, come in a quotation from Isaiah 42:1-4, indicating that the Gentile nations are to be blessed. It would seem that the Old Testament conditions still prevail.

The seventh, in Matthew 20:18-19, records Christ telling the twelve about his impending death.

> "They will condemn him to death and will turn him over to the Gentiles to be mocked and flogged and crucified."

The eighth, in Matthew 20:25-26, comes in Christ's words to His disciples:

> "You know that the rulers of the Gentiles lord it over them, and their high officials exercise authority over them. Not so with you. Instead, whoever wants to become great among you must be your servant."

Apart from Matthew 12:18-21 (the quotation from Isaiah 42:1-4) there is nothing encouraging for the Gentiles in any of these references. It would seem then that the Gospels are more dominated by Israel than the word frequency count would imply. In fact, the place of the people of Israel in the Gospels is no different from their place in the books of the Old Testament. They are first and foremost. The Gentiles are secondary. They are entitled only to the crumbs.

> A Canaanite woman from that vicinity came to him, crying out, "Lord, Son of David, have mercy on me! My daughter is suffering terribly from demon-possession." Jesus did not answer a word. So his disciples came to him and urged him, "Send her away, for she keeps crying out after us." He answered, "I was sent only to the lost sheep of Israel." The woman came and knelt before him. "Lord, help me!" she said. He replied, "It is not right to take the children's bread and toss it to their dogs." "Yes, Lord," she said, "but even the dogs eat the crumbs that fall from their master's table." Then Jesus answered, "Woman, you have great faith! Your request is granted." And her daughter was healed from that very hour. (Matthew 15:22-28)

Christ was sent only to the lost sheep of Israel (Matthew 15:24). He was a servant of the Jews, a minister to the circumcision (Romans 15:8 *KJV*). The Gospels record Christ's dealings with Israel. There are only two or three incidents in which He had any contact with Gentiles, apart from when he was handed over to Pilate: e.g. Matthew 15:21-28 and John 12:20-26. In the former He eventually grants the Canaanite woman her request. In the latter it would seem that He doesn't even grant the Greeks an audience!

> Now there were some Greeks among those who went up to worship at the Feast. They came to Philip, who was from Bethsaida in Galilee, with a request. "Sir," they said, "we would like to see Jesus." Philip went to tell Andrew; Andrew and Philip in turn told Jesus. Jesus replied, "The hour has come for the Son of Man to be glorified. I tell you the truth, unless an ear of wheat ....." (John 12:20-24)

It would appear that the request went unanswered.

The Acts of the Apostles - of whom?

From the frequency table given on the previous page we can see that in the Acts of the Apostles there are many more references to both Israelites/Jews and to Gentiles/Greeks. The figures imply that there was an increase in activity amongst the Gentiles. This was, indeed, the case. However, some have the idea that the Acts of the Apostles starts off with a completely Jewish emphasis, but as it progresses the Jews gradually drift off the scene as the Gentiles take over. So, by the end, Acts is an exclusively Gentile book. This is certainly not the case, as the following frequency table indicates.

Acts chap.	Frequency Jew etc.	Frequency Gentile etc.	Acts chap.	Frequency Jew etc.	Frequency Gentile etc.
1			15	3	7
2	4		16	4	2
3	5		17	5	2
4	3	1	18	10	3
5	3		19	6	2
6	1		20	3	1
7	19	1	21	8	6
8			22	5	1
9	3	1	23	4	
10	5		24	5	
11	2	2	25	7	
12	2		26	6	3
13	11	4	27		
14	6	4	28	4	1

If we group some of the chapters together we get:

Acts chapter	Frequency Jew etc.	Frequency Gentile etc.
1-7	35	2
8-14	29	11
15-21	39	23
22-28	31	5

The above tables reflect what we wrote in the previous chapter concerning the activities of the apostles in Acts. It is exclusively Jewish until Peter goes to Cornelius in Acts 10. However, it is not until Paul and Barnabas embark upon their travels (chapter 13) that there is any significant change in the number of Gentiles approached.

The Acts period letters - of whom?

As mentioned in the previous chapter, Hebrews and the letters of James, Peter, Jude, and John, including his Revelation, were addressed to Israelites. The frequency of words in them is as follows:

Israel/Israelite(s)	6
Jew(s)(ess)(ish)(ry)	2
Circumcis(e)(ed)(ion)(ing)	
Hebrew(s)	2
Abraham, Isaac, Jacob	21
Total	31
Gentiles, Greek(s)	5

This pattern is little different from that displayed in the Gospels and on reading these letters one will find, again, that they deal predominantly with the Jews or Jewish issues.

However, during Acts Paul wrote various letters, seven if we include Hebrews, and it is interesting to consider them and compare them with his seven later letters.

The earlier and later letters of Paul - of whom?

	Earlier letters	Later letters
Israel/Israelite(s)	19	2
Jew(s)(ess)(ish)(ry)	29	2
Circumcis(e)(ed)(ion)(ing)	32	9
Hebrew(s)	1	2
Abraham, Isaac, Jacob	24	-
Total	105	15
Gentiles, Greek(s)	45	11

The pattern in his earlier letters is certainly different from that of the Gospels and reflects his twofold ministry during Acts, to both Israel and the Gentiles (Acts 9:15). In some ways, then, these early letters resemble the second half of Acts, which is entirely taken up with Paul and his travels.

However, the change in pattern seen in Paul's later letters is very significant. Not only are there nearly as many references to Gentiles/Greeks as there are to Israel/Jew, but when we read those passages dealing with Jews we may be surprised at what we find!

The first two are in Ephesians 2:11-12, a passage addressed to Gentiles.

> Therefore, remember that formerly you who are Gentiles by birth and called "uncircumcised" by those who call themselves "the circumcision" (that done in the body by the hands of men) - remember that at that time you were separate from Christ, excluded from citizenship in Israel and foreigners to the covenants of the promise, without hope and without God in the world. But now in Christ Jesus you who once were far away have been brought near through the blood of Christ.

The third, in Philippians 3:2-3, describes Christians, and not Jews, as the true worshippers of God.

> Watch out for those dogs, those men who do evil, those mutilators of the flesh. For it is we who are the circumcision, we who worship by the Spirit of God, who glory in Christ Jesus.

The fourth, fifth, sixth, and seventh references come in Philippians 3:5-7, where Paul describes what *previously* had been important to him.

> Circumcised on the eighth day, of the people of Israel, of the tribe of Benjamin, a Hebrew of Hebrews; in regard to the law, a Pharisee ... But whatever was to my profit I now consider loss for the sake of Christ.

The eighth, ninth, and tenth references occur in Colossians 2:11.

> In him you were also circumcised, in the putting off of the sinful nature, not with a circumcision done by the hands of men but with the circumcision done by Christ.

The eleventh and twelfth references occur in Colossians 3:11.

> Here there is no Greek or Jew, circumcised or uncircumcised, barbarian, Scythian, slave or free, but Christ is all, and is in all.

The thirteenth is in Colossians 4:11 where, writing of Aristarchus, Mark and Justus, Paul says of them:

> These are the only Jews among my fellow-workers for the kingdom of God.

The fourteenth is in Titus 1:10.

> For there are many rebellious people, mere talkers and deceivers, especially those of the circumcision group.

The fifteenth, and last, is in Titus 1:14.

> Pay no attention to Jewish myths or to the commands of those who reject the truth.

When we read through these we can see a clear change. Circumcision, given initially to Abraham as a covenant between him, his sons, and God, and which was previously so important, became irrelevant when compared to the spiritual circumcision carried out by Christ. Circumcision was of great importance for Jews throughout the Old Testament, Gospels, and Acts. It set them apart from other nations and made them different. However, in these later letters it is unimportant. Such differences became irrelevant.

The references cited above stand in direct contrast to the ones from Matthew which were quoted earlier. In those, we saw that, although there were a number of references to Gentiles in Matthew, most had nothing positive to say about Gentiles. So it is with these references to Israelite/Jew/circumcision etc. in Paul's later letters. There are several of them, but not one has anything positive to say about being a Jew or being circumcised. A number are, in fact, quite negative. Comparing Paul's later letters with the Gospels, there is a complete about-turn with respect to Jews and Gentiles.

Faithful and obedient or unfaithful and disobedient?

In the previous sections we have concentrated on racial differences, mainly between Jew and Gentile. However, there are differences of a spiritual and moral nature between people: some have faith, some do not; some who have faith act on it, some do not. We need to distinguish between these different groups and what the Bible says of them.

> For God so loved the world that he gave his one and only Son, that whoever believes in him shall not perish but have eternal life. (John 3:16)

> And without faith it is impossible to please God, because anyone who comes to him must believe that he exists and that he rewards those who earnestly seek him. (Hebrews 11:6)

> For the wages of sin is death, but the gift of God is eternal life in Christ Jesus our Lord. (Romans 6:23)

> For it is by grace you have been saved, through faith - and this not from yourselves, it is the gift of God. (Ephesians 2:8)

Those who have faith in Christ are saved. They do not perish, but have eternal life. However, as well as having the free gift of eternal life, there is a possibility of believers receiving a reward, a prize.

> For no-one can lay any foundation other than the one already laid, which is Jesus Christ. If any man builds on this foundation using gold, silver, costly stones, wood, hay or straw, his work will be shown for what it is, because the Day will bring it to light. It will be revealed with fire, and the fire will test the quality of each man's work. If what he has built survives, he will receive his reward. If it is burned up, he will

> suffer loss; he himself will be saved, but only as one escaping through the flames. (1 Corinthians 3:11-15)

> Do you not know that in a race all the runners run, but only one gets the prize? Run in such a way as to get the prize. Everyone who competes in the games goes into strict training. They do it to get a crown that will not last; but we do it to get a crown that will last for ever. (1 Corinthians 9:24-25)

But will all believers win a crown? Will all win a prize? Will all gain a reward? It would appear not. All believers have the free gift of eternal life, but only those who finish the race, only those who build with gold, silver and costly stones, only those who remain faithful, only those who act upon their faith - they alone will receive some measure of reward.

Thus when we read through the New Testament not only do we need to ask whether the passage is about Jews or Gentiles, we need to know whether it is talking about those who believe or those who do not. And when it is talking about those who believe, we need to ascertain whether it is dealing with believers who are faithful and active or believers who are lacking in these qualities.

Conclusion

We saw in the previous chapter that many of the books of the New Testament were addressed to Jews. In this chapter we have shown that not only were many written *to* Jews, the content of most is *about* Jews. Many of the books were written *to* them, even more were written *about* them.

The Gospels and the first half of the Acts of the Apostles are almost exclusively Jewish. So, too, are the letters of James, Peter, Jude and John (including Revelation) as well as Hebrews.

In the second half of Acts we see a move towards the Gentiles. This is reflected in the letters Paul wrote during that time: Galatians, 1 & 2 Corinthians, 1 & 2 Thessalonians and Romans. These letters, written to churches with a mixture of Jewish and Gentile Christians, dealt with issues that related to either one group or the other or both.

It is not until we get to the last seven letters of Paul that we see a significant change. In Ephesians, Philippians, Colossians, 1 & 2 Timothy, Titus and Philemon, Jewishness becomes irrelevant, as does any other racial qualification. From Acts 28:28 onwards "God's salvation has been sent to the Gentiles" and this new situation is reflected in the letters written after that time. No longer is the Jew first. No longer is more written about the Jew than the Gentile. No longer is more space devoted to Jewish issues. From then on Israel became like any other nation. The situation we have today commenced at that point in time.

6. The Place

Another part of the advice given by Miles Coverdale was that it would help our understanding of Scripture if we asked the question "Where?" That is, we should pay attention to the place mentioned in the passage. Let us look at four examples to illustrate this principle.

The Sabbath - where?

The Israelites were given certain instructions pertaining to the Sabbath day.

> Remember the Sabbath day by keeping it holy. Six days you shall labour and do all your work, but the seventh day is a Sabbath to the Lord your God. On it you shall not do any work, neither you, nor your son or daughter, nor your manservant or maidservant, nor your animals, nor the alien *within your gates*. (Exodus 20:8-10)

Here we must note that non-Israelites were to rest on the Sabbath if they lived in Israel, within their gates. But what of the Israelites living in a foreign land? Were they obliged to keep the Sabbath rest?

> There are six days when you may work, but the seventh day is a Sabbath of rest, a day of sacred assembly. You are not to do any work; *wherever you live*, it is a Sabbath to the Lord. (Leviticus 23:3)

I hope we are beginning to see the value of the advice given by Miles Coverdale. So far we have considered the "who" and "of whom" issues. Now we are beginning to look at "where". When we apply these rules to the Sabbath we see clearly what the teaching was.

(1) Israelites had to rest on the Sabbath wherever they were, whether at home or abroad.
(2) Gentiles had to rest on the Sabbath only if they were in the land of Israel, living amongst the Israelites.

The land - where?

There has been debate among Christians with regard to the boundaries of the land God promised Abraham and whether Israel has ever possessed it all. We shall investigate the matter.

In Genesis 12:1 we read that God said to Abraham, "Leave your country, your people and your father's household and go to the land I will show you."

> They set out for the land of Canaan, and they arrived there. Abram travelled through the land as far as the site of the great tree of Moreh at Shechem. At that time the Canaanites were in the land. The Lord appeared to Abram and said, "To your offspring I will give this land." (Genesis 12:5-7)

> Abram lived in the land of Canaan ... The Lord said to Abram ... "Lift up your eyes from where you are and look north and south, east and west. All the land that you see I will give to you and your offspring for ever ... Go, walk through the length and breadth of the land, for I am giving it to you." (Genesis 13:12-17)

From these passages it is clear that Abraham was promised the land of Canaan. However, there was a second, greater promise made later.

> On that day the Lord made a covenant with Abram and said, "To your descendants I give this land, from the river of Egypt to the great river, the Euphrates - the land of the Kenites, Kenizzites, Kadmonites, Hittites, Perizzites, Rephaites, Amorites, Canaanites, Girgashites and Jebusites." (Genesis 15:18-21)

The land of this second promise is larger, greater, and embraces that of the first promise. The land of the Canaanites was just part of the second promise but it constituted the whole of the first. However, the first promise is repeated.

> "The whole land of Canaan, where you are now an alien, I will give as an everlasting possession to you and your descendants after you; and I will be their God." (Genesis 17:8)

And so, too, is the second promise repeated. In Exodus 23:28 God is to drive the Hivites, Canaanites and Hittites out of the way of the Israelites. And then:

> "I will establish your borders from the Red Sea to the Sea of the Philistines, and from the desert to the River (Euphrates, footnote)." (Exodus 23:31)

We have probably quoted sufficient passages to show the two promises: one concerning the land of Canaan, the other concerning a much larger area, embracing several lands.

Under Moses the Israelites left Egypt and entered the wilderness. Under Joshua they left the wilderness and entered the promised land, but which promised land? We read:

> So the Lord gave Israel all the land he had sworn to give their forefathers, and they took possession of it and settled there. (Joshua 21:43)

Earlier in the chapter we can read of the towns and areas which were given to each of the tribes. A good Bible atlas will show the area and where each tribe was allocated. If we look at such a map we shall see that the region stretches from just east of the Jordan valley to the Mediterranean in the west, and from just north of Dan to just south of Beersheba. That, effectively, was the land of Canaan. What was given to the Israelites at that time was the smaller land, the subject of the first promise. They were not given the larger area, as promised later.

The Antichrist - where?

Some writers on prophecy have seen the Antichrist as coming to attack Christians throughout the world. However, that seems difficult to justify from some of the passages which they quote. Let us consider just two passages, applying the rules we have learnt: "of whom" and "where".

> "So when you see standing in the holy place 'the abomination that causes desolation', spoken of through the prophet Daniel - let the reader understand - then let those who are in Judea flee to the mountains. Let no-one on the roof of his house go down to take anything out of the house. Let no-one in the field go back to get his cloak. How dreadful it will be in those days for pregnant woman and nursing mothers! Pray that your flight will not take place in winter or on the Sabbath." (Matthew 24:15-20)

If we ask "where" this is to happen, we see clearly that it concerns "those who are in *Judea*". Also the "holy place" is part of the Jerusalem temple.

If we ask "who" this is about, it concerns those who may be hindered by the restrictions of the Sabbath Law, i.e. Jews. And it is most relevant for those Jews who live in Judea.

This abomination which is to be set up in the temple is spoken of, again, in Revelation.

> He ordered them to set up an image in honour of the beast who was wounded by the sword and yet lived. He was given power to give breath to the image of the first beast, so that it could speak and cause all who refused to worship the image to be killed. He also forced everyone, small and great, rich and poor, free and slave, to receive a mark on his right hand or on his forehead, so that no-one could buy or sell unless he had the mark, which is the name of the beast or the number of his name. (Revelation 13:14-17)

This gives us the reason why those living in Judea should flee to the mountains. The image of the beast is to be set up in the temple in Jerusalem. People are to be made to worship it and to take a mark in their right hand or forehead. Again, this is not an attack upon Christians, but one upon Jews, those living in and around Jerusalem. They, not Christians, worship in the temple. It was on their hands and foreheads, according to the Law of Moses, that they were to keep their copies of the commandments.

> These commandments that I give you today are to be upon your hearts. Impress them on your children. Talk about them when you sit at home and when you walk along the road, when you lie down and when you get up. Tie them as symbols on your hands and bind them on your foreheads. (Deuteronomy 6:6-8)

The mark of the beast, his number or his name, is to replace the commandments of God.

Eternal life - where?

Revelation chapter 20 ends with resurrection and the judgment of the dead, either to eternal life or to a second death. In the following chapter John paints a beautiful picture of the new creation. "I am making everything new!" declares God (Revelation 21:5) and He makes a new heaven and a new earth, and the former ones pass away. He makes a new Jerusalem, which is to come down from the new heaven to the new earth (Revelation 21:1-3). This new heaven and earth, this new creation, is the home of righteousness (2 Peter 3:13).

> "Now the dwelling of God is with men, and he will live with them. They will be his people, and God himself will be with them and be their

> God. He will wipe every tear from their eyes. There will be no more death or mourning or crying or pain, for the old order of things has passed away." (Revelation 21:3-4)

> "It is done. I am the Alpha and the Omega, the Beginning and the End. To him who is thirsty I will give to drink without cost from the spring of the water of life. He who overcomes will inherit all this, and I will be his God and he will be my son." (Revelation 21:6-7)

> The Holy City, Jerusalem, coming down out of heaven from God. It shone with the glory of God, and its brilliance was like that of a very precious jewel, like a jasper, clear as crystal. It had a great, high wall with twelve gates, and with twelve angels at the gates. On the gates were written the names of the twelve tribes of Israel ... The wall of the city had twelve foundations, and on them were the names of the twelve apostles of the Lamb. (Revelation 21:10-14)

> The nations will walk by its light, and the kings of the earth will bring their splendour into it. On no day will its gates ever be shut, for there will be no night there. The glory and honour of the nations will be brought into it. Nothing impure will ever enter it, nor will anyone who does what is shameful or deceitful, but only those whose names are written in the Lamb's book of life. (Revelation 21:24-27)

From these passages, then, it would appear that many are to spend their eternal life on a new and righteous earth, the centre of which is to be the spectacular new Jerusalem. From what is written of this new Jerusalem it would appear that it is peculiarly Jewish. There are twelve gates, bearing the names of the twelve tribes. There are twelve foundations, bearing the names of the twelve apostles of Christ. And, presumably, somewhere inside there will be twelve thrones upon which those twelve apostles are to sit, in order to judge the twelve tribes of Israel.

> Jesus said to them (the twelve), "I tell you the truth, at the renewal of all things, when the Son of Man sits on his glorious throne, you who have followed me will also sit on twelve thrones, judging the twelve tribes of Israel." (Matthew 19:28)

However, we should not have the impression that every Jew who has ever lived will be there. The context makes it clear that "only those whose names are written in the Lamb's book of life" will have eternal life (Revelation 21:27). But will every Jew who has eternal life be resident in the Heavenly Jerusalem? That may not be the case. Every believing Jew may have eternal life and may spend it on the new and righteous earth, but the book of Hebrews seems to imply that only those Jews who acted upon their faith could hope for a place in the Heavenly Jerusalem; those who had faith and who had been faithful as well.

For example, after writing about Abel, Enoch, Noah and Abraham, Hebrews 11 records that:

> All these people were still living by faith when they died. They did not receive the things promised; they only saw them and welcomed them from a distance. And they admitted that they were aliens and strangers on earth. People who say such things show that they are looking for a country of their own. If they had been thinking of the country they had left, they would have had opportunity to return. Instead, they were longing for a better country - a heavenly one. Therefore God is not ashamed to be called their God, for he has prepared a city for them. (Hebrews 11:13-16)

God, then, had prepared a city for people like Abraham, a heavenly city. Following on from this we read of more people in the Old Testament who acted on their faith: Isaac, Jacob, Joseph, Moses, Rahab, Gideon, Samson, Jephthah, David, Samuel, and the prophets. All these could look forward to an eternity in a heavenly city - and so could the Hebrews, if they were faithful.

> But you have come to Mount Zion, to the heavenly Jerusalem, the city of the living God. (Hebrews 12:22; see also Galatians 4:26)

However, there are some notable absentees from the list given in Hebrews 11. Where is Solomon? He was a man of great faith, but he had not remained faithful. Eternal life for him on the new earth is safe and secure, but there seems no place for him in the Heavenly Jerusalem. Like others of the nations he will be able to enter it (Revelation 21:24-26). However, the ones who are to inherit the heavenly Jerusalem are the ones who overcome, the ones who have faith and are faithful (Revelation 21:7).

It would seem then that as far as Israel was concerned, and the nations to whom they took the message of God, what they hoped for was an eternal life on a new and righteous earth, either in the Heavenly Jerusalem or around it. This state of affairs seems to stretch back before Abraham to Abel, Enoch, and Noah. However, it continues throughout the Old Testament with Abraham, Isaac, Jacob, Joseph, David, and the prophets. It is there in the Gospels, with Christ telling them that the meek will inherit the earth and asking them to pray for God's kingdom to come and His will to be done on earth (Matthew 5:5; 6:10). It is present during the Acts period and we read of it in Revelation, Hebrews, and Galatians.

After Acts, when "God's salvation has been sent to the Gentiles" (Acts 28:28), the distinctions between Jewish and Gentile Christians were done away with. If no such distinctions exist in this life, are they to exist in eternal life? It would seem not.

We have already mentioned that the first letter written after Acts 28:28 was probably Ephesians, a circular letter sent to all the churches. In that letter we are introduced, for the first time in Scripture, to the *heavenly realms*. This is where Christ went when He ascended.

> That power is like the working of his mighty strength, which he exerted in Christ when he raised him from the dead and seated him at his right hand in the heavenly realms, far above all rule and authority, power and dominion, and every title that can be given, not only in the present age but also in the one to come. (Ephesians 1:19-21)

But not only Christ is there. Because Christians are "in Christ" they are considered to be there now, and one day will be there in reality.

> God raised us up with Christ and seated us with him in the heavenly realms in Christ Jesus, in order that in the coming ages he might show the incomparable riches of his grace, expressed in his kindness to us in Christ Jesus. (Ephesians 2:6-7)

Christians are to spend their eternal life in the heavenly realms. In the coming ages God is going to show them there the incomparable riches of His grace. So great are His riches that Paul wrote:

> Praise be to the God and Father of our Lord Jesus Christ, who has blessed us in the heavenly realms with every spiritual blessing in Christ. (Ephesians 1:3)

To sum up then: it would appear that throughout the Old Testament what was offered to believing Israelites, and those of any of the nations who came to God through their ministry, was eternal life on earth. For those who put their faith into practice and acted upon it, there was a reward. That reward was a place in the heavenly Jerusalem which is to come down from heaven and be the centre of the new earth. This hope continued throughout the Gospels and the Acts of the Apostles, including the letters written during that time.

However, following Israel's blindness and deafness at the end of Acts, a new situation arose and a new hope was given. Gone were the national privileges of Israel. All nations were now on the same basis. Jewish and Gentile Christians were now one. Instead of eternal life on a new earth centred around a new Jerusalem, eternal life would be enjoyed in the heavenly realms .

Conclusion

We hope these few examples - the Sabbath, the land, the antichrist and the place for eternal life - are sufficient to show us that we do need to take note of "where" the Bible is referring to. If it says certain things happened or are to happen to Jews in Judea, it would be wrong to say that this applies to Christians throughout the world. Clearly, if the Bible wishes to talk about Christians world-wide then it can do so, and does do so in places. Similarly, if it talks about Egypt, let it mean Egypt. If it talks of the north, let it mean the north. If it talks about the earth, let it mean the earth and not heaven. Similarly, if it talks about the heavenly Jerusalem, let it mean the heavenly Jerusalem and not heaven. If we let the Bible mean what it says and take note of the places written about, we shall have a better and more accurate understanding of what each passage means.

7. The Time

Another part of the advice given by Miles Coverdale was that it would help us to understand Scripture if we marked "at what time" it was written. We shall turn our attention to this and also to the need to pay attention to any references to "time" made in the passage.

The Old Testament - when?

Chronology is the study of time. When applied to the Scriptures it attempts to date each book and the events contained in it. Unfortunately, there is insufficient information to allow us to ascertain exactly when some of the books were written. However, from their contents we can determine the period which they cover. For example, we may not be able to say when the book of Job was written, but it deals with conditions as they were towards the end of Genesis: e.g. Job was a priest in his own home, implying that the situation was before the Levites became priests for the nation of Israel.

What helps us most is to have some idea of the chronological order of the books of the Old Testament. In part this is easy. For example, the following books are in chronological order:

Genesis	
Exodus	
Leviticus	
Numbers	
Deuteronomy	
Joshua	
Judges (Ruth)	
1 Samuel	
2 Samuel	1 Chronicles
1 Kings	
2 Kings	2 Chronicles

I have put Ruth in brackets after Judges because it is set in the time of the Judges.

If we start at Genesis and read through to the end of Kings we have one continuous history of Israel in time order. We should also note that 1 & 2 Chronicles covers the same period as the end of 1 Samuel, the whole of 2 Samuel, and 1 & 2 Kings. In other words we have a second account of that period of history.

So, the first part of the Old Testament is rather easy to read and follow with respect to the timing, or order, of events. However, things begin to get a little more complicated with the rest of the books of the Old Testament.

(a) The Wisdom Literature

Job, Psalms, Proverbs, Ecclesiastes, and Song of Songs are referred to as the *Wisdom Literature*. As mentioned earlier, Job deals with conditions as they were at the end of Genesis.

Many of the Psalms were written by David, who came on to the scene half-way through 1 Samuel and went off it at the end of 1 Kings; see also the parallel passages 1 Chronicles 11-29, which also cover his life. Other Psalms were written by a wide variety of people over quite a period of time.

Proverbs, Ecclesiastes, and Song of Songs contain writings either written by Solomon or for him. His activities occupy 1 Kings 1-11 and 2 Chronicles 1-9.

(b) The Prophets

It is very difficult to date accurately most of the prophets. Basically, they fall into four groups.

i. Jonah, Amos, Hosea.
   Prophets of the Northern Kingdom (Israel).
   Written during the time covered by 2 Kings 14-18 & 2 Chronicles 12-17.

ii. Isaiah, Micah, Nahum, Habakkuk, Zephaniah, Jeremiah, Joel, Obadiah.
   Prophets of the Southern Kingdom (Judah).
   Written during the time covered by 2 Kings 15-25 & 2 Chronicles 26-36.
   Lamentations was written during this time.

iii. Ezekiel, Daniel.
   Prophets in exile.
   Esther was written during the exile.

iv. Haggai, Zechariah, Malachi.
   Prophets to the restored nation.
   Nehemiah and Ezra were written at the start of the restoration.

(c) Esther, Ezra, Nehemiah

These books deal with the history of the Israelites after they had been taken into exile by the Babylonians and after the latter had been taken over by the Medo-Persians. They cover events leading up to and surrounding the nation's return to Jerusalem and Judea.

* * * * *

That is a short over-view of when the books of the Old Testament were written. How does a knowledge of chronology help in understanding the Bible? In what way does our appreciation of the Scriptures improve if we know when a book was written?

The Sabbath - when?

Did Abraham, Isaac, Jacob, and Joseph keep the Sabbath day? Did the Israelites in Egypt rest on the Sabbath day? How could they rest if they were slaves to a foreign power?

If we read through their history (Genesis 12-50) we find no reference to the Sabbath day, no mention of any one of the descendants of Abraham resting, which may come as a surprise to some people.

The Sabbath is mentioned first in Exodus 16. Moses had led the people out of Egypt, through the Red Sea and into the wilderness. There they were in danger of starving, so God sent manna to feed them.

> Each morning everyone gathered as much (manna) as he needed, and when the sun grew hot, it melted away. On the sixth day, they gathered twice as much - two omers for each person - and the leaders of the community came and reported this to Moses. He said to them, "This is what the Lord commanded: 'Tomorrow is to be a day of rest, a holy Sabbath to the Lord.'" (Exodus 16:21-23)

> "Eat it today," Moses said, "because today is a Sabbath to the Lord. You will not find any of it on the ground today. Six days you are to gather it, but on the seventh day, the Sabbath, there will not be any." (Exodus 16:25-26)

> "The Lord has given you the Sabbath; that is why on the sixth day he gives you bread for two days. Everyone is to stay where he is on the seventh day; no one is to go out." So the people rested on the seventh day. (Exodus 16:29-30)

The Sabbath, then, was not introduced to the people of Israel until half-way through the book of Exodus. If we attempt to read Sabbath-keeping and Sabbath Law into books written before this time, we shall be reading error into those earlier books. Therefore, neither Abraham, Isaac, Jacob, Joseph, nor any of their families kept the Sabbath. This special day came onto the scene in Exodus 16. The rules and regulations pertaining to it are given in later parts of Exodus, as well as in Leviticus, Numbers, and Deuteronomy.

The Priests - when?

In Genesis 4:3-5 we read of Cain and Abel bringing their offerings and sacrifices to the Lord. In Genesis 8:20 Noah sacrificed burnt offerings to the Lord on behalf of his family. In Genesis 12:7, and elsewhere, Abraham built an altar to the Lord and offered sacrifices on behalf of his family. In Genesis 31:54 Jacob offered sacrifices and invited his relatives to share in the ceremony. At that time, it would appear that God's people could offer sacrifices for themselves or their families. They did not need a priest to do it for them.

However, we do read of priests in Genesis. There was Melchizedek, king of Salem and priest of God Most High (Genesis 14:18). Egypt had its priests (Genesis 41:45,50; 47:22,26), and so did Midian (Exodus 2:16; 3:1). But it would seem that the descendants of Abraham did not have priests. They sacrificed their own offerings to God. In time, however, Aaron and his tribesmen (the Levites) became priests for the nation of Israel (Exodus 19:22-24). They were officially consecrated in Exodus 28-29.

Therefore, to read a Levitical priesthood back into Genesis will cause us to misunderstand the book and the actions of Abraham, Isaac, Jacob, and Joseph. To be aware of the differences can help us gain a greater appreciation of some of the events. Consider, for example, Jacob's desire to obtain the birthright from Esau.

> He (Esau) said to Jacob, "Quick, let me have some of that red stew! I'm famished!" ... Jacob replied, "First sell me your birthright." "Look, I am about to die," Esau said. "What good is the birthright to me?" But Jacob said, "Swear to me first." So he swore an oath to him, selling his birthright to Jacob. Then Jacob gave Esau some bread and some lentil stew. He ate and drank, and then got up and left. So Esau despised his birthright. (Genesis 25:30-34)

There were three aspects to the birthright: (1) The father's blessing and supremacy; (2) a double portion of the inheritance; (3) the Domestic Priesthood. Thus the priesthood was invested in the firstborn of each family. Later it became vested in Levi for the whole nation (Numbers 3:6,12; 18:1-3).

Jacob wanted the birthright, but Esau despised it. Jacob wanted to be the priest for his family; Esau did not. Jacob wanted to serve God; Esau did not.

The Messiah - when?

We read in Genesis 3:15 of the One special offspring of a woman, Who was to crush Satan. From then on, as far as we are able to tell, that special offspring could have come through any woman.

It is not until we are nearly half-way through Genesis (see Genesis 21:12 and Galatians 3:16) that we learn that this One, this special Offspring or Seed, was to be a descendant of Abraham and Isaac. From that time on, as far as we can tell, that One could come through any female descendant of Abraham and Isaac, and ultimately Jacob.

Later, however, we learn that this Messiah was to be of the seed of David (Isaiah 11:1,10; Jeremiah 23:5; John 7:42). From that time on it was clear that the woman who was to bear the Messiah not only had to be descended from Adam, Abraham, Isaac, and Jacob, but also from David. We also learn that the Baby was to be born in Bethlehem (Micah 5:2).

The point to be made here is that we cannot read teaching that the promised seed is to come through David's line into the earlier promises given in Genesis and the other early books. We may know this to be the case, but the people to whom those books were written did not. The information given in later books tells of the necessity of the Davidic line, but there is no such information in the earlier books, and we are wrong to read it into them.

The New Testament - when?

Again, it can be difficult for us to know exactly when any particular New Testament documents were written. However, the contents of the writings do fall into three distinct time periods.

(a) The Gospel Period

The events written about in Matthew, Mark, Luke, and John cover this period. Traditionally, people have held the view that Mark was written first, then Matthew and afterwards Luke - Luke completing his book towards the end of Acts. Then, some time after, came John, towards the end of the first century. However, modern research has suggested that instead of being the last and latest, John's Gospel was probably written much earlier (see Appendix 2). This makes much sense for, as we read earlier, John's ministry was to the twelve tribes of Israel and he had agreed, together with Peter and James, to minister to the Jews. Thus there would have been little point in John writing for Jews after the end of Acts, when the nation had been blinded and deafened, and a large and growing majority of Christians were Gentiles.

All the Gospels deal with Christ's time on earth and were distributed during the Acts period: that is, within a relatively short time of His ascension.

(b) The Acts Period

The main book of this period is "The Acts of the Apostles", probably published at the end of Paul's two year house arrest in Rome (Acts 28:30). Luke's Gospel, being his former book to Theophilus, must have been completed some time before that. Thus Luke, probably the last of the gospels, was published during Acts.

The other books written during Acts were all letters. There were those written specifically for Jews: i.e. Hebrews, James, 1 & 2 Peter, 1,2 & 3 John, Jude, and Revelation. It is, however, very difficult to know exactly when each of them was written. Traditionally, James' letter was thought to be the first and John's last, but modern research has suggested that John's may have been earlier: (see J. A. T. Robinson's *A Redating of the New Testament* and *The Priority of John*). We can get ourselves bogged down in going into unneccesary details. The possibility is that all were written within the space of a few years, during a time covered by the third quarter of Acts (chapters 14-21).

The same is true of the earlier letters which Paul wrote for the Jews and Gentiles in various churches, though it is somewhat easier to date and order these, as we know much more of Paul's life and movements. Many commentators suggest the following order: Galatians, 1 & 2 Thessalonians, 1 & 2 Corinthians, Romans - although some place 1 & 2

Thessalonians before Galatians. These, too, were probably written during the time covered by the third quarter of Acts.

(c) The Post Acts period

It was during this time that Paul wrote his last seven letters, and the majority view of the order is as follows: Ephesians, Colossians, Philemon, Philippians, Titus, 1 & 2 Timothy. Some suggest that Colossians may come before Ephesians or 1 Timothy before Titus. However, suffice it to say that all these letters were written within a period of about five years.

* * * * *

But, in what way does it help our understanding of the New Testament to know the (approximate) order of the books? We give a couple of examples to illustrate this point.

Jew/Gentile equality - when?

In earlier chapters we have shown that the promise given to Abraham in Genesis 12:1-3, and built upon through the Old Testament, was that Gentiles were to receive God's blessings through Israel, and that Israel was to be the premier nation upon earth, the head and not the tail. This was the situation during the period covered by the Gospels. It continued throughout the Acts of the Apostles and can be seen in the letters written during that time (e.g. Acts 13:46, 18:6; Romans 1:16; 2:9-10; 3:1).

We have suggested that this situation changed after national blindness and deafness came upon Israel, when God's salvation was sent to the Gentiles (Acts 28:25-28). After this, various letters were written which show that there was no longer any advantage in being a Jew and that Israel was no longer the premier nation (Ephesians 2:14-16; 3:6). This situation came about because of Christ's work on the cross (Ephesians 2:16). However, it did not come into effect at the cross, as our reading of Acts and the earlier letters shows.

That something was achieved *on the cross*, but did not come into operation *at the cross*, should not surprise us. On the cross Christ defeated sin, death, and Satan, but all these remained active afterwards and are still active today. However, there is coming a day when, thanks to what Christ achieved on the cross, all three will be done away with.

Equality between Jewish and Gentile Christians, then, came about after Israel lost its privileged position as the first nation before God. This happened at the end of Acts, when national blindness and deafness set in. This does not mean that individual Jews had not put their faith in Christ; many had. But those who had done so, and those who subsequently did so, no longer had a prior position. They had no advantages and no privileges. They were one with Gentile Christians. They were on a complete equality in all things. However, this came about at the end of Acts and references to its effects are contained only in the last letters written by Paul. To read this situation back into the Gospels will only cause confusion. To read it back into the Acts, back into the letters written during that time, back into Paul's earlier letters, will lead to misunderstanding.

The Law abolished - when?

This point is related to the previous one. It is not until we get to Ephesians 2:14-15 and Colossians 2:14-16 that we read that the Law with its commandments and regulations was abolished for Israel. There we learn that the written code with its regulations was cancelled. From then on there was no longer any need for Jewish Christians to observe the dietary regulations. No longer had they to keep the religious festivals, the new moon celebrations, and the Sabbath day (Colossians 2:16). Earlier, however, in Acts, Paul was most zealous to keep the Sabbath (e.g. Acts 13:14; 16:13; 18:4), to attend the religious festivals (e.g. Acts 20:6,16) and to keep the Law (Acts 16:3; 18:18; 21:20-26; 23:5; 24:18).

Again, the abolition of the Law was made possible by what Christ had achieved on the cross (Ephesians 2:15; Colossians 2:14). The Law could have been cancelled any time after the cross. However, it was not abolished at the cross. It was abolished for Israel after they had lost their national privileges because of national blindness and deafness. This was at the end of Acts.

Therefore we need to realise that the Jews to whom Christ spoke in the Gospels, the Israelites to whom Peter, James, John and Jude ministered, the Jews whom Paul and Barnabas visited and taught in Acts, were all Jews who observed the Law. They were not under the Law for righteousness (Romans 3:21), but they upheld the Law and were zealous for it (Romans 3:31; Acts 21:20).

For us to read freedom from the Law into the Gospels, the Acts or the letters written during Acts will cause confusion. If we do so we are bound to misunderstand the passage and its teaching.

To sum up - the Law was introduced to Israel by Moses in the second half of Exodus and we are wrong to read it into Genesis and the first part of Exodus. The Law went out for Israel at the end of Acts, and we are wrong to read freedom from it into the Gospels, the Acts, and the earlier letters.

About - when?

So far we have paid attention to when a book was written. However, when reading any passage of Scripture we should also note if it has anything specific to say about time in the context. The following example may help to illustrate the point.

The Promise of Canaan - when?

We have seen how the Lord promised Abraham and his descendants both the land of Canaan and a much larger land, but Abraham, himself, never enjoyed the fulfilment of that promise. It is doubtful if he ever expected to.

> Then the Lord said to him (Abraham), "Know for certain that your descendants will be strangers in a country not their own, and they will be enslaved and ill-treated four hundred years. But I will punish the nation they serve as slaves, and afterwards they will come out with great possessions. You, however, will go to your fathers in peace and be buried at a good old age. In the fourth generation your descendants will come back here, for the sin of the Amorites has not yet reached its full measure." (Genesis 15:13-16; see also Acts 7:6)

This tells us when the promise would be granted. Abraham's descendants would have to wait until the four hundred years were up.

Prophecy - when?

The Scriptures contain many prophetic statements. Some of them relate to the return of the Lord Jesus Christ. In Christian circles there is a wide and healthy variety of opinions as to what is to happen before Christ returns. The order of these events and their timing are much discussed in some groups, but extra-special care should be taken with such prophetic events. Consider, for instance, the four prophecies recalled and fulfilled in Matthew 2.

> But you, Bethlehem, in the land of Judah, are by no means least among the rulers of Judah; for out of you will come a ruler who will be the shepherd of my people Israel. (v 6)

> Out of Egypt I called my son. (v 15)

> A voice is heard in Ramah, weeping and great mourning, Rachel weeping for her children and refusing to be comforted, because they are no more. (v 18)

> He will be called a Nazarene. (v 23)

It may be easy for us in retrospect, as it was for Matthew, to connect these four prophecies together and to put them in the correct chronological order. With hindsight it is not difficult. However, before the event would we have included the third one, about Rachel weeping for her children, with the birth of the Messiah?

Not only that, even if we had put all four prophecies together, would we have got them in the correct order? And what period of time would we have placed between them?

The chronological order of events was (1) the birth at Bethlehem; (2) Rachel weeping for her children; (3) the coming out of Egypt; (4) the living in Nazareth. But what was the length of time between these?

Between the first and second was under two years. However, we cannot say with certainty how long it was between the second and third; a few years for sure. The time between the third and the fourth would depend upon how long it took to travel from Egypt to Nazareth, but as we do not know exactly where they went in Egypt, we cannot tell how long the journey would have taken; possibly something like a year.

The point to be made, with respect to the unfulfilled prophecies surrounding the return of Christ, is that it is difficult for us to know (1) exactly how they will be fulfilled, (2) the order in which they will be fulfilled, and (3) the time-gap between successive events. We can learn a lesson from those alive when Christ was born. They could see and understand things and work them out much better than their ancestors could have done. Similarly, those alive in the days leading up to the return of Christ will have a much better understanding and a more accurate scenario of prophetic events than past and present writers.

Conclusion

We have provided a few examples of when the books of the Old and New Testament were written, when the Sabbath and the Priesthood were established, when the promises of the pedigree of the Messiah were given, when Jew/Gentile equality came in, and when the Law was abolished for Israel. We have shown how we can greatly increase our understanding and interest in what the Scriptures say just by noting when the various books were written and when the information in them was first given. I hope this has shown us the danger of reading teaching given in later books back into earlier ones. Knowing *when* something was first revealed by God does help us.

The two examples of time details given in a passage - when the promise of Canaan would be fulfilled, and the timing of prophetic events - have shown us the need to pay special attention to when something is going to happen. When we do that we may be disappointed (especially in prophecy) that insufficient detail is given and we find we are unable to draw up a timetable of future events!

8. What is said

We turn our attention now to what is, perhaps, the most obvious part of Miles Coverdale's advice. We must mark not only what is spoken or written, but with what words, with what circumstances, considering what goes before and what follows. I suppose most of us think we take note of "what" is said, and take note of the preceding and following verses in order to get the passage in its context. Here, I think Miles Coverdale is trying to tell us to note "*exactly* what" is said. It is equally easy for us to read something into a passage or to miss the point of what is there. To avoid these errors we need to note the words. We need to know the circumstances. This will mean considering far more than just the preceding and following verses.

The Sabbath - what was said?

We have already been helped in our understanding of the Sabbath by concentrating on "Who?", "Where?", and "When?" We have seen in Chapter 6 that it was for all Israelites, wherever they lived, but for only those Gentiles who happened to be living with the Israelites in Palestine. We saw in Chapter 7 that the Sabbath was not given to Israel until halfway through Exodus and, together with the rest of the Law, was abolished after Acts. But what was involved in the weekly Sabbath? What did the Israelites have to do, or not do? We read that they, their household, their slaves and servants, their animals, and any Gentile visitors had to rest. But that was only part of the Sabbath Law.

> There are six days when you may work, but the seventh day is a Sabbath of rest, a day of sacred assembly. You are not to do any work; wherever you live, it is a Sabbath to the Lord. (Leviticus 23:3)

The Sabbath, then, was a day of sacred assembly, but what were they to do when they assembled together?

> "Take fine flour and bake twelve loaves of bread, using two-tenths of an ephah for each loaf. Set them in two rows, six in each row, on the table of pure gold before the Lord. Along each row put some pure incense as a memorial portion to represent the bread and to be an offering made to the Lord by fire. This bread is to be set out before the Lord regularly, Sabbath after Sabbath, on behalf of the Israelites, as a lasting covenant." (Leviticus 24:5-8)

Representatives from the nation of Israel had to supply these loaves every Sabbath. The bread was prepared and baked before the Sabbath, but was taken to the Tent of Meeting, the Tabernacle, on the Sabbath. It was for the priests.

> "On the Sabbath day, make an offering of two lambs a year old without defect, together with its drink offering and a grain offering of two-tenths of an ephah of fine flour mixed with oil. This is the burnt offering for every Sabbath, in addition to the regular burnt offering and its drink offering." (Numbers 28:9-10)

Not only did the Israelites have to rest on the Sabbath, they had to take twelve loaves to the Tent of Meeting and gather together for a sacred assembly. At this, three offerings were made: a drink offering, a grain offering and an offering of two lambs. This was what Israel had to do on the Sabbath day.

The Land - what was said?

We have already mentioned that the promises of a land made to Abraham for his posterity are twofold. Some relate to Canaan: e.g. Genesis 12:6-7; 13:12-17; 17:8; Joshua 21:43. Others relate to a much larger area which takes in Canaan and other lands: e.g. Genesis 15:18-21; Exodus 23:31. Thus we need to note carefully in any passage which land is under consideration.

Gifts and Rewards - what was said?

The New Testament records a number of gifts which God freely gives to those who have faith in the Lord Jesus Christ. For example:

> The wages of sin is death, but the gift of God is eternal life in Christ Jesus our Lord. (Romans 6:23)

> For it is by grace you have been saved, through faith - and this not from yourselves, it is the gift of God. (Ephesians 2:8)

> Now when a man works, his wages are not credited to him as a gift, but as an obligation. However, to the man who does not work but trusts God who justifies the wicked, his faith is credited as righteousness. (Romans 4:4-5; see also 3:21-24 and 4:23-25)

From the above we can see that three of the gifts which God freely gives to those who have faith in Christ are salvation, eternal life, and righteousness. These cannot be earned by works of any kind. They are gifts from God. They are not the result of any merit anyone may have. They are not given to people because of any good works they may have done. This ensures "that no-one can boast" (Ephesians 2:8-10).

However, as well as talking about free gifts from God, the New Testament also speaks of certain rewards or prizes which God may or may not give to those who believe in the Lord Jesus. The distribution of these is not according to faith, but according to actions.

> For the Son of Man is going to come in his Father's glory with his angels, and then he will reward each person according to what he has done. (Matthew 16:27)

Matthew has much to say about rewards (e.g. 5:11-12,44-46; 6:1-6,16-18; 10:41-42); and so do other New Testament writers.

> Whatever you do, work at it with all your heart, as working for the Lord, not for men, since you know that you will receive an inheritance from the Lord as a reward. (Colossians 3:23-24)

It would appear that unlike the gifts, which are safe and secure, the reward is not. It is possible for some people to obtain a full reward, whereas others, it seems, could lose out on the prize.

> Watch out that you do not lose what you have worked for, but that you may be rewarded fully. (2 John 8)

> Do not let anyone who delights in false humility and the worship of angels disqualify you for the prize. (Colossians 2:18)

Therefore when we read through the Bible we need to distinguish whether the passage is talking about faith and its related gifts (such as salvation, eternal life, and righteousness), or works with their related rewards, prizes, and crowns. The gifts cannot be lost or taken back. The rewards can. Failure to distinguish between faith and works, failure to notice the difference between the gifts and the rewards, can cause confusion.

Some Christians believe people are saved by works; others that we are saved by faith but kept by works. However, it seems that the true teaching of the Bible is that to please God man requires faith. If we have that faith God will give us salvation, eternal life, righteousness, and various other gifts. These gifts are ours for eternity and God never takes them back. However, having placed our faith in God, He wants us to act on it. If we do so we will receive some measure of reward, a prize or a crown, but it is possible for us to lose these should our faith become cold and our actions selfish. One passage which distinguishes most clearly between these two different lines of teaching is the following.

> Each one should be careful how he builds. For no-one can lay any foundation other than the one already laid, which is Jesus Christ. If any man builds on this foundation using gold, silver, costly stones, wood, hay or straw, his work will be shown for what it is, because the Day will bring it to light. It will be revealed with fire, and the fire will test the quality of each man's work. If what he has built survives, he will receive his reward. If it is burned up, he will suffer loss; he himself will be saved, but only as one escaping through the flames. (1 Corinthians 3:10-15)

It is possible for believers to receive a reward from God. On the other hand, they may not gain that reward. None the less they will be saved and have eternal life, but only as one escaping from the flames. That is, as people escape from a burning house with nothing but their lives.

This teaching runs throughout the whole of Scripture. God's people of all ages, of all times, in all situations, and of all races and nationalities are required to have faith and to act upon it. Earlier we referred to Hebrews 11.

> By faith Moses, when he had grown up, refused to be known as the son of Pharaoh's daughter. He chose to be ill-treated along with the people of God rather than to enjoy the pleasures of sin for a short time. He regarded disgrace for the sake of Christ as of greater value than the treasures of Egypt, because he was looking ahead to his reward. (Hebrews 11:24-26)

Moses forsook all the treasures of Egypt because he looked forward to his reward, a place in a heavenly city, the new Jerusalem (Hebrews 11:16; 12:22). However great the treasures of Egypt may have been, they were worthless when compared with those of that heavenly city which is to come upon the new earth (see Revelation 21:10-21).

Earlier we suggested that the Scriptures teach that some people will be granted eternal life on earth, whereas others will be in heaven. The reward for those on earth seems to be a place in the new Jerusalem with some measure of administration over part of God's new and perfect earth. It is likely that there is a parallel for those in the heavenly realms. Any who are granted a reward may have a measure of administration over some part or aspect of the new heaven.

Throughout the Scriptures we get the consistent teaching that all men have sinned, that none are righteous. We see throughout the Scriptures that faith is essential, and if any place their faith in God He gives them free gifts - e.g. salvation, eternal life, righteousness. If any who have faith exercise it and act upon it, putting God's wishes into practice, then He rewards them.

These lines of teaching occur throughout Scripture. Where eternal life will be spent and what the reward will be may vary, but the fact of them does not change.

Jew/Gentile - what is said?

Again we need to note carefully what is said about Jews and what is said about Gentiles. This is especially true in the second half of Acts and the letters Paul wrote during that time, when the first Gentile Christians were coming onto the scene.

Hebrews, James, 1 & 2 Peter, 1,2 & 3 John, Jude, and Revelation were written for Jews and are mainly about Jews. These say little about Gentiles.

Paul's later letters - Ephesians, Philippians, Colossians, 1 & 2 Timothy, Titus, and Philemon - were written after the differences between Jewish and Gentile Christians had been abolished. Therefore, when studying these letters we may not need to pay so much attention to whether something is said to a Jew or a Gentile.

The problems come with the second half of Acts and Paul's earlier letters - Romans, 1 & 2 Corinthians, Galatians, 1 & 2 Thessalonians.

Jew/Gentile and the Law - what is said?

In Acts 15 some Jewish Christians stated that "Unless you are circumcised, according to the custom taught by Moses, you cannot be saved" (v 1). Then some of the Pharisees who had become Christians said, "The Gentiles must be circumcised and required to obey the law of Moses" (Acts 15:5).

The elders and the apostles met in Jerusalem to consider this question and their conclusion was voiced by James.

> "It is my judgment, therefore, that we should not make it difficult for the Gentiles who are turning to God. Instead we should write to them, telling them to abstain from food polluted by idols, from sexual immorality, from the meat of strangled animals and from blood." (Acts 15:19-20)

This was written in a letter and sent to Antioch with Paul and Barnabas, Judas and Silas (Acts 15:22-29).

When it comes to the Law we need to be careful of the context, noting whether the people in question are Jewish Christians or Gentile ones. For example, in Acts 21 James informs us that "thousands of Jews have believed, and all of them are zealous for the law" (v 20). However, he adds, "As for the Gentile believers, we have written to them our decision that they should abstain from food sacrificed to idols, from blood, from the meat of strangled animals and from sexual immorality" (v 25). If James is so careful to distinguish between Jewish and Gentile Christians, we should exercise similar care.

Jew/Gentile and circumcision - what is said?

As we have seen, a number of the Jewish Christians thought Gentile believers either had to be circumcised to be saved or should have been circumcised in obedience to the Law of Moses. This was not the ruling of the Jewish Council. That ruled in favour of the Jewish Christians continuing to keep the Law, but of Gentile Christians needing to obey just four rules, which did not include being circumcised.

Titus, who was a Greek, was not compelled to be circumcised when he visited Jerusalem with Paul (Galatians 2:3). Timothy, on the other hand, whose mother was a Jewess (and Jews could take their racial status from their mother) was circumcised by Paul (Acts 16:1-3). Timothy, having had a Greek father, had not been circumcised on the eighth day as he should have been. Paul corrected this omission.

Again, if Paul at that time was so careful to distinguish between Jewish and Gentile Christians, so should we be.

Conclusion

In this chapter we have tried to show that it is important to look at exactly what is said. We have tried to show how it helps us to consider not only what is written, but also the words, the circumstances and the wider context.

We have considered examples relating to the Sabbath and the Land, gifts and rewards, Jews and Gentiles, the Law and circumcision. Naturally, more could have been said, and many more examples could have been brought before the reader. However, perhaps those given have been sufficient to show us (1) how careful we need to be with the words, (2) what a great help it is to understand the circumstances of the people, and (3) the value of considering the wider context.

9. The reason why

We have considered each part of Miles Coverdale's exhortation save one: "to what intent?" In other words, he is suggesting that we find out the intention, the reason behind what is spoken or written. Sometimes this is very easy to do, as the reason is given in the near context. At other times it is harder. The reason may be found in some other part of Scripture. On some occasions the Scriptures give no reason, but from their overall view of Scripture, commentators and expositors are able to suggest one. However, sometimes we have to admit that we do not know the reason for a certain statement or action in Scripture and are unable to think of one. That is a reflection upon *our* limitations, not upon the integrity of Scripture.

We shall now, by way of example, consider some issues in the Bible and see if we can find out the reason for what was said or done.

The Sabbath - why?

The Israelites were given the Sabbath for two reasons.

(1) So that they, their sons and daughters, their slaves and servants, their animals and Gentile visitors, could rest and be refreshed (Exodus 23:12).
(2) So that they could gather together in a sacred assembly, to worship and offer sacrifices to the Lord (Leviticus 23:3; 24:5-8; Numbers 28:9-10).

The Land - why?

Why was the promise that Abraham's descendants were to inherit the land of Canaan delayed for 400 years? The Lord gives the reason.

> "For the sin of the Amorites has not yet reached its full measure." (Genesis 15:16)

At the time the promise was given, the Amorites were living in the land of Canaan. What, exactly, they were like does not matter. The fact is God did not consider them sinful enough to be removed and the land given to Israel. However, in time their sin became greater and in the end it was right for God to remove the Amorites and give the land to the Israelites.

Abraham willing to sacrifice Isaac - why?

In his old age Abraham was given a son, Isaac. Some time later God told Abraham to sacrifice Isaac as a burnt-offering. This Abraham set about doing, and would have done had God not stopped him (Genesis 22). But why was Abraham willing to sacrifice his son to God?

> By faith Abraham, when God tested him, offered Isaac as a sacrifice. He who had received the promises was about to sacrifice his one and only son, even though God had said to him, "It is through Isaac that your offspring will be reckoned." Abraham reasoned that God could raise the dead. (Hebrews 11:17-19)

The reason seems to be that God had told Abraham that the promise of a nation as numerous as the stars in the sky and as plentiful as the sand on the sea shore would come through Isaac. If God then instructed Abraham to sacrifice Isaac, Abraham reasoned that God would raise Isaac from the dead in order to keep His former promise.

Moses gave up the treasures of Egypt - why?

In Exodus we read of the baby Moses being found by Pharaoh's daughter. He was brought up in the palace and could have enjoyed an easy and pleasant life. Yet he gave up the pleasures and treasures for a rough and tough time. Why?

> By faith Moses, when he had grown up, refused to be known as the son of Pharaoh's daughter. He chose to be ill-treated along with the people of God rather than to enjoy the pleasures of sin for a short time. He regarded disgrace for the sake of Christ as of greater value than the treasures of Egypt, because he was looking ahead to his reward. (Hebrews 11:24-25)

Father forgive them - why?

While he was hanging on the cross, the Lord Jesus cried, "Father forgive them". Was his prayer for the Jews, who had handed him over to be crucified, or for the Romans, who had placed him on the cross? Peter placed the blame for the crucifixion on both the Jews (Acts 2:22-23; 5:30; 10:39) and, albeit to a lesser extent, upon the Gentiles (Acts 4:27).

However, we are fortunate in this instance. Christ gave the reason for his prayer.

> "Father, forgive them, for they do not know what they are doing." (Luke 23:34)

The statement "they do not know what they are doing" may seem to apply only to the Romans. Some think it does, stating that surely the Jews knew what they were doing. However, this is not the case. When speaking to the people of Israel about their rejection and crucifixion of Christ, Peter said:

> "Now, brothers, I know that you acted in ignorance, as did your leaders. But this is how God fulfilled what he had foretold through all the prophets, saying that his Christ would suffer." (Acts 3:17-18)

Under the Law of Moses a sin committed in ignorance was forgivable (Numbers 15:24-29). The nation of Israel had rejected Christ in ignorance. He knew this and He prayed for their forgiveness. This may explain why the nation was given the opportunity to repent during Acts and why Israel was still at the centre of God's plans during that time.

However, this leads us to ask why it was that Israel acted in ignorance. One possible reason why Israel did not receive Jesus of Nazareth as the Messiah is that in their Scriptures, our Old Testament, they saw two pictures of the Messiah. One they termed Messiah-ben-David, the all powerful and great King, and the other Messiah-ben-Joseph, the lowly and humble suffering One. Some schools taught that the Messiah-ben-Joseph was a picture, not of the Messiah Himself, but of His people, Israel. He and His people were seen as one. They were considered so close that when they suffered, He suffered.

The people of Israel had had a hard time for centuries, first under the Babylonians and then under the Medo-Persians. After that came the Greeks and finally the Romans. Israel had suffered. It was small compared to these superpowers. It was lowly. It was humble. This interpretation fitted their history. Not only that, they could not see how it was possible for the Messiah to suffer. As a result they looked only for the Messiah-ben-David, the mighty King. This was the One they wanted. The One who would release them from the Romans.

When Jesus came "gentle and riding on a donkey" (Zechariah 9:9), the vast majority of Israel simply did not see Him as their Messiah. They were not looking for the meek and lowly One. They were not looking for a carpenter from Nazareth.

Jew/Gentile and the Law - why?

Why did the Jews continue to observe the Mosaic Law during Acts? One straightforward reason is quite simply that God did not tell them to stop doing so. That instruction came after Acts (Ephesians 2:14-15; Colossians 2:14-16).

That being the case, why did God want them to continue to observe the Law during Acts? And observe it they did! There is every indication that Jews were more zealous of the Law after conversion to Christ than before (Acts 21:20; Romans 3:31).

We must bear in mind that the risen Christ told His disciples that "repentance and forgiveness of sins will be preached in his name to all nations, *beginning at Jerusalem*" (Luke 24:47). He told them that they were to be his "*witnesses in Jerusalem*, and *in all Judea* and Samaria, and to the ends of the earth" (Acts 1:8). As pointed out earlier, these verses show the centrality of Jerusalem and Judea at that time.

If the disciples were to be witnesses in Jerusalem, if they were to preach repentance and forgiveness of sins in Jesus' name in Judea, who would have listened to them if they had ceased to observe the Law? Any Jew who stopped keeping the Mosaic Law would be considered a backslider by his fellow countrymen. He would be seen as unspiritual. Any who continued in such non-observance would be treated as unclean. They would be viewed as Gentile dogs. Certainly they would not be listened to on any matters relating to God. If the disciples were to be an effective witness to their fellow-countrymen they had to continue observing the Law. The more zealous they were for that Law, the more effective would be their ministry.

However, a problem was caused for the Christian Jews when Gentiles started to believe in Christ. It was against their custom for a Jew to associate with a Gentile or visit him (Acts 10:28). But if the Jewish Christians were to help the new Gentile converts, how could they do so without offending their fellow Jews, to whom they had a prior duty to witness concerning Christ (Romans 1:16)?

The problem for Jews meeting and associating with Gentiles was that the visit could render them unclean. It need not do so, but it could. It depended on what the Gentile had been doing. Hence the four rules given in Acts 15:19-20. Provided that the Gentiles abstained from food polluted by idols, from sexual immorality, from the meat of strangled animals and from blood, then Jews could visit them without becoming unclean. If the Christian Gentiles of that period observed these four rules it enabled the

Christian Jews to associate with them and, at the same time, allowed the Christian Jew to maintain his integrity in the eyes of his fellow Israelites.

Of course, once the Jewish nation had hardened its heart, shut its ears, and closed its eyes to Christ (Acts 28:26-27), God's salvation was sent to the Gentiles (Acts 28:28). From then on there was no longer the need for Jewish Christians to observe the Law. Neither need Gentile Christians be so concerned about rendering their Jewish brothers unclean. We read in Ephesians 2:14-15 and Colossians 2:14-16 that the Law with its commandments and regulations was abolished, the written code with its regulations was cancelled. Colossians 2:16 goes on to specifically mention food and drink: "Do not let anyone judge you by what you eat or drink". The dietary restrictions of the Mosaic law were abolished for the Christian Jews. The food regulations for Christian Gentiles, announced in Acts 15:20, were cancelled.

> For he himself is our peace, who has made the two one and has destroyed the barrier, the dividing wall of hostility, by abolishing in his flesh the law with its commandments and regulations. His purpose was to create in himself one new man out of the two, thus making peace, and in this one body to reconcile both of them to God through the cross, by which he put to death their hostility. (Ephesians 2:14-16)

This passage tells us the reason why God abolished the Law. It was to make Jewish and Gentile Christians one. However much they may have been one in Adam with respect to sin and death - all sin and all die; however much they may have been one in Christ - by faith in His sacrifice for sin - there were still big differences between Jewish and Gentile Christians during the Acts. One has only to read through the Acts of the Apostles, and some of the letters written during that time (e.g. Romans 3:1-2; 9:3-5) to see this. The Jew was first. He was dominant. He was the leader. Gentiles received God's blessings, including the gospel of Christ, through the Jews.

At that time, when the Christian Jews' primary duty was to their fellow countrymen, it was right and correct to keep the Law. But as more and more of their nation heard about Christ and the majority of those who heard rejected, so the Christian Jews became isolated from their fellow Israelites. Finally, at the end of Acts, it was time to close the door on the nation of Israel and to open wide a new door. However, there was something hindering this which had to be cleared out of the way. That something was the Law. God took it out of the way. This not only freed Christian Jews from their need to observe the Law, it also made them one with Christian Gentiles. The Law had been the barrier between them. The Law had resulted in differences. The Law had given the Jews privileges and priorities because they were descended from Abraham. Now physical descent from that man was irrelevant. What was important now was to have faith like Abraham, faith in Christ. All who had faith in Christ were the same, no matter what their nationality, race, culture, or social status. This is the situation which we have today, a situation that started at the end of Acts.

Peter's reluctance to go to Cornelius - why?

We have mentioned earlier that to get Peter to visit Cornelius God gave him a vision and spoke to him through the Holy Spirit (Acts 10:9-20). When he met Cornelius' men he asked them "Why have you come?" and to Cornelius himself he addressed the question, "May I ask why you sent for me?" (Acts 10:21,29).

We may be right in stating that the reason Peter was reluctant to visit Cornelius was, in his own words, "You are well aware that it is against our law (custom) for a Jew to associate with a Gentile or visit him" (Acts 10:28). However, Christ had told them, "You will be my witnesses in Jerusalem, and in all Judea and Samaria, and to the ends of the earth" (Acts 1:8). If that purpose was in Peter's mind then it does seem strange that he asked Cornelius and his men "Why have you sent for me? Why have you come?" These are hardly the words of someone eager to fulfil Christ's commands!

But Peter *was* eager to carry out Christ's commands. One can never accuse him of lack of zeal. Christ had stated that "repentance and forgiveness of sins will be preached in his name to all nations, *beginning at Jerusalem*" (Luke 24:47). It would seem, then, that the apostles understood their mission to mean that first they were to witness in Jerusalem. When Jerusalem had responded and believed they were to go to Judea, and when Judea had responded there would be a believing nation of Israel. This nation would go first to Samaria and then to the ends of the earth. This, certainly, was the gist of the Old Testament. Israel was to be a kingdom of priests to the other nations of the world. They were to be a holy nation with a missionary role (Exodus 19:5-6; Zechariah 8:23).

When persecution broke out against the church at Jerusalem, all were scattered except the apostles (Acts 8:1). They dutifully stayed there and continued to witness to Christ. There can be little doubt that Peter would have willingly gone to the Gentiles once his own nation had repented. As it was, neither in Jerusalem nor in Judea were things going too well.

Some who were scattered went to Samaria and many there believed. Peter, together with John, went there to see what had happened. They stayed there for some time teaching the people and then returned to Jerusalem, preaching the gospel in many Samaritan villages (Acts 8:25). This must have been quite a step for Peter, but not too big a one. The Samaritans were related to the Jews, being the descendants of the ten tribes of the Northern Kingdom who had returned from their Assyrian exile, albeit somewhat mixed up with other races. Christ had been to Samaria and had spoken to a Samaritan woman. It may not have been too difficult for Peter to have followed His example. But Christ had never visited a Gentile. He had had few dealings with them.

All this, and more, explains why Peter had difficulty going to Cornelius. First, it was against custom for a Jew to associate with or visit a Gentile. Second, although he knew that at some time he and the other apostles would go to the Gentiles, it could not be until Israel had repented as a nation.

Even after Peter had visited Cornelius, spoken to him and seen him and his household accept Christ, he still seems unhappy about having dealings with the Gentiles. There is no record of him visiting any other Gentile and we read in Galatians that at times he withdrew from Gentile Christians.

> When Peter came to Antioch, I opposed him to his face, because he was clearly in the wrong. Before certain men came from James, he used to eat with the Gentiles. But when they arrived, he began to draw back and separate himself from the Gentiles because he was afraid of those who belonged to the circumcision group. The other Jews joined him in his hypocrisy, so that by their hypocrisy even Barnabas was led astray. (Galatians 2:11-13)

Peter withdrew from the company of the Gentile Christians because he was afraid of how the Jewish Christians from Jerusalem might react. This was after his vision of the sheet, after words from the Holy Spirit, after his visit to Cornelius, and after explaining to the Christians in Jerusalem what had happened (Acts 11:1-18). It would seem that Peter was over-cautious with respect to his fellow Jews, but in this section perhaps we can see why he was like that. His understanding was that he was to go first to Jerusalem and Judea. His mission was to preach repentance to his nation (Galatians 2:7-8). When they had responded to Christ then, as a kingdom of priests, they would take the message of the Messiah to the other nations of the world.

Gentile salvation in Acts - why?

Above we have tried to give some background to how the Christian Jews of the Acts period would have seen things. They knew their Scriptures and knew that a day was to come when all Gentiles would be blessed through Israel. They knew that the centre of those blessings was forgiveness, salvation, and righteousness in Christ. They knew that they were to take that message to the ends of the earth. Yet as we read through Acts we note a severe reluctance to do that.

From Acts 1 to Acts 7 they remained in Jerusalem. Persecution forced all but the apostles out of Jerusalem and the rest were scattered throughout Judea and Samaria. The Samaritans responded. But when the apostles in Jerusalem heard about this they sent Peter and John to investigate (Acts 8:14). After a while they returned to Jerusalem, preaching in many Samaritan villages on the way.

After Saul's conversion the Church throughout Judea, Galilee, and Samaria enjoyed a time of peace. Peter travelled about the country, visiting such places as Lydda and Joppa (Acts 9:31-36). It was while he was at Joppa that he had the vision of the sheet, heard the words from the Holy Spirit, and received the visit from Cornelius' men. Peter went to Caesarea to see Cornelius, later returning to Jerusalem to give an account of his behaviour to the Jewish Christians there (Acts 11:1-18).

However, there is no more reported activity amongst Gentiles in the land of Judea, or anywhere else, for some time. The Jewish Christians who had been scattered travelled as far as Phoenicia, Cyprus, and Antioch, "telling the message only to Jews" (Acts 11:19). But then some of the Christian Jews from Cyprus and Cyrene went to Antioch and began to speak to the Greeks there, and a great number of them believed (Acts 11:19-21). When the Christian Jews in Jerusalem heard of this, they sent Barnabas to investigate.

When Barnabas was in Antioch he went to Tarsus to fetch Saul back to Antioch. They stayed there a whole year before visiting Jerusalem (Acts 11:25-30; 12:25). It may have been during this visit that Paul and Barnabas met James, Peter, and John (Galatians 2:1-10). At this meeting it was agreed that Peter, James, and John would go to the Jews and Paul and Barnabas would go to the Gentiles, or better, (literally) go to the *nations*. They were to visit the Jews and Gentiles who lived in different countries.

However, as God's purpose was that the people of Israel, as a nation, were to repent first and then, as a nation of priests, be witnesses of Christ to all other nations, why did Peter go to Cornelius? Why did

Barnabas sanction the preaching of the good news to Gentiles at Antioch? And why was it agreed that he and Paul should visit the nations, speaking to both Jews and Gentiles? What was the point of preaching to Gentiles before the nation of Israel had repented? Wouldn't it have been better to have concentrated their efforts upon the Israelites?

There is a section of Romans which answers these questions. It is a very difficult passage to understand if taken out of its historical context.

> Again I ask: Did they (Israel) stumble so as to fall beyond recovery? Not at all! Rather, because of their transgression, salvation has come to the Gentiles to make Israel envious. (Romans 11:11)

In this section of Romans, Paul is dealing with the problem of why Israel, as a nation, had not repented and turned to Jesus as their Messiah and Saviour. However, he is at pains to explain that, at that time, the plight of the nation was not beyond recovery. It could still be restored. He also deals with the situation that we have been discussing, namely the salvation of certain Gentiles. Paul states that "salvation has come to the Gentiles to *make Israel envious*". This, he says, is the reason why God turned to the Gentiles in Acts. God's plan was to save the people of Israel and then use them to be His witnesses to the world. However, not all were responding.

> I do not want you to be ignorant of this mystery (secret), brothers, so that you may not be conceited: Israel has experienced a hardening in part until the full number of the Gentiles has come in. (Romans 11:25).

Here there was a hardening *in part*. Later, at Acts 28:25-27, there was to be a *total* hardening. However, at this point in the middle of Acts it was not total, it was in part. As such there was hope. Recovery was possible. One means of aiding recovery was provocation and one way of provoking Israel was Gentile salvation.

> I am talking to you Gentiles. Inasmuch as I am the apostle to the Gentiles, I make much of my ministry in the hope that I may somehow arouse my own people to envy and save some of them. (Romans 11:13-14)

How could arousing the Israelites to envy save some of them? Paul went on to explain what he meant in Romans 11:17-21. There Israel is pictured as a cultivated olive tree, and the Gentiles as a wild olive.

However, the olive tree of Israel was not bearing fruit. What could be done about it?

In olive-farming there was the practice of grafting into a cultivated olive tree a branch of a wild olive. When olive trees became very old and the amount of fruit they bore decreased, the farmers were reluctant to cut them down and plant new trees. It takes many, many years for an olive tree to grow to maturity and bear fruit. The farmers developed a method by which they could inject new life into a flagging tree, to cause it to crop again. This they did by cutting off one of the natural branches of the olive tree and grafting into its place a branch from a young wild olive. The life and vigour from this new limb would revive the old olive tree and cause it to crop abundantly again for many years to come.

What was man's practice in olive-farming was, so to speak, now being done by God. Israel was the old olive. It was not repenting and turning to Christ. It was not bearing fruit. The Gentiles were a young and wild olive. If a group of Jews did not believe, then Paul turned to the Gentiles of that area. These verses in Romans explain Paul's actions in Acts. They give us the reason for Gentile salvation in Acts, salvation ahead of the Jews, before the nation had been saved.

> On the next Sabbath almost the whole city gathered to hear the word of the Lord. When the Jews saw the crowds, they were filled with jealousy and talked abusively against what Paul was saying ... they (Paul and Barnabas) spoke so effectively that a great number of Jews and Gentiles believed. But the Jews who refused to believe stirred up the Gentiles and poisoned their minds against the brothers. (Acts 13:44-45; 14:1-2)

From these, and various other passages in Acts, we can see that the Jews were stirred up and provoked, were roused and envious; but, sadly, not sufficiently to bear fruit, to repent, and to believe in Christ. The partial hardness in Israel at that time (Romans 11:25), became total by the end of Acts (28:25-27).

The purpose of Gentile salvation today is very different from what it was in Acts. It may best be summarised by the following:

> Although I am less than the least of all God's people, this grace was given me: to preach to the Gentiles the unsearchable riches of Christ, and to make plain to everyone the administration of this mystery, which for ages past was kept hidden in God, who created all things. His intent was that now, through the church, the manifold wisdom of God should be made known to the rulers and authorities in the heavenly realms. (Ephesians 3:8-10)

Conclusion

In this chapter we have tried to show how beneficial it is to our understanding of Scripture if we are able to ascertain the reason why God has said something or done something. On occasion the reason is given us in the close context. In other places it may be in another part of Scripture. Sometimes no reason is given and it may require an overall understanding of God's plans and purposes to be able to suggest a reason. Now and then, however, we are unable to suggest any reason and we have to admit our limitations.

We have considered the Sabbath, the Law, Abraham's willingness to sacrifice Isaac, Moses' willingness to leave Egypt, Christ's prayer from the cross, Jews and Gentiles and the Law, Peter's reluctance to go to Cornelius, and the reason why Gentiles were being saved in Acts before the whole nation of Israel had repented. These have been sufficient to show us the value of stopping and meditating upon the reason why something was said or done.

10. The application

We have now dealt with each part of the advice given by Miles Coverdale. To summarise:

1) We have considered the necessity to take each part of the Bible in its context.
2) We have seen the need to find out to whom each part is addressed and which people it is about.
3) We have looked into when each book was written and have seen the benefit of paying attention to anything a passage may say concerning the timing of its events.
4) We have seen the need to note the place written about. We have tried to find out the circumstances of the people who are the subject of the passage.
5) We have considered how valuable it can be to our understanding if we are able to ascertain why something was written, said or done.

If we approach the Bible along these lines then we can establish the interpretation of the passage: its historical-grammatical interpretation. We mentioned in chapter 2 the danger of leaving things at this point, for we may see little that is relevant to ourselves and our age in some parts of the Bible. Thus, having established the historical-grammatical interpretation, we should seek a valid application of the passage to our lives today. However, if we do not establish a clear understanding of the passage first, then we will be in danger of making wrong applications. The interpretation must come first. We must start off with the advice given by Miles Coverdale, after which seeking an application must follow. With this in mind, we now consider some applications.

The Sabbath - application?

We have read that under Sabbath Law the Israelites were not to work on the Sabbath day. This ran from evening to evening. We might say from sunset on Friday to sunset on Saturday. Not only were they not allowed to work, neither were their sons and daughters, slaves and servants, domestic animals and aliens (anyone of another nation who happened to be living amongst them). The Israelites had to keep this Sabbath rest wherever they lived, but aliens did not. They had to observe it only if they were in Palestine.

The rules included not lighting a fire, and not picking up sticks for a fire. If any Israelite broke the Sabbath Law then the punishment was death (Exodus 35:2-3; Numbers 15:32-36). It was a day of rest and relaxation.

On the Sabbath the Israelites were also to gather together for a sacred assembly. At this, twelve loaves of bread were set before the Lord in the Tent of Meeting and three offerings had to be made: two lambs, a drink offering, and a grain offering.

Sabbath Law continued throughout the Old Testament and Gospels and into Acts, where we have a number of references to Paul observing the Sabbath; but when the Christian Jews met to discuss the problems of the Gentile Christians in Acts, keeping the Sabbath was not one of the things the Gentiles were asked to observe (Acts 15:20). Not only that, after the Jewish nation had rendered itself blind and deaf and God's salvation had been sent to the Gentiles (Acts 28:25-28), the Law was abolished for the Christian Jews. This meant they no longer needed to observe Sabbath days and other religious festivals (Ephesians 2:14-15; Colossians 2:14-16). That being the case, is there any application for today that we can make from all this teaching on the Sabbath?

First, there is the need for rest and relaxation. This is desirable for all people, and all domestic work animals. Not only should Christians ensure that they have a day of rest and relaxation for themselves and their family, they should do as much as they can to ensure that all people in their community and country have the opportunity of one day's rest in seven. We may not be able to persuade others to take that rest, but we should do our utmost to ensure that our society provides the opportunity to rest for others. Which day of the week it is, does not matter. Even if there are different days for different people, it does not matter. The point is, to rest and relax on one day in seven; this seems to be the application. It makes no difference on which day people rest.

Second, there is the religious aspect. As well as resting and relaxing, Israel also gathered together for a sacred assembly at which they worshipped God and offered sacrifices. We may not want to offer sacrifices as they did, but Christians should want to meet together to worship God. The day upon which this is done is of secondary importance. However, whereas rest can be taken by individuals at different times, it would seem sensible if Christians arranged matters so that they could meet on the same day and at the same time; and this, by and large, is what does happen today.

Circumcision - application?

In Genesis 17:10-14 we read of the covenant of circumcision, made between God and the descendants of Abraham. In this every male child had to be circumcised on the eighth day. Is there any application of this for today?

It would appear not, for circumcision prefigures the putting off of our sinful nature in the circumcision (crucifixion) of Christ and has nothing to do with infant baptism or dedication.

> In him (Christ) you were also circumcised, in the putting off of the sinful nature, not with a circumcision done by the hands of men but with the circumcision done by Christ. (Colossians 2:11)

> For it is we who are the circumcision, we who worship by the Spirit of God, who glory in Christ Jesus, and who put no confidence in the flesh. (Philippians 3:3; cf. Deuteronomy 10:16; 30:6)

None the less, some see infant baptism or dedication as a valid application of circumcision. However, a child was brought and presented to the Lord, not when he was eight days old, but when the days of his mother's purification were complete.

> On the eighth day, when it was time to circumcise him, he was named Jesus, the name the angel had given him before he had been conceived. When the time of their purification according to the Law of Moses had been completed, Joseph and Mary took him to Jerusalem to present him to the Lord (as it is written in the Law of the Lord, "Every first-born male is to be consecrated to the Lord"), and to offer a sacrifice in keeping with what is said in the Law of the Lord: "a pair of doves or two young pigeons". (Luke 2:21-24)

Only first-born males had to be presented to the Lord (Exodus 13:2). This took place when the mother had completed her days of purification, at the end of which she took a burnt offering and a sin offering to the priest. This period of purification was forty days after the birth in the case of a male child, and eighty days after the birth in the case of a female (Leviticus 12:1-8).

A baby boy was circumcised and named on the eighth day. This was probably performed at home and was a private affair, as the mother was still ceremonially unclean according to the Law. It was not until the end of another thirty-three days that she was considered purified. This was marked by taking a burnt offering and sin offering to the priest. This was a much more public occasion, a time of worship and celebration. Perhaps making infant dedication an application of this ceremony would be more sensible than trying to base it upon the rite of circumcision.

The Law - application

We have mentioned that, from the time of Moses to the end of Acts, the people of Israel were subject to the Law. On the other hand Gentiles were not, although there may have been parts of it which certain Gentiles had to keep. For example: Gentiles living in Israel had to rest on the Sabbath; Christian Gentiles in Acts were told to "abstain from food polluted by idols, from sexual immorality, from the meat of strangled animals and from blood" (Acts 15:20).

At the end of Acts, when the nation of Israel hardened itself by closing its eyes and shutting its ears to Christ, the Law was abolished (Ephesians 2:14-15; Colossians 2:14-16). Jewish Christians were then free to eat what they liked and observe whichever days they wished. But what of the four rules given to the Gentiles in Acts? It would seem that they could now eat what they wanted, even meat offered to idols and meat which had been strangled. They could drink what they wanted, even blood! But what of sexual immorality? Adultery, fornication and the like were totally banned under the Mosaic Law. Were the Gentiles, and the Christian Jews, for that matter, free to indulge in such practices? No!

> Put to death, therefore, whatever belongs to your earthly nature: sexual immorality, impurity, lust, evil desires and greed, which is idolatry. (Colossians 3:5)

> But among you there must not be even a hint of sexual immorality, or of any kind of impurity, or of greed, because these are improper for God's holy people. (Ephesians 5:3)

We may simplify the Law of Moses by depicting it as having three parts; the Ceremonial Law, the Civil Law and the Moral Law. What we find in the letters written after Acts 28:25-28 is the abolition of the Law. It would appear that this refers mainly to the Ceremonial Law, with its commandments and regulations. It may also refer to the Civil Law, which related to how Israel was to be run and governed and which may have little relevance for other countries and cultures. However, it does not refer to the Moral Law. The second halves of both Ephesians and Colossians contain many "do's" and "don'ts" which correspond with the

Moral Law. In fact, as we go through Scripture we find few changes in what God tells us to be morally right and wrong.

When it comes to reading the Old Testament (be it the Law of Moses or the proclamation of the prophets), when we study the New Testament (whether it be the Sermon on the Mount, the letters written to Jews or Paul's earlier or later letters), we find the moral teaching is the same. We cannot dismiss the whole of the Mosaic Law as having no application to us today. The Ceremonial Law may have been abolished. The Civil Law may be irrelevant. But the Moral Law is still operative.

As for the rest of the Law, there may be many lessons we can learn from it. Paul wrote to Timothy telling him that "the law is good *if a man uses it properly*" (1 Timothy 1:8). He also said, "All Scripture ... is useful for teaching, rebuking, correcting and training in righteousness, so that the man of God may be thoroughly equipped for every good work" (2 Timothy 3:16-17).

The Heavenly Jerusalem - application?

Earlier, we referred to Hebrews 11 and the people there, who not only had faith in God but who were faithful and who acted upon their faith. One of these was Moses.

> By faith Moses, when he had grown up, refused to be known as the son of Pharaoh's daughter. He chose to be ill-treated along with the people of God rather than to enjoy the pleasures of sin for a short time. He regarded disgrace for the sake of Christ as of greater value than the treasures of Egypt, because he was looking ahead to his reward. (Hebrews 11:24-26)

The reward that Moses looked ahead to was a place in a heavenly city, the New Jerusalem (Hebrews 11:16; 12:22) whose glories far outshone and outweighed those of Egypt (Revelation 21:18-21). What motivated Moses to give up any claim to being an Egyptian and what encouraged him to walk out on the treasures of Egypt, was his heavenly reward.

Because of the Jewishness of the New Jerusalem, and the change in God's administration at the end of Acts, a reward in that heavenly city may not be open to Christians today. Nevertheless, God can still reward us, in the heavens rather than on earth, should our works merit it.

> Whatever you do, work at it with all your heart, as working for the Lord, not for men, since you know that you will receive an inheritance

from the Lord as a reward. It is the Lord Christ you are serving. (Colossians 3:23-24)

Not only can we make a valid application of Hebrews 11:24-26, we may find it a positive encouragement when we are faced with difficult decisions which may involve our losing out on something which the world has to offer. We may find it a spur to help us make sacrifices in this life. Let us learn from Moses. Let us look ahead to a reward in the heavens and not worry about what we may miss on earth.

Gentile salvation in Acts - application?

We read in Romans 11:11 that "salvation has come to the Gentiles to make Israel envious". This verse was dealt with at length in the previous chapter. However, we are now considering possible applications. What application can be made from this section of Romans? The answer may well have to be, "None!"

This particular section of Romans deals with a unique situation which was peculiar to that time. Nothing like it exists today. None of us were saved to make a Jew jealous! In fact, there probably wasn't even one around at the time and many Christians don't know any Jews personally.

Certainly we are not being grafted into the olive tree of national Israel. That tree was cut down at Acts 28:25-28 with Paul's final statement involving the last pronouncement of the prophecy from Isaiah 6:9-10 (note verses 11-13, which talks of trees having been cut down).

On occasion we have to admit that there may be no valid application of a particular passage of Scripture for us in our time, the situation and issues dealt with being so very special to the people, the place, and the time when they were written.

Conclusion

In this section we have extended the advice of Miles Coverdale by looking for valid applications of passages which we have considered previously and for which we have obtained the historical-grammatical interpretation. We have looked at the Sabbath and Circumcision, the Law, the Heavenly Jerusalem, and Gentile Salvation in Acts.

We have seen clear and obvious applications of the Sabbath and of the reward associated with the Heavenly Jerusalem. We have seen that the Moral Law is as applicable today as it was when Moses gave it. There may be no valid application of circumcision, for the purification ceremony with its public offering of sacrifices may lend itself more readily to be applied to infant dedication. On the other hand, when it comes to the Gentile's position in Acts, one of being grafted into the Olive Tree of Israel in an attempt to provoke Israel, there really is no such situation today. There is no application.

These few examples show us that we can gain better and more accurate applications of passages after we have ascertained their historical-grammatical interpretation. Such an approach to the Bible will greatly enrich and expyand our Christian lives.

Part III

Using the Approach

In chapter 1 we asked the question "What is your approach to the Bible?" and we set out four different approaches, possibly the four most commonly used today.

In chapter 2 we asked, "Which approach should we use?" and suggested that the historical-grammatical one was best, as it tended to be objective rather than subjective. This has the advantage of tending to converge views, rather than causing them to diverge. We also suggested that one of the best ways of obtaining a valid interpretation is to follow the advice given by Miles Coverdale. We added, however, that we thought that once the interpretation had been established we should attempt to make a valid application of the passage to our own situation.

In chapters 3-10 we set about describing in more detail each of the statements of advice given by Miles Coverdale, summarised by the five words "Who?", "Where?", "When?", "What?", and "Why?". To these we added the injunction "Apply!". By looking at different examples from the Bible, we were able to see both the wisdom of and the need for what we were doing.

To help us further we now need to consider some subjects and passages of Scripture in detail. That is, we need to take these subjects and passages and study them along the lines set out above, dealing with "Who?", "Where?", "When?", "What?", "Why?", "Apply!". This we shall now do, dealing first with a number of subjects before we go on to consider some passages.

11. Approaching subjects

The Sabbath

If we wish to study the weekly Sabbath then we need to know everything the Bible says about it. We need to know:

Who was to observe it?
Where were they to keep it?
When were they to keep it?
What were they to do, or not do?
Why were they to observe it?
Is there any application to ourselves of what we have learnt?

To help up discover all that the Bible teaches on this subject the first, and most valuable, aid is a concordance. We can look up the words *sabbath* and *sabbaths* and arrange them in order. For example:

References to the Sabbath before Abraham

None

References to the Sabbath from Abraham to the giving of the Law

None.

References to the Sabbath in the Law

Exodus	16:23,25,26,29
	20:8,10,11
	31:13,14,15,16
	35:2,3
Leviticus	16:31
	19:3,30
	23:3,11,15,16,24,32,38,39
	24:8
	25:2,4,6,8
	26:2,34,35,43
Numbers	15:32

	28:9,10
Deuteronomy	5:12,14,15

By reading the above verses, and surrounding passages, we can learn most of what the Mosaic Law has to say on the subject of the Sabbath. We may find some of the references do not relate to the weekly Sabbath, but to special Sabbaths associated with the Feast of Trumpets or the Feast of Tabernacles. That being the case, they can be put on one side. However, if we study these and note what is said about the people of Israel and what is said about the Gentiles, considering where the people have to observe them and what they have to do and why, we shall discover that:

1) The Sabbath was a sign between the Lord and the nation of Israel for generations to come. It was to be observed on the seventh day from evening to evening.
2) No work was to be done in Israel on the Sabbath. This day of rest extended to sons and daughters, servants, slaves and all animals, as well as strangers from other countries who were in Israel. However, the Israelites had to observe the Sabbath rest wherever they lived.
3) The Sabbath day was a day for sacred assembly. On each Sabbath twelve loaves of bread were to be set before the Lord in the Tent of Meeting, the Tabernacle. Three offerings had to be made: two lambs, a drink offering, and a grain offering.
4) No-one was to light a fire on the Sabbath day and anyone who broke the Sabbath Law was to be put to death by the whole assembly.

It is essential to have a good grasp of what the Law of Moses states on a subject as it forms the basis not only of the rest of the Old Testament, but also much of the New.

References to the Sabbath in the Prophets

Amos	8:5
Hosea	2:11
Isaiah	1:13
	56:2,4,6
	58:13
	66:23
Jeremiah	17:21,22,24,27
Lamentations	1:7
	2:6
Ezekiel	20:12,13,16,20,21,24

22:8,26
23:38
44:24
45:17
46:1,3,4,12

Sometimes it is best to consider what the prophets have to say in chronological order. In that case we would consider Amos first, then Hosea, Isaiah, Jeremiah, and Lamentations. Ezekiel was a prophet who spoke to the people of Israel when they had been exiled to the land of Babylon.

The role of the prophets was to turn Israel back to God and to bring them back to keeping His Law. If we read the above references and surrounding passages we find that a nominal observance of the Sabbath by the people of Israel did not satisfy the Lord. Neither did a slavish obedience to it if it was not accompanied by an equally zealous attitude towards the civil part of the Law, with its moral obligations towards the widows, the fatherless, and the poor.

References to the Sabbath in the Wisdom Literature

Psalm 92	title

References to Sabbath in the Historical Books

2 Kings	4:23
	11:5,7,9
	16:18
1 Chronicles	9:32
	23:31
2 Chronicles	2:4
	8:13
	23:4,8
	31:3
	36:21
Nehemiah	9:14
	10:31,33
	13:15,16,17,18,19,21,22

In such passages as 2 Kings 11:5-8 and 2 Chronicles 23:4-8, we see that even at exceptional times, crisis points, the people of Israel were still to keep the Sabbath. The only ones allowed to do anything on the Sabbath were the Levites and the priests, those who normally had duties to perform on that day.

Nehemiah was written after the people of Israel returned from the seventy years of captivity in Babylon. We can see that he is keen for the Israelites to return to the Mosaic Law. Not only were they to keep the Sabbath day holy by resting on it, but so were their animals and any Gentiles who lived amongst them.

References to Sabbath in the Gospels

Matthew	12:1,2,5,8,10,11,12
	24:20
	28:1
Mark	1:21
	2:23,24,27,28
	3:2,4
	6:2
	15:42
	16:1,2,9
Luke	4:16,31
	6:1,2,5,6,7,9
	13:10,14,15,16
	14:1,3,5
	18:12
	23:54,56
	24:1
John	5:9,10,16,18
	7:22,23
	9:14,16
	19:31
	20:1,19

Above we have all that the Gospels have to say on the subject of the Sabbath, although in some places the Greek word *sabbitos* has been translated "week". However, before considering what is said, we need to note a statement Christ made about the Law in general.

> "Do not think that I have come to abolish the Law or the Prophets; I have not come to abolish them but to fulfil them. I tell you the truth, until heaven and earth disappear, not the smallest letter, not the least stroke of a pen, will by any means disappear from the Law until everything is accomplished. Anyone who breaks one of the least of these commandments and teaches others to do the same will be called least in the kingdom of heaven, but whoever practises and teaches these

commands will be called great in the kingdom of heaven." (Matthew 5:17-19)

Here Christ completely upholds the Mosaic Law. We see Him keeping the Sabbath in such passages as Mark 1:21; 6:1-2; Luke 4:16,31. That being the case, why was He, at times, in conflict with the Pharisees over His *apparent* breaking of the Sabbath? See, for example, Matthew 12:1-8; Mark 2:23-28 and Luke 6:1-5. The point seems to be that the Law forbade the harvesting of produce on the Sabbath, but not the picking of food to eat for oneself. Leviticus 23:39-40 specifically told the Israelites to take choice fruit from the trees on one of their Sabbaths. The Pharisees had added extra restrictions to the Law and it was these, not the actual Law of Moses, that the Lord Jesus broke.

Making the seventh day separate and different (holy) was for the benefit of mankind, to ensure that all had a day of rest and an opportunity to worship God. To pick food and eat it was not harvesting the crops. To carry a mat for sitting on was not transporting goods for sale. To make mud for the eyes of a blind man was not ploughing a field. If freeing a trapped animal on the Sabbath saved it from undue and prolonged stress and was good, then healing people was even more so. It did not contravene the Law.

References to Sabbath in Acts and the Early Letters

Acts	1:12
	13:14,27,42,44
	15:21
	16:13
	17:2
	18:4

There appear to be no references to the Sabbath in any of the early letters, but this throws the spotlight on two problems which we need to consider.

First: Hebrews 4:9 has "rest" in the *KJV*, "Sabbath-rest" in the *NIV*. This shows us the vagaries of translations and of using English-based concordances. Better ones to use are George V. Wigram's *The Englishman's Hebrew and Chaldee Concordance of the Old Testament* and *The Englishman's Greek Concordance of the New Testament*. These require little, if any, knowledge of the language involved. First we find out the Hebrew, Chaldee or Greek word for the English subject we are studying from the back of the book. Then we look up every reference to this word. We can see also the different ways in which that word has been translated.

Second: we must be aware that passages in the Bible dealing with the subject we are considering may not contain the word we are looking up. For example, there are at least two passages which deal with the subject of the Sabbath but which do not contain the word. They are:

Galatians	4:8-11
Romans	14:5-6

Such passages as these are found with the help of commentaries or cross-reference Bibles.

For completeness we may also want to consider such expressions as:

The first day of the week: Matthew 28:1; Mark 16:2,9; Luke 24:1; John 20:1,19; Acts 20:7; 1 Corinthians 16:2

The Lord's Day or *The Day of the Lord*: 1 Thessalonians 5:2-3; 2 Thessalonians 2:1-3; 2 Peter 3:10; Revelation 1:9-11.

To obtain a consistent line of teaching from all these references we need to note the people concerned in each passage. The Jewish Christians observed the Sabbath. The Gentile Christians did not. In fact, the Gentile Christians in Acts were asked to observe just four parts of the Law.

"It seemed good to the Holy Spirit and to us not to burden you with anything beyond the following requirements: You are to abstain
from food sacrificed to idols,
from blood,
from the meat of strangled animals and
from sexual immorality.
You will do well to avoid these things." (Acts 15:28-29)

The Sabbath was not one of the listed items. The Jewish Christians, in contrast, were rightly zealous for the Law. As James said to Paul:

"You see, brother, how many thousands of Jews have believed, and all of them are zealous for the law. They have been informed that you teach all the Jews who live among the Gentiles to turn away from Moses, telling them not to circumcise their children or live according to our customs. What shall we do? They will certainly hear that you have come, so do what we tell you. There are four men with us who have made a vow. Take these men, join in their purification rights and pay

> their expenses, so that they can have their heads shaved. Then everybody will know there is no truth in these reports about you, but that you yourself are living in obedience to the law ..." The next day Paul took the men and purified himself along with them. Then he went to the temple to give notice of the date when the days of purification would end and the offering would be made for each of them. (Acts 21:20-26)

Here we see Paul, for the second time in Acts (cf. 18:18), undertaking the Nazirite vow of the Law of Moses (Numbers 6:1-21). He had never told the Jewish Christians that they were not to keep the Law and should not circumcise their children. He had, however, told the Gentiles this. It would seem that what he was doing had got twisted and turned round by the time the reports reached Jerusalem.

Clearly the Gentile Christians did not keep the Sabbath, but the Jewish ones did, including Paul himself - see Acts 13:14; 16:13; 17:2; 18:4. Nowhere, at that time, did Paul tell Jews not to observe the sabbath, but that was soon to change.

References to Sabbath in the Later Letters

Colossians 2:16

Following the final pronouncement of the deafness and blindness of Israel in Acts 28:25-27, it was announced that God's salvation was to be sent to the Gentiles and that they would listen (v 28). This heralded a change and for the following two years Paul was under house-arrest in Rome from where he probably wrote, amongst others, the letters to the Ephesians and Colossians. In these letters he told the Christian Jews that they no longer needed to keep the Law, in general, and to observe the Sabbath regulation, in particular.

> He forgave us all our sins, having cancelled the written code, with its regulations, that was against us and that stood opposed to us; he took it away, nailing it to the cross ..... Therefore do not let anyone judge you by what you eat or drink, or with regard to a religious festival, a New Moon celebration or a Sabbath day. (Colossians 2:13-16; see also Ephesians 2:14-16)

So after the Jewish nation hardened its heart against Christ and became blind and deaf to the gospel, it lost its privileged position as God's special people on earth. As a result Christian Jews were freed from their obligation to keep the Law.

Application

Once we have considered all the references to Sabbath and looked at all related passages which deal with the subject; once we have noted what was to be done, by whom, where and when, we may then be in a position to make a useful application. If we find conflicting things taught, then by noting what is said *to whom*, or by considering what was said *when*, we may be able to resolve that conflict. With respect to the latter, it does seem sensible, where there is a seeming conflict, to give greater weight to teachings given later in the Bible, rather than to ones given earlier. That being the case, what, if any, applications of the Sabbath can we make which are relevant for Christian living today?

Clearly, we would not consider it right or proper to sacrifice two lambs, or to make a drink offering and a grain offering. Neither would it seem appropriate for us to set twelve loaves of bread somewhere. Not to light fires would be impracticable. It would be impossible to close down certain industrial processes, like electricity generation, for one day a week and we would not want to put to death those who keep them going. However, these are the details and in concentrating on them we can miss the two main principles: rest and worship.

Rest: People need one day a week to be different and separate from the others. They need a day when no work is done. This allows the body time to recover and recharge itself, ready for another week of work. This, Christians can advocate not only for themselves but for the whole of mankind, and for animals which work.

Worship: for six days we may need to work to earn a living for food, clothing, shelter. However, in biblical times, those who knew the Lord gathered together to read the Law and the Prophets, to sing the Psalms and to pray. This can apply equally to Christians today. We will not want to bring sacrifices and offerings, but it is good if we can meet together once a week, to have fellowship together, to pray, sing, and hear the Word of God. However, on which day we do so is of secondary importance (Romans 14:5-6; Colossians 2:16).

12. Approaching subjects

Circumcision

We shall approach the subject of circumcision in the same way as the Sabbath. We need to ask such questions as "Who?", "Where?", "When?", "What?", and "Why?", obtaining answers to these before considering if there is a valid application of circumcision for ourselves today.

References to circumcision before Abraham

None

References to circumcision from Abraham to the giving of the Law

Genesis	17:10,11,12,13,14,23,24,26,27
	21:4
	34:14,15,17,22,24
Exodus	4:26
	12:44,48

Genesis 17 is the chapter which introduces the covenant of circumcision to Abraham. It was a covenant God made with Abraham and his descendants after him. All males had to be circumcised and new-born boys had to be circumcised on the eighth day. This covenant extended not only to the descendants of Abraham, but also to any slaves they might own. It did not include any foreigners, Gentiles, living amongst them.

Only those who had been circumcised could participate in the Passover. If any Gentile living amongst the Israelites wanted to celebrate the Lord's Passover, then all the males in his household had to be circumcised. In effect, he became an Israelite.

References to circumcision in the Law

Leviticus	12:3
Deuteronomy	10:16

30:6

Leviticus reinforces the rule that all male Israelites were to be circumcised on the eighth day. However, by using the term figuratively of the heart, Deuteronomy shows that God wanted the people to circumcise their hearts, to turn to Him and be cut off from the world.

References to circumcision in the Wisdom Literature

None

References to circumcision in the Historical Books

Joshua 5:2,3,5,7,8

Here Joshua ensured that the whole male population of Israel was circumcised before they entered the promised land.

References to circumcision in the Prophets

Jeremiah 4:4
9:25

The prophets were also concerned that the people had not only been circumcised physically, but also morally and spiritually.

However, this is, again, the time to point out the deficiency of studying just one word, rather than the subject. On occasion circumcision is referred to simply as "the *covenant*". For instance, in Isaiah 56:6:

> And foreigners who bind themselves to the Lord to serve him, to love the name of the Lord, and to worship him, all who keep the Sabbath without desecrating it and who hold fast to my covenant - these I will bring to my holy mountain and give them joy in my house of prayer.

Any Gentile could become part of the nation of Israel and bind himself to God by being circumcised and observing the Sabbath and the rest of the Law. Such Gentiles were known as Proselytes.

References to circumcision in the Gospels

Luke 1:59
2:21

John	7:22,23

Both the Lord Jesus Christ and John the Baptist were circumcised when they were eight days old.

References to circumcision in the Acts and Early Letters

Acts	7:8
	10:45
	11:2
	15:1,5
	16:3
	21:21
Galatians	2:3
	5:2,3,6
	6:12,13,15
1 Corinthians	7:18,19
Romans	2:25,26,27,28,29
	3:1,30
	4:9,10,11,12
	15:8

By New Testament times the people of Israel were often called "the circumcision" and the Gentiles "the uncircumcision", or the "circumcised" and "uncircumcised". Some translations, like the *NIV*, sometimes use "Jew" to translate the Greek word for circumcision (e.g. Colossians 4:11).

One of the main issues of the period covered by the Acts of the Apostles, a time when Gentiles were being saved and sharing in Israel's blessing, was whether these Gentile Christians had to be circumcised to be saved (Acts 15:1,5). This was discussed at a big council meeting in Jerusalem and the ruling was that it was not necessary (Acts 15:24-29). Titus, for example, who was a Greek, was not circumcised when he went to Jerusalem (Galatians 2:3).

However, in order for the non-Christian Jews to listen to the Christian Jews, it was necessary for the latter to continue their observance of the Law and its practices, including circumcision. It was for this reason that the Christian Jews continued observing the Law and Paul circumcised Timothy (Acts 16:3; 21:21). On the other hand, Gentile Christians did not need to be circumcised and Jewish Christians were wrong to try to reverse their circumcision (1 Corinthians 7:18-19; Galatians 5:6). With respect to salvation and righteousness, circumcision was irrelevant and any who thought that it was necessary were wrong

(Galatians 6:12-15). At that time there were advantages in being a Jew (Romans 3:1-2), but those advantages were not in the realm of forgiveness of sins and salvation by grace through faith in the Lord Jesus Christ.

References to circumcision in the later Letters

Ephesians	2:11
Philippians	3:3,5
Colossians	2:11
	3:11
	4:11
Titus	1:10

In these letters Paul distinguishes between a circumcision done by men (Ephesians 2:11) and that done by Christ for all Christians, whether Jews or Gentiles (Colossians 2:11). Physical circumcision prefigured the cutting off of our sinful natures achieved by Christ being cut off on the Cross.

Paul refers also to a circumcision done in the flesh (Philippians 3:5) in contrast to the true circumcision: worshipping God by the Spirit, glorying in Christ Jesus and putting no confidence in the physical rite (3:3).

At the end of Acts the nation of Israel, by and large, had hardened their heart against the message that Jesus was their Messiah. With their nation in such a blind and deaf state, the prior responsibility of Jewish Christians was no longer towards their fellow countrymen. It was now towards Gentile Christians. God's salvation was sent to the Gentiles, who were to listen (Acts 28:25-28). The Law, with its commandments and regulations, was abolished for the Jewish Christians (Ephesians 2:15). The written code with its regulations was taken out of the way (Colossians 2:14). Jewish Christians were no longer subject to what they ate or drank, or which days and festivals they kept (Colossians 2:16). In this way the differences that had existed between Jewish and Gentile Christians in Acts, including circumcision, were abolished. These two groups were made one (Ephesians 2:11-18).

Application

Having now considered all the relevant passages, we are in a position to make an application of circumcision. I am inclined to the view that there is no physical or ritualistic application. Some appeal to circumcision as a justification for infant baptism, or dedication. This seems highly unlikely as circumcision was a very private affair, the mother still being unclean (Leviticus 12:1-8). However, at the end of her days of purification offerings were then made at the Tent of Meeting (the Tabernacle) and this occasion may give us grounds for a rightly felt need for some form of service for thanking God for the birth of a new child and for the health of the mother.

At the same time, circumcision was also used in a figurative sense. Just as any Israelite in the Old Testament or New, a Christian today needs to be cut off from worldly influences and turn to God with all his heart, mind and body.

13. Approaching subjects

Fasting and Tithing

Fasting

In the Old Testament fasting is sometimes referred to as "afflicting your souls" (*KJV*) or "denying yourselves" (*NIV*). That being the case, we will need to pay attention to these expressions, as well as passages which speak of fasting.

References to fasting before Abraham

None

References to fasting from Abraham to the giving of the Law

None

References to fasting in the Law

Leviticus	16:29,31 23:27,32
Numbers	29:7
	30:13

On the tenth day of the seventh month, the Day of Atonement, the Israelites were to rest and fast, and so, too, were any aliens living amongst them. This day was also one of the special Sabbaths on which Israel was to hold a sacred assembly and present to the Lord an offering of one young bull, one ram, and seven male lambs a year old, all without defect.

The fast and the Sabbath rest were to be held from the evening of the ninth day until the following evening and the Israelites were to observe them wherever they lived. Any who did not fast and any who worked were to be cut off from the nation or destroyed.

As well as this annual national occasion, any individual could make a pledge to fast at any time.

References to fasting in the Historical books

Judges	20:26
1 Samuel	7:6
	31:13
2 Samuel	1:12
	12:16,21,22,23
1 Kings	21:9,12,27
1 Chronicles	10:12
2 Chronicles	20:3
Esther	4:3,16
	9:31
Ezra	8:21,23
Nehemiah	1:4
	9:1

The only regular fast was on the Day of Atonement. However, on certain occasions the nation, or part of it, or individuals within it, chose to fast. This was either as a sign of mourning or as an accompaniment for ascertaining the will of the Lord.

The Israelites fasted for a day when they sought God's will as to whether or not they should fight the Benjamites. Similarly Jehoshaphat declared a fast when seeking the Lord's will concerning battle against the Moabites and Ammonites who were about to attack. And David fasted when pleading with the Lord for the life of the child born to Bathsheba.

The nation fasted under Samuel, when they threw out their Baals and Ashtoreths, repented, and turned again to the Lord.

The people of Jabesh Gilead fasted for seven days when they heard what the Philistines had done to King Saul. David and all the men with him fasted until evening when mourning the death of Saul and Jonathan. Ahab tore his clothes and put on sackcloth and ashes when he heard how Jezebel had cheated Naboth of both his vineyard and his life.

In the later Historical Books, the Jews fasted and mourned when they heard of Haman's edicts to destroy the Jews. Esther and her maids fasted for three days and nights when they heard that news.

Ezra declared a fast when the Israelites were about to return to Jerusalem and Judea after the seventy year exile. They humbled themselves before the Lord, and asked for a safe journey. Then, when back in the land, the Israelites gathered together, fasted and wore sackcloth. They confessed their sins and worshipped the Lord.

Nehemiah fasted and prayed when he heard that the walls of Jerusalem had been broken down and its gate burned.

References to fasting in the Prophets

Isaiah	58:3,4,5,6
Jeremiah	14:12
	36:6,9
Daniel	6:18
	9:3
Joel	1:14
	2:12,15
Jonah	3:5
Zechariah	7:5
	8:19

Isaiah 58 is a marvellous chapter dealing with *true* fasting. Simply denying themselves food for a day was not what the Lord wanted. If, at the end of the day, there were quarrels and strife, fighting and continued exploitation, what was its value? True fasting entailed loosing the chains of injustice, breaking the yoke which held the workers, setting the oppressed free, sharing food with the hungry, providing the poor wanderer with shelter, clothing the naked, and providing for one's own flesh and blood. The purpose of the fast was an opportunity to appreciate all that they had, and to humble themselves before the Lord. However, if their attitude was not right, the Lord would not listen to their cries and prayers, even if they fasted. If their attitude was right then, as in the case of Darius and Daniel, the Lord responded.

In addition, certain days were declared days of fasting. In anticipation of the great and terrible day of the Lord, the prophets called for a fast, and for Israel to repent and turn back to the Lord.

At the cry of Jonah, Nineveh repented. The people put on sackcloth, fasted, and averted the Lord's judgment.

By Zechariah's time extra annual fasts had been incorporated into the calendar of Israel, each marking disasters in their history. These are referred to as fasts of the fourth, fifth, seventh and tenth months. The fourth month was Tammuz and on the ninth day of the month the nation remembered when the city had been broken up (Jeremiah 52:6-7). The fifth month was Ab and on the tenth day the Temple and the houses had been burned (Jeremiah 52:12-13). On the third day of Tisri, the seventh month, Gedaliah had been slain by Ishmael, the son of Nethaniah (Jeremiah 40:8; 41:1-3, 15-18). And on the tenth of Tebeth, the tenth month, the king of Babylon had set his face against Jerusalem (Ezekiel 24:1-2). All these fasts had been appointed by man, and not by God. Indeed He is quite crictical of them in Zechariah 7, asking, "When you fasted and mourned in the fifth and seventh months for the past seventy years, was it really for me that you fasted?" (verse 5). It would seem that these were simply external acts and therefore irrelevant.

References to fasting in the Wisdom literature

Psalm	35:13
	69:10
	109:24

David refers to putting on sackcloth, humbling himself and fasting when praying.

Summary of the Old Testament

The only fast decreed by the Lord for the nation of Israel was on the Day of Atonement, on which they had to eat no food, do no work and worship the Lord. The Israelites had to observe these wherever they lived. The no work and fasting edicts for the Day of Atonement also fell upon any Gentile living amongst the Israelites in Israel. By Zechariah's time other national fast days had been introduced, but none of these had been decreed by the Lord.

As for individuals, they could pledge themselves to fast whenever they felt it appropriate and many did so when they wished to repent or seek the Lord's will. This sometimes happened on a national scale when the religious leaders called on the entire population to mourn or repent, to seek the Lord's will or to avert judgment.

Fasting in the Gospels

Matthew	4:2
	6:16,17,18
	9:14,15
	15:32
	17:21
Mark	2:18,19,20
	8:3
	9:29
Luke	2:37
	5:33,34,35
	18:12

We read of the Lord fasting for forty days and forty nights before being tempted in the wilderness. This is the only occasion when we read of His fasting and this might have been an enforced fast as the first temptation implies there was no food there.

The Lord's disciples never fasted when He was on earth, even though John's did. However, their failure to perform certain healings was because prayer and fasting (*KJV*) were necessary, but the *NIV*, and most Greek texts, omit any reference to the need for fasting.

When referring to the personal fasts which individuals could undertake, the Lord told them not to make it obvious to others that they were fasting. There were some who did so to win the approval of men. Such fasts, no doubt, would be as efficacious as those of Isaiah 58. The Pharisees were guilty of this. They were proud that they fasted twice a week, on Mondays and Thursdays. In contrast to them stood Anna, who frequently fasted and prayed in the temple.

References to fasting in the Acts and Early Letters

Acts	10:30 (*KJV*)
	13:2-3
	14:23
	27:9
1 Corinthians	7:5 (*KJV*)
2 Corinthians	6:5
	11:27

In Acts 10:30 we read of Cornelius praying and fasting (*KJV*), although the reference to fasting is omitted in the *NIV* with most Greek texts. The prophets and the teachers worshipped, fasted, and prayed before sending Paul and Barnabas off on their first journey. Paul and Barnabas, themselves, prayed and fasted before taking their leave of the elders at various churches. The fast on the Day of Atonement is also referred to (Acts 27:9) and it would appear that Paul often fasted, although in 2 Corinthians 6:5 and 11:27 he may be referring to hunger (*NIV*), rather than fasting (*KJV*).

Husbands and wives were told not to keep themselves from one another, except by mutual consent for prayer and fasting (*KJV*), although, again, fasting is omitted in the *NIV* and most texts.

References to fasting in the Later Letters

None

Application

There are four strands to the biblical teaching on fasting. The first involved the whole nation of Israel on the Day of Atonement and was to embrace any Gentiles living amongst them. Such a national fast as this cannot be applied to any secular society.

The second was the calling of the whole nation to fast as part of repentance and mourning, or as an accompaniment to special prayers for guidance. This, again, cannot be applied to the secular nations of today.

The third was when a section of Israel mourned or wanted answers to their prayers. Whether this could be applied to individual churches or groups of Christians in this age is hard to say. There are no examples of it in the New Testament, although during the Acts period certain of the Christian leaders, who were Jews, fasted when appointing elders and when sending off Paul and Barnabas.

The fourth was the individual's desire to pledge himself or herself to fast, for whatever reason, but usually as a sign of sorrow or repentance and as an accompaniment to prayer. Again, whether this should be applied to individual Christians today is a matter for each individual, but it is unlikely. Fasting was not included in the instructions the Jerusalem Council issued for Gentiles (Acts 15:20) and little, if anything, is said concerning it in the early letters and none in the later ones.

Certainly the disciples, who we must remember were Jews, would have fasted on the Day of Atonement, but Christ did not instruct them to fast at other times. He was aware of the danger in fasting, with its tendency to encourage spiritual pride, as it did in the Pharisees. For Him individual fasting was a very private affair and there is but one possible reference to it in the earlier letters (1 Corinthians 7:5 *KJV*, but not *NIV*) and none in the later ones.

Some Christian groups have made fasting compulsory and attached a superstitious merit to it. Others claim that it brings them nearer to God, to Whom they feel closer and Whom they sense through a feeling of well-being. However, such a feeling is a physical phenomenon rather than a spiritual one, as various health food books testify and to which many, who for health reasons practise fasting, will attest. This has caused the majority of Christians to conclude that the teaching on fasting has no application to today. Whatever a Christian's attitude to it may be, Isaiah 58 is of utmost importance. It can be summed up in the following words: "An habitual self-denial is doubtless the spirit of fasting, rather than the mere occasional abstinence from food" (George Morrish, *New and Concise Bible Dictionary*). That is the primary application for today.

Tithing

Most Christians are aware that the biblical tithe was a tenth, but of what was it a tenth? In our studies, as well as considering the word "tithe", we will also need to take into account the word "tenth".

References to tithing before Abraham

None

References to tithing from Abraham to the giving of the Law

Genesis	14:20
	28:22

Abraham gave Melchizedek, who was both the king of Salem and priest of God Most High, a tenth of everything he possessed. This appears to be a one-off tithe and was never repeated.

Jacob made a vow to give one tenth of all that he had to God if He would be with him and watch over him, and give him food to eat and clothes to wear. This, again, seems to be referring to a one-off gift.

References to tithing in the Law

Leviticus	27:30,31,32
Numbers	18:21,24,26,28
Deuteronomy	12:6,11,17
	14:22,23,28
	26:12

The tithe was of everything from the land and of the entire herd and flock: that is, grain from the soil, fruit from the trees, and every tenth animal. All these belonged to the Lord. They were to be given to the Levites for the work they did while serving the Lord. However, the Levites had to present a tenth of those tithes as the Lord's offering. This was to be given to the priests and it had to be the best and holiest part of all the tithes.

If they wished to redeem their animals from the tithe they could do so, but a fifth of the value had to be added to the monetary gift.

Animals could be slaughtered and eaten in their towns, but the tithes of the grain, the new wine, the oil, and the firstborn of the flocks, were to be eaten in the presence of the Lord at a place He chose: i.e. Jerusalem. The offering of the tithes took the form of a ritual meal in which the Levites were to share.

If the tithes were too large to carry, they could be sold for silver and the silver taken to the special place where cattle, sheep, wine, and other things could be purchased and given as tithes.

Every three years tithes were to be offered in each person's own locality. A tenth of that year's produce was to be stored in the towns so that the Levites, the aliens, the fatherless, and the widows who lived there would have food to eat. It may be that this tithe was in addition to the regular one.

References to tithing in the Prophets

Amos	4:4
Malachi	3:8,10

Amos reminded the people to bring their tithes and Malachi chastened them for not bringing the full tithe into the storehouse.

References to tithing in the Historical Books

Nehemiah	10:37,38
	12:44
	13:5,12

On returning to their home country after the seventy year exile, the people of Israel agreed to give a tithe of their wine, the fruit of their trees, and the crops of their ground to the Levites. They, in turn, took a tenth of the tithe to the house of the Lord, to the storerooms; all this to be in accord with the Law of Moses.

References to tithing in the Gospels

Matthew	23:23
Luke	11:42
	18:12

Here the Lord chastened the Pharisees for paying attention to some of the additions to the Law (such as giving a tenth of their spices and herbs -

mint and rue, dill and cummin), but for neglecting the more important matters of the Law: justice, mercy, and faithfulness.

Other Pharisees gave in excess of that demanded by the Law, teaching that everything that is eaten and everything that grows out of the earth had to be tithed. "I fast twice a week and give a tenth of *all* I get" (Luke 18:12). However, the Law never asked for people to fast twice a week. Neither did it demand a tenth of everything. It was a tenth of certain things. By doing more and by giving in excess some Pharisees considered themselves righteous, and not sinners.

References to tithing in Acts and the Earlier Letters

Hebrews 7:2,4,5,6,8,9

This passage refers to Abraham giving a tenth of all that he had to Melchizedek, and to what the Law of Moses teaches on tithing. Thus there is almost a complete silence on tithing in the literature referring to the Acts period.

References to tithing in the Later Letters

None

Application

Basically the New Testament says nothing about tithing, although one imagines that the Jews continued to practise it in some form or another. However, no Gentile was ever instructed to tithe and it formed no part of the decisions made by the Jerusalem Council conerning Gentiles (Acts 15:24-29). Although we may not read of tithing, we do read about *giving* and the attitude, rather than the quantity, is the main point.

In Luke 21:1-4 a widow offered two copper coins. Christ considered she had given more than all the wealthy because "out of her poverty she put in all that she had". And He considered it "more blessed to give than to receive" (Acts 20:35). This may have been because God "gives you the ability to produce wealth" (Deuteronomy 8:18). Thus any who had wealth should share it with those who were less fortunate. All came from God and all belonged to Him. "Command those who are rich ... to do good, to be rich in good deeds, and to be generous and willing to share" (1 Timothy 6:17-18).

When it came to how much to give, Paul wrote, "Each man should give what he has decided in his heart to give" (2 Corinthians 9:7). He did not say how much this should be, but added that this should be given "not reluctantly or under compulsion, for God loves a cheerful giver". He also stated that "if the willingness is there, the gift is acceptable according to what one has, not according to what he does not have" (2 Corinthians 8:12).

An overview of the New Testament shows that tithing has no application today. Naturally, people need to give to keep Christian work alive. How much they give to their local church and how much to other Christian work is for them to decide. Should they decide to give a tenth, then how that tenth is divided between local and other organisations is up to them. However, there are two points which may be of help.

First, the debate as to whether Christians should give a tenth of all they earn (i.e. before taxes, national insurance or social security, and the like have been deducted) or a tenth of what they have left after these have been deducted, may be resolved by noting that Israel were *not* obliged to give a tenth of everything.

Second, the idea that all giving should come out of the tenth, (i.e. giving to famine relief and social charities as well as Christian work) was not the idea in the Law. There the tithe was given for the Levites and priests and for the local stores where the aliens, widows, fatherless, and poor could eat. However, there was also the command that they be open-handed towards their brothers and towards the poor and needy in their land (Deuteronomy 15:11). This would imply that giving to such people was on top of their tithes and what Christians give for famine relief and the like should be on top of what they have decided to give to Christian work.

14. Approaching subjects

Healing

Sometimes it may be appropriate for us to concentrate our studies solely on the New Testament. This could be because the Old Testament has nothing to say about the subject under consideration or its teaching on the subject is so different. As an instance of this, let us consider the subject of healing. There certainly are healings in the Old Testament, but they are few and infrequent, so very different from the ministry of Christ in the Gospels and the Apostles in Acts.

We find that there are three Greek words translated "heal" in the New Testament. These are:

therapeuo;

iaomai, and its relatives *iama* and *iasis*;

sozo and its relative *diasozo*.

According to the *Englishman's Greek Concordance to the New Testament*, the occurrences of these words are as follows:

References in the Gospels

	therapeuo	*iaomai, iama, iasis*	*sozo, diasozo*
Matthew			1:21
	4:23,24		
	8:7,16	8:8,13	8:25
	9:35		9:21,22
	10:1,8		10:22
	12:10,15,22	13:15	
	14:14		14:30,36
	15:30	15:28	16:25
	17:16,18		18:11
	19:2		19:25
	21:14		24:13,22
			27:40,42,49
Mark	1:34		
	3:2,10,15		3:4
	5:29		5:23,28,34

Mark	6:5,13		6:56
			8:35
			10:26,52
			13:13,20
			15:30,31
			16:18
Luke	4:23,40	4:18	
	5:15	5:17	
	6:7,18	6:18,19	6:9
	7:21	7:7	7:3,50
	8:2,43	8:47	8:12,36,48,50
	9:1,6	9:2,11,42	9:24,56
	10:9		
	13:14	13:32	13:23
	14:3	14:4	
		17:15	17:19,33
			18:26,42
			19:10
		22:51	23:35,37,39
John			3:17
		4:47	
	5:10	5:13	5:34
			10:9
			11:12
		12:40	12:27,47

References in Acts and the Early Letters

	theraypeuo	*iaomai, iama, iasis*	*sozo, diasozo*
Acts			2:21,40,47
		3:11	
	4:14	4:22,30	4:9,12
	5:16		
	8:7	9:34	
		10:38	11:14
			14:9
			15:1,11
			16:30,31
	17:25		23:24
			27:20,31,43,44
	28:9	28:8,27	28:1,4
Romans			5:9,10
			8:24

Romans			9:27
			10:9,13
			11:14,26
1 Corinthians			1:18,21
			3:15
			5:5
			7:16
			9:22
			10:33
		12:9,28,30	15:2
2 Corinthians			2:15
1 Thessalonians			2:16
2 Thessalonians			2:10
Hebrews			5:7
			7:25
		12:13	
James			1:21
			2:14
			4:12
		5:16	5:15,20
1 Peter		2:24	3:20,21
			4:18
Jude			5,23
Revelation	13:3,12		21:24

References in the post Acts letters

	therapeuo	*iaomai, iama, iasis*	*sozo, diasozo*
Ephesians			2:5,8
1 Timothy			1:15
			2:4,15
			4:16
2 Timothy			1:9
			4:18
Titus			3:5

Therapeuo

We shall consider each of these words in turn. According to E W Bullinger's *A Critical Lexicon and Concordance*, *therapeuo* means:

> To serve as a *therapon* (an attendant, higher than *doulos* [slave], as implying free and honourable service); to be an attendant, to do service:

> then, to take care of, especially one's person, to dress, wash etc., then, especially, to take care of the sick, tend them and treat them medically.

Therapeuo gives us the English therapeutic and occurs 44 times in the New Testament. In all references, except Acts 17:25 where it is translated "worship" in the *KJV* and "serve" in the *NIV*, it is translated "heal" or "cure". For example, we read that:

> Jesus went throughout Galilee, teaching in their synagogues, preaching the good news of the kingdom, and *healing* every disease and sickness among the people ... people brought to him all who were ill with various diseases, those suffering severe pain, the demon-possessed, those having seizures, and the paralysed, and he *healed* them. (Matthew 4:23-24)

> Jesus went through all the towns and villages, teaching in their synagogues, preaching the good news of the kingdom and healing every disease and sickness. (Matthew 9:35)

> Many followed him, and he healed all their sick. (Matthew 12:15)

Throughout His ministry, the Lord Jesus Christ healed every kind of illness in everyone, immediately and completely. Healing was one of the signs which showed Israel that He was their Messiah (Isaiah 35:4-6; Acts 2:22). He gave this ability to His disciples, so that their testimony about Him would carry the same weight (Matthew 10:1; Hebrews 2:3-4). Thus this instant, immediate, and complete healing continued into the Acts period.

> Crowds gathered also from the towns around Jerusalem, bringing their sick and those tormented by evil spirits, and all of them were healed. (Acts 5:16)

> When this had happened, the rest of the sick on the island came and were cured. (Acts 28:9)

Iaomai, iama and *iasis*

Bullinger's *A Critical Lexicon and Concordance* defines these words as follows:

> *iaomai*: to heal, to cure: properly of surgeons: to cause to live, revive or recover from illness.

> *iama*: healing (the termination denoting the complete act: the result or product of the act).
>
> *iasis*: healing (the termination denoting the action as incomplete and in progress).

These words occur some 34 times in the New Testament and are generally translated "heal", or "made whole" (in the *KJV*). For example we read:

> A large crowd of his disciples was there and a great number of people from all over Judea, from Jerusalem, and from the sea-coast of Tyre and Sidon, who had come to hear him and to be healed of their diseases. Those troubled by evil spirits were cured, and the people all tried to touch him, because power was coming from him and healing them all. (Luke 6:17-19)
>
> He welcomed them and spoke to them about the kingdom of God, and healed those who needed healing. (Luke 9:11)
>
> Immediately her bleeding stopped and she felt in her body that she was freed from her suffering ... In the presence of all the people, she told why she had touched him and how she had been instantly healed. (Mark 5:29; Luke 8:47)
>
> And his servant was healed at that very hour ... And her daughter was healed from that very hour. (Matthew 8:13; 15:28)

Again, we see that throughout His ministry the Lord Jesus Christ healed every kind of illness in everyone immediately and completely. If we continue our study into the period covered by the Acts of the Apostles, this situation does not change. We find the apostles performing all sorts of healings in accordance with the promise of Mark 16:18.

> Taking him by the right hand, he helped him up, and instantly the man's feet and ankles became strong. (Acts 3:7)
>
> "Aeneas," Peter said to him, "Jesus Christ heals you. Get up and tidy up your mat." Immediately Aeneas got up. (Acts 9:34)

Again, immediate and complete healing is seen during Acts. However, it is, perhaps, significant that none of these words (*therapeuo*, *iaomai*, *iama* or *iasis*) occur after Acts. In fact *therapeuo* does not occur in any of the epistles, neither the earlier ones nor the later ones. If we search those letters written after Acts (Ephesians, Colossians, Philemon, Philippians, Titus, 1 & 2 Timothy) we read nothing of such healings. Rather we find that people are given advice or left sick.

> Stop drinking only water, and use a little wine because of your stomach and your frequent illnesses. (1 Timothy 5:23)

In Acts Paul would have sent an apron or handkerchief to heal Timothy (see Acts 19:11-12). Afterwards he sent only advice. It would seem that something had changed.

> I left Trophimus sick in Miletus. (2 Timothy 4:20)

In Acts Paul left no one sick on Malta (see Acts 28:8-9). After Acts he left one of his closest friends ill at Miletus. It would seem that things were now different.

> He (Epaphroditus) longs for all of you and is distressed because you heard he was ill. Indeed he was ill, and almost died. But God had mercy on him, and not on him only but also on me, to spare me sorrow upon sorrow. (Philippians 2:26-27)

During the Acts period there would have been no need for the Philippians to have been concerned about the ill-health of one of their number. But afterwards there was. In Acts there would have been no need for Paul to have sorrowed. But afterwards there was. Thankfully, in His own good time, God restored Epaphroditus to health, but there was nothing instant and immediate about it, as there was throughout the Gospels and Acts. Healing was no longer guaranteed, as Timothy and Trophimus learned.

The instant and immediate healing, which during the Gospels and Acts was open to all, eventually ceased. This probably happened just after the announcement that Israel were to be left in their blind, deaf, and hardened condition, following which God's salvation was to be sent to the Gentiles (Acts 28:25-28). Healing, as a sign, was of great significance to the Jews, though it often confused the Gentiles. For example, when Paul healed a man in Lystra, the Gentiles thought Paul and Barnabas were Hermes and Zeus (Acts 14:8-13). On Malta the Gentiles thought Paul was a god when he did not die from a snake bite (Acts 28:6). Thus, in our study of healing, we can learn a lot about the subject by paying attention to whether the people involved were Jews or Gentiles and by noting what their reaction was. We can also learn from observing the change in the apostles' ability to heal which took place at the end of Acts

Sozo and *diasozo*

We must now turn our attention to the third column, the occurrences of *sozo* and *diasozo*. *A Critical Lexicon and Concordance* defines them as follows:

> *sozo*: to save, to rescue, to preserve, save from danger, loss and destruction.
>
> *diasozo*: to bring safely through danger or sickness.

These words occur about 114 times in the New Testament and in the vast majority of cases (about 90%) *sozo* is translated "save". In most of the others it is rendered "heal", but in some of these the translators are unsure and have supplied the alternative "save" in the margin or footnote. One place where it is rightly rendered "heal" is Matthew 14:35-36.

> People brought all their sick to him and begged him to let the sick just touch the edge of his cloak, and all who touched him were healed.

In our study of *sozo* and *diasozo* we will find nothing that contradicts what we have discovered so far about the subject. Healings during the Gospels and Acts were immediate and complete and open to all. After Acts nothing is said about healing. Where *sozo* occurs after Acts it is rightly translated "save". For example:

> It is by grace you have been saved ... For it is by grace you have been saved, through faith - and this not from yourselves, it is the gift of God - not by works, so that no-one can boast. (Ephesians 2:5,8)

After Acts it is never found in the context of illness or sickness, whereas it is in the earlier epistle of James (see 5:15).

Faith! For healing or salvation?

We mentioned earlier that we can learn much by paying attention to who was involved in the healings and their reactions to them. We can also learn much by noting *what* is being said. In practically all the cases of healing in the Gospels and Acts nothing is ever said about faith being necessary. However, a common view today is that great faith is needed by the sick person if he is to be healed. This is erroneous and is based upon a misunderstanding of a few verses which, seemingly, link faith and healing.

> In Lystra there sat a man crippled in his feet, who was lame from birth and had never walked. He listened to Paul as he was speaking. Paul looked directly at him, saw that he had faith to be healed (*sozo*) and called out, "Stand up on your feet!" At that, the man jumped up and began to walk. (Acts 14:8-10)

Should this expression be translated "Paul saw that he had faith to be *healed*?" Would it not have been better to have given *sozo* its primary meaning, *saved*? Paul was preaching the good news, the gospel of salvation (verses 6-7). We are told that the man listened to what Paul was saying (verse 9). Did the man believe the gospel Paul was preaching? Most likely he did, for Paul looked at him and saw that he had the faith to be ... *saved*. This is possibly a better translation and is consistent with the overall teaching of the New Testament, which is that our faith *saves* us. Both *Young's Literal Translation* of the Bible and the margin of the *Revised Version* have "saved" instead of "healed" in Acts 14:9.

I have dealt with this problem fully in the chapter on healing in *The Miracles of the Apostles*, to which the reader is referred. The following is taken from pages 110 and 111 of that book:

> Blind Bartimaeus was told "Your faith has healed (*sozo*) you," (Mark 10:52). Here even the translators of the *KJV* add, in the margin, "Thy faith hath *saved* thee," and this does seem more appropriate for we read that "Immediately he received his sight and followed Jesus along the road." Again both *Young* and the *RV* margin have "saved", and in the parallel account in Luke 18:42 the *KJV* has "Receive thy sight, thy faith hath *saved* (*sozo*) thee", which is more appropriate as verse 43 tells us, again, that "Immediately he received his sight and followed Jesus, praising God."
>
> In Luke 17:11-19, ten lepers were healed, but only one returned: a Samaritan, to whom the Lord said, "Your faith has made you well (*sozo*)". The other nine had no faith, yet they were cured. The one who returned praised God in a loud voice and worshipped Christ. So again, it is more fitting to translate Christ's words by "Your faith has *saved* (*sozo*) you," - as done by *Young* and the margin of the *RV*.

The book deals with all such passages but the above is sufficient to demonstrate the point.

Faith and the healer

We have shown above that faith was not required in a sick person for healing to be effective, neither during the Gospels nor in the Acts. If we read the various passages carefully, we see that it was the *healer* who was required to have faith. As Peter said:

> "By faith in the name of Jesus, this man whom you see and know was made strong. It is Jesus' name and the faith that comes through him that has given this complete healing to him, as you can all see." (Acts 3:16)

Peter is not referring to the man's faith. He had no faith, except, possibly, in money (Acts 3:5). Neither here, nor in Acts 4:9-10, does Peter mention anything about the faith of the sick man. That man had asked for money, not healing. He did not believe in the Lord Jesus, and certainly did not believe that Peter could heal him. Nothing could have been further from the man's thoughts.

In these passages Peter is referring to his own faith. He says that such a miracle of healing could be performed only by those who had faith in the Lord Jesus Christ. It was the miracle worker who had to have the faith, not the sick. This was in accordance with what the Lord Jesus Christ had told them after His resurrection.

> "These signs will accompany *those who believe* (in me) ... they will place their hands on sick people, and they will get well." (Mark 16:17-18)

Again, we read:

> Is any one of you sick? He should call the elders of the church to pray over him and anoint him with oil in the name of the Lord. And the prayer offered in faith will make the sick person well; the Lord will raise him up ... The prayer of a righteous man is powerful and effective. (James 5:14-16)

Here it was the elders who were to pray for the healing of the sick. It was their prayers which saved the sick - and their prayers did, if they were offered in faith. Faith was required by the elders, not by the sick person.

It was the prayer of a righteous man that was powerful and effective. If the sick person was not cured, then the prayers of the elders had not been offered in faith. If there was any failure to heal, then doubt must be cast upon the faith of the elders, not on that of the sick.

This was the situation during the Gospels and Acts. However, this was no longer the case after Acts. Paul's faith certainly was not suspect, yet he did not heal Timothy, Trophimus or Epaphroditus. This, again, indicates that there had been a change.

Application

Throughout the Lord's ministry while on earth, and throughout the ministry of the apostles during Acts, we have a clear line of teaching. Healing was open to all but a few (see chapters 15 and 16 for the exceptions). It was effective, immediate, and comprehensive. They were healed of whatever was wrong with them, immediately and completely. All that was required was faith in Christ - not faith on the part of the sick person, but faith on the part of the healer.

However, after the Acts things changed. There is no evidence of any instant and immediate healing, although Epaphroditus did get well after nearly dying. For us today it makes more sense to receive as truth for today the latest situation revealed in the Bible, rather than an earlier one. We learn that our faith guarantees our salvation. It does not mean that we will be cured of our illnesses or that we will be able to cure sickness in others.

15. Approaching passages

Jesus Christ is the same yesterday and today and forever (Hebrews 13:8)

We have looked at several subjects - the Sabbath, circumcision, and healing - and approached them in an objective manner by considering all that the Bible says about them. We have noted if and when the teaching changed and whether God was dealing with Jews differently from Gentiles.

We turn our attention now to some specific passages from the Bible. The first we shall consider is Hebrews 13:8. The words from that verse are quoted by some Christians to support the view that nothing has changed since the days when our Lord Jesus Christ walked this earth. He may be in heaven, they say, but He is the same yesterday and today and for ever, and they quote Hebrews 13:8 to support their view. He healed people when He was on earth, as the Gospels record. He healed people through the apostles, as the Acts records. Thus He should heal through Christians today, just as He did in Acts, for He never changes. He is the same yesterday and today and forever.

A closer look at this view reveals a number of difficulties. During His time on earth the Lord Jesus healed *all* who asked, immediately and completely - with the exception of the blind man at Bethsaida, who was healed in two stages, but in less than five minutes (Mark 8:22-26). All people were healed, no matter whether they had faith or not.

Similarly, during the period covered by the Acts of the Apostles we have numerous accounts of people being healed immediately and completely, and a casual reading of Acts may convince us that nothing has changed. However, 1 Corinthians 11:30, a letter written during Acts, records that some of the Christians at Corinth were weak and sick. Indeed, some died because they unworthily ate the bread and drank the wine when remembering the Lord's death.

James, too, was concerned about Christians who were sick because they had sinned. He told them they needed to confess their sins to the elders who were to pray for them. Then they would be forgiven and healed - James 5:14-16.

John instructed his readers to pray for a Christian brother who had committed a sin, but not if he had committed "a sin that leads to death" - 1 John 5:16-17; cf. Acts 5:1-10.

So although healing in the Gospels is similar to healing in Acts, to say that nothing has changed - to say it was the same yesterday and today and for ever - would be a dangerous over-simplification. In the Gospels *all* were healed. In Acts some Christians, those who had sinned in certain ways, were not healed.

But what, then, of the healings that are claimed for today? Does anyone heal as Christ did? He healed all who asked, whatever their physical, spiritual or moral condition. That does not happen today. So, has He changed?

Or perhaps He heals from heaven as He did during the Acts of the Apostles? Or is healing, today, more like that in the later parts of the New Testament, as it is in Paul's last letters?

Certainly there is no recorded instance of immediate healings in any of those letters - Ephesians, Colossians, Philemon, Philippians, Titus, 1 & 2 Timothy. In fact, in them, we have examples of keen Christians who were not healed immediately and completely: Epaphroditus in Philippians 2:25-27; Timothy in 1 Timothy 5:23, and Trophimus in 2 Timothy 4:20.

There is nothing to indicate that the illnesses of these people were the result of some sin. Timothy is called "my true son in the faith" (1 Timothy 1:2) and Paul gives him advice on how to cope with his condition. He does not tell him to stop sinning.

By comparing the Gospels with the Acts and letters written during Acts, and then by comparing these with the letters written after Acts, we see changes. The healings when Christ was on earth were different from those which happened during the Acts of the Apostles which, in their turn, were very different from what went on after Acts. And when we look at healing ministries today, we can only conclude that they have very little in common with what is recorded in the Gospels and Acts. So, Jesus Christ the same? Yesterday and today and forever?

Clearly, the way in which Christ works does change, and we should be glad that it does. When He sent out the Twelve He told them:

> "Do not go among the Gentiles or enter any town of the Samaritans. Go rather to the lost sheep of Israel." (Matthew 10:5-6)

However, in Matthew 28:19 He instructs the same group to "make disciples of all nations". In Luke 24:47 His words are:

> "Repentance and forgiveness of sins will be preached in his name to all nations...."

while in Acts 1:8 He tells them:

"You will be my witnesses in Jerusalem, and in all Judea and Samaria, and to the ends of the earth."

The One Who told the Canaanite woman that He "was sent only to the lost sheep of Israel" (Matthew 15:24) certainly appears to have changed His purposes. That being the case, what do we make of the words of Hebrews 13:8, "Jesus Christ is the same yesterday and today and forever"? Clearly the interpretation put on them by some Christians cannot be correct. What, then, is Hebrews talking about? We shall answer that question by first asking "Who?", "Where?", "When?", "What?" and "Why?", and then by seeking a valid application.

Who?

The letter to the Hebrews was clearly written to Hebrew Christians, as its title and contents makes clear. This may explain why many (Gentile) Christians today have difficulty understanding some parts of it.

Where?

The Hebrew Christians to whom this letter was sent may have been living in Jerusalem or Judea, but it may have been for those living in one of the countries of the eastern half of the Roman Empire, possibly in Galatia. The Jews who were scattered amongst these countries were known as the dispersion. They attended the local synagogue and tried to get to Jerusalem as often as they could to celebrate one of the major feasts of the Law.

When?

This letter was probably written during the second half of the period covered by the Acts of the Apostles. Certainly it makes sense placing it before Israel became blind and deaf due to their hard heartedness at the end of Acts (Acts 28:25-27). It seems unlikely to have been after this for it was written at a time when the old Mosaic covenant was ageing and soon to disappear (Hebrews 8:13). By the time Ephesians and Colossians were written that Law, together with its covenant, had been abolished (Ephesians 2:14-15; Colossians 2:14).

What?

Although we have considered "Who?", "Where?", and "When?", none of these has been a great help to us. As we have already mentioned, the suggested interpretation that Jesus Christ never changes in any of His dealings with men is simply not correct. As we have shown, there were some differences between the healings Christ did when on earth and the healings He did from heaven (through the apostles) during the Acts period. He also changed His instructions to the twelve when He was on earth.

This view that Christ never changes in the way He deals with mankind is caused by tearing Hebrews 13:8 from its context, which has nothing to do with healing or related miraculous subjects. The opening words of the chapter are:

> Keep on loving each other as brothers. Do not forget to entertain strangers, for by so doing some people have entertained angels without knowing it. Remember those in prison as if you were their fellow prisoners, and those who are ill-treated as if you yourselves were suffering. Marriage should be honoured by all, and the marriage bed kept pure, for God will judge the adulterer and all the sexually immoral. (Hebrews 13:1-4)

These verses are exhortations for the Hebrew Christians to keep on loving each other as brothers (v 1), to entertain strangers (v 2), to remember those in prisons (v 3), to remember those who have been ill-treated (v 3), to honour marriage and to keep the marriage bed pure (v 4). Then we read:

> Keep your lives free from the love of money and be content with what you have, because God has said,
>
> "Never will I leave you; never will I forsake you."
>
> So we say with confidence,
>
> "The Lord is my helper; I will not be afraid. What can man do to me?"
>
> Remember your leaders, who spoke the word of God to you. Consider the outcome of their way of life and imitate their faith. *Jesus Christ is the same yesterday and today and forever.* (Hebrews 13:5-8)

Money was then, as it is even now for some, a fatal attraction. The Hebrew Christians are told to be content with what they have for they have God and God will never leave them, nor forsake them. That is not true of money.

As God will never leave them nor forsake them, they should have said with the Psalmist, "The Lord is with me; I will not be afraid" (Psalm 118:6-7). To encourage them in this attitude, these Hebrew Christians were reminded of the lives of their leaders, which they were told to imitate. Whether this referred to their present leaders - Peter, James and John - or to past leaders (those recorded in Hebrews 11) matters not. Both sets spoke the word of God. Both sets of lives were notable and worthy of imitation. Both past and present leaders had had great faith and had been rewarded by the Lord for their faithfulness. And the Hebrew Christians, too, could be rewarded for their faithfulness because *Jesus Christ was the same yesterday and today and forever.* He would reward the Hebrew Christians being addressed here just as He had rewarded past and present leaders.

The Lord wanted them to love each other, to entertain strangers, to remember those in prisons and those who were being ill-treated. He wanted them to honour their marriages and to be faithful to their partners. He did not want them to give in to sexual desires or to the love of money. They would require help in doing all this and *He was the same yesterday and today and forever.* He would not leave them nor forsake them, just as he had not left or forsaken His people in the past (Deuteronomy 31:6) . He would be their helper, just as He had helped His people in the past (Psalm 118:6-7). He would help them, just as much as He had helped their leaders - past and present, and future.

There was no need for them to be afraid. Let them consider the lives of their leaders. Even though many of them had suffered in this life, the Lord would reward them in eternity. And *He was the same yesterday and today and forever.* He would reward the Hebrew Christians also.

Hebrews 13, then, is not dealing with healings or aspects of the miraculous. It is dealing with fundamental, unchanging aspects of the spiritual life. Clearly Christ changed His commands. Obviously a number of things changed during the years covered by the Old and New Testaments, but not everything. The Lord's nearness to His people has never changed, nor will it ever change. His willingness to help, strengthen, and encourage His people has been consistent. His ability to free them from fear has never altered. *How* He has helped, strengthened, encouraged, and freed His people may have changed, but not His desire, willingness, and ability to do so. This is what Hebrews 13 is dealing with and this is what verse 8 is emphasising when it states that "*Jesus Christ is the same yesterday and today and forever.*"

Why?

Hebrew Christians during the period covered by the Acts of the Apostles had a difficult time. If they lived in Jerusalem and Judea they would be surrounded by many of their fellow countrymen who rejected the claims that Jesus was the Messiah, the Son of God.

There were persecutions from the high priests and temple authorities and, at one time, all except the apostles were forced to flee from Jerusalem (Acts 8:1). The Sadducees, who did not believe in resurrection or any life after death, would have been the hardest opponents. There was oppression under Herod (Acts 12:1-4). There was famine (Acts 11:28).

For those Hebrew Christians living outside the land of Israel there would have been other difficulties. The Jewish communities were small and close knit. They formed an homogenous, comfortable clique. They would have been disturbed by the claims that Jesus of Nazareth was the Messiah. Some believed, but some did not. Those who did not believe made it very difficult for those who did, and in some places the Hebrew Christians were driven from the synagogue (Acts 18:1-7).

It is very enlightening to read through the Acts of the Apostles with the Hebrew Christians in mind. Things were difficult for them and their families, whether they lived in Israel or outside it. Some gave up Christianity and went back to Judaism. Others were beginning to falter. The writer to the Hebrews had to remind them that "it is impossible for the blood of bulls and goats to take away sins" (Hebrews 10:4).

Hebrews seems to have been written to correct and encourage the Hebrew Christians of the Acts period. It may have been hard for them, but it had been hard for their past leaders, and it was hard for their present ones. However, the Lord was there, and always had been there, and always will be there. He was there for them that day. He would be there for them tomorrow. He would not leave them. He would not forsake them. He would help and comfort them because *He was the same yesterday and today and forever.*

Application

If we keep in mind that Hebrews 13:1-8 is not talking about the ministry of healing or the ability to work certain miracles, but is concerned with God being near and helping His people as they try to live godly lives, then it can be applied to our lives today. If we realise that it is not talking about the way in which God helps people (for that did change from the Gospels to the Acts and beyond to the post-Acts) but is dealing with the fact that He still does help, then what was written to encourage the Hebrew Christians can encourage us.

God wants us to live lives worthy of the name of Christ. However, we all know how difficult that is. We have all been tempted at one time or another, in one way or another, to compromise our Christian principles, but we should never yield to such temptation. We need to hold fast and firm to them, realising with Paul that "I can do all things through Christ which strengtheneth me" (Philippians 4:13, *KJV*); the "all things" being defined by the context (Philippians 4:6-12) and including contentment (cf. Hebrews 13:5).

When concluding his letter to the Philippians, Paul reminded them that "God will meet all your needs according to his glorious riches in Christ Jesus" (Philippians 4:19). And again, "all needs" must be understood in the context of the letter, which is primarily to do with contentment, peace of mind, and the inner needs of man.

So for us Gentile Christians today, as for the Hebrews, *Jesus Christ is the same yesterday and today and forever*. He will never leave us nor forsake us, although the way in which He helps us may be different from the way in which He helped them.

We can say with the Psalmist of old, "God is our refuge and strength, an ever present help in trouble" (Psalm 46:1). However, the way in which He helps us may be different from the way in which He helped the Psalmist.

Thus *Jesus Christ is the same yesterday and today and forever* is not a statement that the Lord will never change anything that He is doing. Clearly He has done so. It is a statement concerning His unchanging care and concern, His unfailing love and help. These have never changed, but the way in which they have been manifested has changed. We need to distinguish between the "*what?*" and the "*how?*". The "What?", His love, never changes. The "How?", how that love is manifest, does.

16. Approaching passages

Sins - Unforgivable and Unto Death

In Romans 3:23 Paul wrote that "all have sinned and fall short of the glory of God". The *all* shows that there is no difference between people, and the statement itself emphasises what he had just written, namely "There is no-one righteous, not even one" (v 10). Thankfully, from this sad predicament mankind has a happy release, for "God made you alive with Christ. He forgave us *all* our sins" (Colossians 2:13). But are all sins forgivable? The Bible does talk about an unforgivable sin, and about a sin that leads to death. Is that death a physical one or a spiritual one? In this chapter we shall look first at the unforgivable sin and then at the sin that leads to death.

The unforgivable sin

In Psalm 25 David prayed that the Lord would look upon his affliction and distress and take away (forgive) *all* his sins (v 18). This prayer was answered, but what if David had committed the unforgivable sin? What is the unforgivable sin? And was it possible for people in David's day to commit it?

In his first letter John wrote "If we confess our sins, he is faithful and just and will forgive us our sins and purify us from *all* unrighteousness" (1:9). But what if some of the people John was writing to had committed the unforgivable sin? Could they be purified from its effects? What is the unforgivable sin? And was it possible for people in John's day to commit it?

And what of people today? Some on the fringe of Christian circles may have heard something or other about something which cannot be forgiven. They fear that things done in their past life may have included it. They worry because they fear they can never receive forgiveness. What is the unforgivable sin? And is it possible for people today to commit it?

We shall attempt to answer these questions by approaching the passages which deal with this subject first, by asking the questions "Who?", "Where?", "When?", "What?", "Why?", and then by seeking an application.

Who? and Where?

There are only two passages in the Bible which mention the subject of the unforgivable sin.

> Anyone who speaks a word against the Son of Man will be forgiven, but anyone who speaks against the Holy Spirit will not be forgiven, either in this age or in the age to come. (Matthew 12:32)

> And everyone who speaks a word against the Son of Man will be forgiven, but anyone who blasphemes against the Holy Spirit will not be forgiven. (Luke 12:10)

The context of the first is Matthew 12:22-37. Some people brought to the Lord Jesus a demon-possessed man and He healed him. On seeing this miracle the people began to wonder whether or not Jesus was the Son of David, that is the Messiah. However, the Pharisees, on hearing what the people were saying and after seeing what Christ had done, said:

> "It is only by Beelzebub, the prince of demons, that this fellow drives out demons." (v 24)

Then follows the passage which deals with the unforgivable sin, and the words are addressed to the Pharisees (Matthew 12:24).

Luke 11:14-26 deals, again, with those who accuse Christ of casting out demons by the power of Beelzebub. In verse 29 they are described as a wicked generation for demanding a miraculous sign, and verses 37-52 contain six "woes", aimed at the Pharisees and the experts in the Mosaic Law. Luke 12:1 opens with the Lord talking to His disciples and warning them about the hypocrisy of the Pharisees and, again, His comments in verse 10 about the unforgivable sin concern the Pharisees.

This is all that the Bible has to say on the subject and it would seem, then, that these words were spoken by Christ in Judea and were a response to a certain attitude adopted towards His miracles by some of the Pharisees.

What?

From the start of His ministry, the Lord Jesus Christ healed every disease and sickness. News of Him spread far and wide. People brought to Him all those who were ill, including the demon-possessed, and He healed every one (Matthew 4:23-25). This situation continued for quite some time. A large company began to follow Christ, much to the distress of the Sadducees, the Pharisees, and the experts in the Law. They started to oppose what Christ taught. They had a hard time, for His teaching had authority and was validated by the miraculous signs which He did. If their arguments against what Christ taught were to carry weight, then they had, in some way, to discredit what He was doing. In order to do this they were prepared to go to some extreme lengths.

The episode before us starts off with a demon-possessed man being healed before a crowd of people. They responded by asking whether this Jesus was the Son of David, their Messiah. This was too much for the Pharisees, but what could they do about it? They had seen the miracle with their own eyes, and not only *that* miracle, but many, many more. For quite some time Christ had been going about the country healing all manner of sicknesses, casting out demons, feeding people. Everyone was talking about this Man and what He was doing and saying. The religious leaders went to see for themselves, to hear what He was teaching and see what He was doing. Did they believe what He taught? Did they accept the testimony of the miraculous signs that He was performing right in front of their own eyes? It would seem not. They were at a loss to explain them and, on this occasion, attributed Christ's power to Beelzebub. But who was Beelzebub?

We read of Baal-Zebub, the god of Ekron, in 2 Kings 1:2,3,16. *The Companion Bible* is helpful on this verse.

> Baal-zebub = Lord of flies. Later Jews polluted it by changing it to Beel-zebul (Lord of dung or dunghills). In Matthew 12:24 it is in Greek Baal-zebul = Lord of abominable idols; the prince of idols and idolatry; the worst and chief of all wickedness. Imagine the blasphemy.

Thus the Pharisees attributed Christ's miracle, not to the power of the Holy Spirit, but to the power of the prince of demons, the worst and chief of all wickedness. They were eyewitnesses of what Christ had done, not only on that occasion, but on others also. Yet they would not accept the clear testimony of what was staring them in the face. The Scriptures told them that when the Messiah came the eyes of the blind would be opened and the ears of the deaf unstopped. The lame would leap like a deer and the tongue of the dumb shout for joy (Isaiah 35:4-6). They saw all this, and more, with their own eyes. The ordinary people saw it and asked "Could this be the Son of David?" The more informed Pharisees saw it and said "It is only by Beelzebub, the prince of demons, that this fellow drives out demons" (Matthew 12:23-24). Christ's answer, in verses 25-37, shows the sheer stupidity of such a comment. However, it also shows the seriousness of it.

First the Lord told them that if He was driving out demons by the Spirit of God, then the kingdom of God had come upon them. Next He told them that to attribute the miracles that He was doing to Beelzebub, rather than to the Spirit of God, constituted blasphemy against the Holy Spirit and that this could not be forgiven, neither in this age nor in the one to come. It was unforgivable.

When?

This teaching concerning the unforgivable sin was given by Christ when He was on earth. His words seem to be a comment on and a condemnation of certain people who were there at that time, who were eye-witnesses of what He was doing. These people stood there before Him and were obstructing Him, and trying to discredit Him and the source of His power.

Christ's words on the subject of the unforgivable sin do not seem to describe any people of either the past or the future. They are concerned with that unique situation which was peculiar to His time on earth. They were said to people who were there at the time when He was on earth, who saw what He was doing and who attributed His miraculous signs not to the Holy Spirit but to Beelzebub.

Why?

Blasphemy, today, is usually connected with swearing or uttering oaths which abuse the names of God and Christ. Many of us have been distressed by people with whom we work blaspheming in this way. It is, however, interesting that blasphemies which abuse the Spirit do not exist in the English idiom. One etymologist has suggested that blasphemous expressions abusing the name of the Holy Spirit (or Holy Ghost) do not exist because in the past people were afraid that to use them would be committing a sin which could not be forgiven, neither in this age nor in the age to come. However, a consideration of what the Bible has to say on the subject of the unforgivable sin reveals that this type of blasphemy (i.e. swearing abusively) is nowhere in the context. The use of the Spirit's name in a derogatory way is as wrong as using the names of God and Christ in a similar fashion, but it is not unforgivable. What was unforgivable was attributing Christ's power to Beelzebub rather than to the Spirit.

The root-meaning of the Hebrew word for blasphemy is "an act of effrontery in which the *honour* of God is insulted by man" (*New Bible Dictionary*). In these passages from Matthew and Luke we have seen that, instead of attributing Christ's miracles to the Spirit of God, the Pharisees said that the power came from Beelzebub, the prince of demons, the chief of all wickedness. Could there be any greater effrontery than that? Could God's *honour* be more seriously abused?

These people knew their Scriptures. They knew what the prophets said the Messiah would do. They saw what the Lord Jesus was doing. If they had opposed Christ simply by rejecting what He said and did and said nothing, they could have been forgiven and given another opportunity later to repent, just as the majority of Israel were during the Acts period. However, to oppose Christ by attributing the source of His power to the worst of all wickedness was unforgivable. It was blasphemy against the Holy Spirit and could not be forgiven.

Application

It is impossible for anyone, other than those who heard what Christ taught and saw the miracles that He did, to blaspheme against the Holy Spirit in the unforgivable way described in Matthew 12 and Luke 12. The special position they were in has never been repeated. It was a unique time. They were a highly privileged people. Thus no one at any other time can commit this unforgivable sin.

The words which Christ uttered were to, and about, a very specific group of people, at a very special moment in time. It was when He was on earth, teaching and preaching, healing and helping. What He said concerned a certain group of people who heard what He preached and taught, and who saw how He healed and helped. They were eyewitnesses of God's power exhibited in Christ's miracles. If they had rejected it all, and left it at that, they could have had another chance. If they attributed these works to the prince of demons, the chief of all wickedness, that was unforgivable. There was no second chance.

People today cannot be eyewitnesses to Christ's miracles and so they are not in the same position as those Pharisees of old. I doubt if any today would attribute Christ's miraculous powers to Beelzebub. The vast majority wouldn't even know who Beelzebub was!

Maybe some people today do not believe the biblical record concerning Christ's miracles. That is sad, but it is not unforgivable. We should try to convince them of the truth of what the Bible says about

Jesus of Nazareth. His miracles show not only that He was the Messiah of Israel, but that He was also the Saviour of the World.

In conclusion

There are some Christians today who attribute certain extreme charismatic manifestations, the frothing at the mouth and rolling on the floor, to the power of Satan, rather than the power of the Spirit. These Christians are charged by such charismatics with committing the unforgivable sin, but such a charge is not sustainable for a number of reasons.

First, these charismatics are not Christ and only He has the authority to say what is forgivable and unforgivable.

Second, Christ's words concerning the unforgivable sin were aimed not at those who believed in Him, but at those who did not and who actively opposed Him. Thus they can have no application to Christians.

Third, Christians have been guaranteed eternal life by grace, through faith in Christ's death on the cross, through His being a sacrifice for their sins. That being the case, nothing can separate them from the love of God that is in Christ Jesus (Romans 4:16; 6:5; 8:35-39). As a result it is impossible for any Christian to commit any sin which is unforgivable. To attribute certain unusual phenomena of today to Satan, rather than emotion, may be wrong, but it is not unforgivable.

* * * * *

The sin that leads to death

Although it is impossible for Christians to commit any sin that is unforgivable, the Bible does speak of their committing sins that lead to death.

> If anyone sees his brother commit a sin that does not lead to death, he should pray and God will give him life. I refer to those whose sin does not lead to death. There is a sin that leads to death. I am not saying that he should pray about that. All wrongdoing is sin, and there is sin that does not lead to death. (1 John 5:16-17)

Here John writes about two different types of sin. One led to death. The other did not. He encouraged his writers to pray for those who committed the latter. However, he discouraged them from praying for those who committed the former. What then was this sin, or these sins, which led to death? And can Christians, today, commit them and die in the same way?

When?

The majority of commentators date John's writings towards the end of the first century, making him the last contributor to the New Testament. However, E.W. Bullinger, in *The Companion Bible*, states that "The character of the contents indicates a much earlier date than is usually supposed". J.A.T. Robinson in *Redating the New Testament* and *The Primacy of John* dates John's writings early. The implication is that John wrote for Hebrew Christians during Acts and this agrees with the internal evidence of the Bible. Christ told John that he was to be one of the twelve who were to sit on twelve thrones judging the twelve tribes of Israel (Matthew 19:28). Then, in Galatians 2:7-9, we read of the task given Paul and Barnabas, on the one hand, and Peter, James and John, on the other.

> On the contrary, they saw that I (Paul) had been given the task of preaching the gospel to the Gentiles, just as Peter had been given the task of preaching to gospel to the Jews. For God, who was at work in the ministry of Peter as an apostle to the Jews, was also at work in my ministry as an apostle to the Gentiles. James, Peter and John, those reputed to be pillars, gave me and Barnabas the right hand of fellowship when they recognised the grace given to me. They agreed that we should go to the Gentiles, and *they to the Jews.*

As God's salvation was sent to the Gentiles at the end of Acts, following Israel's blindness, deafness and hardness, it seems clear that John's ministry to Israel must be kept within the period covered by the Acts of the Apostles.

Who? and Where?

Both Peter and James wrote during the Acts of the Apostles to those Israelites who were scattered amongst the cities of the Roman Empire (1 Peter 1:1; James 1:1). It would seem that John did the same, for he shared in this ministry with them (Galatians 2:7-9). Also, he is the only other New Testament writer to use the word *diaspora*, a technical term referring to the dispersed or scattered Israelites (John 7:35).

As stated previously, there would have been little point in John writing to the nation of Israel after it had hardened its heart, closed its ears, and shut its eyes - a situation reached at the end of Acts (Acts 28:25-28). From then on God's salvation was sent to the Gentiles. The ministry of Peter, James, and John to the Jews seems confined to the Acts period. In fact, Josephus informs us that James was stoned to death in Jerusalem at the end of the Acts period (see *The Antiquities of the Jews; 20,9,1*).

These verses in John's first letter are the only ones which specifically talk about people committing the sin that leads to death. However, we can learn much about this subject by comparing it with other passages written during Acts.

> Is any one of you sick? He should call the elders of the church to pray over him and anoint him with oil in the name of the Lord. And the prayer offered in faith will make the sick person well; the Lord will raise him up. If he has sinned, he will be forgiven. Therefore confess your sins to each other and pray for each other so that you may be healed. The prayer of a righteous man is powerful and effective. (James 5:14-16)

Here the confession of sin is not by an unsaved person for salvation. Rather it is by the believer for healing. Note: "Therefore confess your sins to each other ... *so that* you may be healed."

At that time, during the Acts period, it was possible for Christians to be afflicted with ill-health because they had sinned. But are John, and James, writing about illnesses which can result from extremely bad behaviour? For example, a person may develop venereal diseases or AIDS as a result of sexual promiscuity, or cirrhosis of the liver from consuming excessive alcohol. Are these in the category of the "sin that leads to death", as we might be tempted to think? A passage from one of Paul's Acts period letters may help us here.

> Therefore, whoever eats the bread or drinks the cup of the Lord in an unworthy manner will be guilty of sinning against the body and blood of the Lord. A man ought to examine himself before he eats of the bread and drinks of the cup. For anyone who eats and drinks without recognising the body of the Lord eats and drinks judgment on himself. That is why many among you are weak and sick, and a number of you have fallen asleep (died). (1 Corinthians 11:27-30)

It would appear, then, that the reason why some of the Corinthian Christians were weak and sick, and why others had died, was not because of any sexual immorality. Rather it was because they had eaten the bread and drunk the cup in an unworthy manner, possibly by being drunk (1 Corinthians 11:21). So drunkenness at the Lord's Supper may have been a "sin that leads to death".

Acts records other incidents of a person's sin leading to death. In Acts 5:1-10 first Ananias, and then his wife Sapphira fell down dead because they told lies to Peter and the rest of the apostles. In Acts 12:21-23, Herod was struck dead when, following a great speech, the people said:

> "This is the voice of a god, not of a man." Immediately, because Herod did not give praise to God, an angel of the Lord struck him down, and he was eaten by worms and died.

What?

Some have suggested that in 1 John 5:16-17 the writer is dealing with what they term *mortal sin*, that is sin which results in spiritual death. However, the concept of *believers* committing sins which lead to the spiritual death, and hence to losing their eternal life, is foreign to the Bible. It may have been possible for *unbelievers* to commit sins which were unforgivable, and so ensure that they could never gain eternal life (see the earlier part of this chapter), but for believers to lose their eternal life and suffer spiritual death is not the teaching of the Bible.

It seems most likely that John had in mind one of the sins we have mentioned above. It may have been lying to fellow believers, not giving praise to God, being drunk at the Lord's supper or, possibly, it may have been some other sin. However, we can be sure that the death he was talking about was not a spiritual one but a physical one: death in this world. He wanted his readers to pray for Christians who had committed certain sins, the sins that did not lead to death. Maybe those who had committed such sins were weak and sick. Confession of those sins to the elders followed by prayers offered in faith by righteous men would restore them (James 5:15-16).

On the other hand, if the sin committed was one that was to lead to death, John stated that there was no point in praying for them to be healed (1 John 5:16).

Why?

During the period covered by the Acts of the Apostles it is easy to forget that the Jews were still subject to the Law of Moses. This was not only true of the ordinary Jews, those who had not come to believe Jesus was the Messiah, but it was also the case for Christian Jews. They may not have been *under* the Law for righteousness, but they continued to observe it as the right way of life (Acts 21:20-24).

Part of that Law consisted of blessings for obedience and judgments for disobedience (Deuteronomy 28; see vs 1-14 for blessings and vs 15-68 for judgments and note especially v 22). During the Acts the Jewish Christians received many great blessings from the hand of the Lord. Healings, for instance, abounded. However, the other side of the coin was judgment, and it is interesting to note that where judgment did fall, it appears to have fallen only upon Jews. Ananias and Sapphira (Acts 5) were both Jewish Christians. Elymas the sorcerer, who was struck with blindness in Acts 13:6-12, was a Jew. Herod was King of the Jews (Acts 12:1,21-23). The letter to James was addresses to "the twelve tribes scattered abroad" and John's ministry, as we have seen from Galatians 2:7-9, was also to the Jews. But what about 1 Corinthians? True, there were Gentiles in the Corinthian church, but some of the letter is addressed to Jewish Christians, some to Gentile Christians and some to them both. 1 Corinthians 10:1 starts a section aimed at the Jewish Christians which seems to continue throughout chapters 10 and 11. However, 1 Corinthians 12:1-2 commences a new section, one for the Gentile Christians who had been pagans.

Those verses in 1 Corinthians 11 which deal with weakness, sickness and death, due to an abuse of the Lord's supper, are within a Jewish section of the letter. This would make sense as the Jews were the people to whom the new covenant was promised; compare 1 Corinthians 11:25 with Jeremiah 31:31-34. For Jewish Christians to abuse the cup which symbolised the blood of the new covenant was serious indeed.

There does not seem to be any record of any Gentile Christian during Acts, or afterwards, being subject to direct judgment from God, either in death or by illness.

However, for Jews during the Acts period the situation seems to have been a little more complicated. Some sins were punished with death, others with sickness or illness, while still others were not penalised at all. By this God was guiding and protecting, disciplining and purifying the faithful remnant of the nation of Israel, those who had accepted the Lord Jesus as their Messiah.

Application

As mentioned above, there is no record in the New Testament, either in the Gospels, during the Acts period or afterwards, of any Gentile

Christians suffering direct judgment from the hand of God for any of the sins they may have committed. Such judgments fell upon the Jews, whether Christian or not, as part of the promises of Deuteronomy 28. However, once the nation of Israel had lost its primary place and special privileges at the end of Acts, promises of temporal blessings and immediate judgments ceased. The law with its commandments and regulations was abolished (Ephesians 2:15; Colossians 2:14).

The Gentiles now came to the fore. The salvation of God was sent directly to them and a new period, "the administration (dispensation) of God's grace", commenced (Acts 28:26-28; Ephesians 3:2). It is true that God's grace had always been on earth, from Adam's time onwards. However, grace had not *characterised* any previous age as there had always been the possibility of judgments, some of which were catastrophic, like the flood. In contrast to this, the age in which we live, which was heralded at the end of Acts, is characterised by grace. The destruction of Jerusalem and its temple in AD 70, a few years after the end of Acts, may be seen as God's outward act of demonstrating to Israel that the Law had, indeed, been abolished, that the door had been firmly closed on Israel (Ephesians 2:14-15; Colossians 2:14).

Grace characterises this age. It is how God deals with all people. Throughout this time He has not directly and immediately judged anyone on earth for any wrong they may have done. Thus there is no "sin that leads to death" today. Neither are there any sins which, as a result of God's immediate judgment, cause Christians to be weak and sick.

Of course, if we abuse our bodies then there is a natural law that still operates. "A man reaps what he sows", says Galatians 6:7. A person who gets drunk may feel ill with a hangover. A person who indulges in fornication may catch a venereal disease. Homosexual activity may result in AIDS and, ultimately, death. These, and many others, are the natural consequences of the world in which we live. They are *natural* judgments, not direct judgments from God.

As for Christians today, many commit sins and suffer nothing physically from doing so. However, such behaviour has a detrimental effect upon our Christian lives. It also grieves the Holy Spirit with Whom we are sealed (Ephesians 4:30). We may not be subject to direct judgment for our sins in this age of grace, but that does not mean that God views them as any less serious. To use grace as an excuse for continuing in sin is untenable.

> What shall we say, then? Shall we go on sinning, so that grace may increase? By no means! We died to sin; how can we live in it any longer? (Romans 6:1-2)

When we believed in the Lord Jesus we were given a new nature. We were identified with Christ in His death, in His burial and in His resurrection, and we were sealed with the Holy Spirit. Our responsibility as believers is to live in a new way, one appropriate to all that God has done for us in Christ and to the position in which He has placed us in Christ.

In conclusion

This approach to these passages has taught us a number of important lessons about sin. It is true that even today all people sin and come short of God's glory. However, no one today can commit the unforgivable sin and so forgiveness is open to all. Also today there are no sins which lead to death, for God no longer judges people instantly. None the less, our behaviour is of great concern to our Saviour and, if selfish and immoral, can grieve the Holy Spirit with whom we are sealed. That being the case let us endeavour to shun all sin.

17. Approaching passages

I will do whatever you ask in my name
John 14:13-14; see also John 16:23-24

There are many problems associated with promises such as these and it is difficult to know where to begin. It may be best to start with ourselves and our fellow-believers. All of us have presented petitions to God and have *not* received what we have asked for. All of us have made intercessions for others, only to wait in vain for something to happen. Initially, we think our form of prayer may be incorrect and not acceptable. We learn to end our prayers with "This we ask in the name of our Lord and Saviour, Jesus Christ". But even that formula does not work. Many of our petitions go unanswered. Did we read the promise correctly in the first place?

> "I tell you the truth, anyone who has faith in me will do what I have been doing. He will do even greater things than these, because I am going to the Father. And I will do whatever you ask in my name, so that the Son may bring glory to the Father. You may ask me for anything in my name, and I will do it." (John 14:12-14)

> "In that day you will no longer ask me anything. I tell you the truth, my Father will give you whatever you ask in my name. Until now you have not asked for anything in my name. Ask and you will receive, and your joy will be complete." (John 16:23-24)

We did read it correctly, so what is the problem? We tend to think the reason why our prayers are not answered lies with us. Our attention turns to such passages as Matthew 21:22. There the Lord said:

> "If you believe, you will receive whatever you ask for in prayer."

But is Christ speaking about faith in Him as Saviour, which we have? Or is He talking about the need to believe that He has the ability to do what we ask, which we also have? Or do we need to believe that He not only has the ability, but also that *He will do* what we ask? This faith we may have had, at one time. However, we may no longer possess it because so many of our requests have not been granted. We have not had what we asked for in His name.

Alternatively, we may look to the other writings of John, where we read:

> We have confidence before God and receive from him anything we ask, because we obey his commands and do what pleases him. (1 John 3:21-22)

We may be tempted to conclude that the reason our requests have not been granted is because we do not please Him. Our petitions are not fulfilled because our level of obedience is below that which He requires for answering prayers. Our worthy walk may be far from worthy. But is that true of all the saints who have experienced this problem before us?

Then there are the words of 1 John 5:14-15.

> This is the assurance we have in approaching God: that if we ask anything according to his will, he hears us. And if we know that he hears us - whatever we ask - we know that we have what we have asked of him.

We may conclude that even though our form of prayer is correct, being asked in Christ's name, and even though we obey His commands, what we have asked for was not in accordance with His will. That may be correct, but that does leave us rather puzzled as to why so many seemingly good and proper things, for which Christians intercede on behalf of others, are not God's will. Are we more humanitarian than He is? More loving? More caring? Of course not! But how does it appear to unbelievers?

As usual we have created many problems for ourselves because we have not approached the passages in a systematic and objective manner. We shall now attempt to do so, asking the questions "Who?", "Where?", "When?", "What?", and "Why?" before seeking an application for Christians today.

Who? and Where?

We need to appreciate first of all that the Lord's promises in both John 14 and 16 were made to the twelve disciples. He had just washed their feet (John 13:1-17), forecast Judas' betrayal (13:18-30), and told Peter of his impending denials (13:31-38). Then, in chapter 14, He spoke to the remaining eleven, Judas having left (13:30). He replied to questions put by Thomas (verse 5), Philip (verse 8) and Judas, not Iscariot (verse 22). All of chapters 14, 15 and 16 are addressed to the remaining eleven.

This is also true of the words of Matthew 21:22, where we read, "If you believe, you will receive whatever you ask for in prayer". These were addressed to the disciples - see verse 20.

When?

Now it would be unwise to suggest that these promises were given exclusively to the eleven and for them alone. John's first letter shows that others did share in the promise of having their prayers answered. Thus it is pertinent to ask when the promise was given and for what time, or times, it was operative. The former is easy to answer: It was given by Christ on the night of His arrest. The latter is not so easy to answer.

It is quite obvious to many believers that this promise is not true for Christians alive today. Some think it was meant for the years following His ascension into heaven: that is the period covered by the Acts of the Apostles. However, even that view has problems. For example, James was imprisoned and executed by Herod in Acts 12:1-2. Didn't anyone think to pray for James' safekeeping and release? Didn't they believe God could free him and save him? Didn't any of them obey God's commands sufficiently well to have their prayers answered? Wasn't it God's will to free James?

All this stands in contrast to Peter's situation, described just a few verses later. He had been arrested a little while after James' execution and placed in prison. Although the believers prayed for him (Acts 12:5), it was hardly believing prayer (verses 15-16). When Peter was released by an angel, the disciples did not believe it!

A study of Acts and the letters written during that time can lead only to the conclusion that the disciples and believers of that age did *not* receive whatever they asked for in Christ's name. On three occasions Paul pleaded with God to remove his "thorn in the flesh", but his request was refused (2 Corinthians 12:7-9). Because of this, some commentators have suggested that the promise given by Christ has not yet been fulfilled, but will be in the future, after Christ's return, during the millennial kingdom. That may or may not be correct. However, the difficulties we have with the teaching of these verses may be due to our misunderstanding of the exact meaning of the words and phrases used.

What?

When we look at John 14:13-14 and 16:23 there are two sets of words which require comment. First there is *whatever* and *anything*. And then there is *in my name*. We shall deal with *whatever* and *anything* first.

There are various words in any language which, in their literal sense, are all-embracing: for example everybody, everything. However, in normal use they seldom take that literal meaning. We may ask before the commencement of a meeting, "Is everybody ready?", meaning not every person in the world, but everyone of an understood, limited, and restricted group. Similarly before a meal we may ask, "Is everything ready?"

The words *whatever* and *anything* fall into this category. They seldom take their literal meanings. That being the case, when the Lord Jesus said to the disciples, "I will do *whatever* you ask in my name ... you may ask *anything* in my name and I will do it", He was not giving them a blank cheque.

Sometimes, where such words occur, the context makes it clear what is the *everything*, and who is meant by *everybody*. However, John 14-16 does not seem to define for us what the Saviour meant by *whatever* and *anything*. On the other hand, it would be wrong for us to insist upon their literal meaning when quite clearly neither Thomas, nor Philip, nor any of the disciples ever received everything they asked for, and it is doubtful whether they expected to. No doubt Christ's words to them were spoken in a context in which they would have understood what He meant by *whatever* and *anything*, even if we do not.

But what did Christ mean when He told them about asking *in my name*? I suppose many of us have held the simplistic view which imagines that provided we end our prayers, "And this we ask in the name of our Lord and Saviour, Jesus Christ" we have asked in His name. However, this cannot be what Christ meant by it.

In *Jesus, Then and Now*, Metropolitan Anthony writes:

> To ask in Christ's name means to ask with the intention that my prayer should be that of Christ if he were here in my place. It is not a way of forcing God's hand. When Christ says, "Whatever you ask in my name it shall be done to you", it does not mean we can force his hand by saying, "It is in Christ's name that I will do it, and therefore you must". It means that from within my oneness with Christ these are the words I speak. If there is no oneness in Christ in what you ask, then you are not speaking in Christ's name. I think any Christian prayer should be such that Christ could have said it in our place.

Thus, to ask anything in Christ's name means to ask what He would ask if He was in our situation. If we do that, then the prayer will be answered. If we ask for something different, then it will not. That being the case, we return to the problem of James' imprisonment and death in Acts 12:1-2. Maybe the disciples did obey God's commands. Perhaps they did believe that God had both the power to save and free James, and that He would do so. However, to have prayed for his release would not have been *in Christ's name*. It was not something Christ would have asked for if He had been there, possibly because He had predicted that James, and his brother John, were to be martyred (Mark 10:38-40).

Why?

On the night of His arrest, the Lord Jesus told His disciples that He was going away and that He would be leaving them (John 14:1-4,28). The time was coming when they would be without Him, when they would not see Him. However, they had seen His power and heard His prayers, and had seen them answered. How were they going to manage without Him?

In John 14 Christ told them that they, too, could have their prayers answered, just as He had had His answered. They had only to ask *in His name*. In other words, if they asked for what He would have asked for if He had been there, then they would receive it. This He would do "so that the Son may bring glory to the Father" (John 14:13). In His life on earth He sought not to please Himself, but the Father Who sent Him (John 5:30). Following His resurrection and ascension He wanted only to bring glory to the Father and this could be achieved by the disciples praying for what Christ would have prayed for and by God granting their requests.

Application

It may be the case that this passage was true for the disciples and their associates during the time covered by the Acts of the Apostles and has little application to Christians today. Accepting the limitations on *whatever* and *anything*, there are some outstanding answers to prayers in Acts and so one can see how that promise was fulfilled at that time.

In conclusion

There may, nevertheless, be an application of these passages to this age in which we live. It is this:

If Christians of the Acts period asked for what Christ would have asked for if He had been there, then their prayers were answered. So too for us today. If we ask for what Christ would ask for if He were here in our place, then our prayers will be answered also. However, we need to recognise that in this age Christ may well want and ask for something different from what He would have wanted and asked for during Acts.

18. Approaching passages

666 - The Mark of the Beast

> He ordered them to set up an image in honour of the beast who was wounded by the sword and yet lived. He was given power to give breath to the image of the first beast, so that it could speak and cause all who refused to worship the image to be killed. He also forced everyone, small and great, rich and poor, free and slave, to receive a mark on his right hand or on his forehead, so that no-one could buy or sell unless he had the mark, which is the name of the beast or the number of his name. This calls for wisdom. If anyone has insight, let him calculate the number of the beast, for it is man's number. His number is 666. (Revelation 13:14-18)

The above passage, and its context, has caught the imagination of many great writers throughout the centuries, George Orwell's *1984* presenting, perhaps, the outstanding example of an all-knowing, oppressive government.

Recently, it would seem, some Christian writers and film makers have allowed their imaginations to run wild as they have considered and commented upon this chapter and these verses from Revelation. Many books have been written, dramatising the terrible effects of such an oppressive ruler upon the citizens of this world. Films such as *Thief in the Night* and its sequel, *Distant Thunder*, are centred on a family in a typical town in America. There the people have to swear allegiance to a poster of this world ruler and receive his mark, 110 110 110 - 666 in binary. If they refuse to do this, they are guillotined! The message of this film is that this situation is to happen everywhere in the world to everyone. The choice for the entire population is between death and the mark of the beast. Yet is this scenario correct?

The Bible tells us that the downfall of this great ruler is brought about by the return of the Lord Jesus Christ, Who will destroy him by the splendour of His coming (2 Thessalonians 2:8). Christ then sets up His kingdom upon this earth; but who is to be part of this kingdom? We learn that the names of those who worship the beast and who receive his mark will not be written in the book of life and that the wrath of God is poured out upon them (Revelation 13:8; 14:9-11; 16:2). These people, therefore, cannot enter the kingdom Christ is to set up. However, those who refuse to receive the mark are to be killed. They will be raised from the dead when Christ returns and will reign with Him over His kingdom for a thousand years (Revelation 20:4). But over whom will they reign? Who will be in this kingdom, other than a few people who have managed to escape the clutches of this mighty ruler and who have, somehow or other, managed to survive without food and drink?

Another problem is that the Scripture teaches us that if a man does not provide food for his family, he has denied the faith and is worse than an unbeliever (1 Timothy 5:8). Could a man stand by and watch his wife and children die of starvation, thinking that he is doing the will of God? The sight of the skeletal children of Sudan, Ethiopia and other parts of Africa, strikes hard at our hearts. What if these were our *own* children, our *own* flesh and blood? Many might be tempted to take the mark of the beast in order to obtain food and drink for them. However, does the Bible teach that the entire world is to be placed in such a situation? The scenario which sees this beast, his image, and his mark covering the whole wide world is suspect.

Where?

When we read Revelation 13 we note that only *one* image of the beast is to be set up, not many throughout the world. That being the case, we need to search the Scriptures to find out where this image is to be.

> He will confirm a covenant with many for one 'seven', but in the middle of that 'seven' he will put an end to sacrifice and offering. And one who causes desolation will place abominations *on a wing of the temple* until the end that is decreed is poured out on him. (Daniel 9:27)

> His armed forces will rise up to desecrate *the temple fortress* and will abolish the daily sacrifice. Then they will set up the abomination that causes desolation. (Daniel 11:31)

> So when you see standing *in the holy place* 'the abomination that causes desolation', spoken of through the prophet Daniel - let the reader understand - then let those who are *in Judea* flee to the mountains. (Matthew 24:15-16)

> He opposes and exalts himself over everything that is called God or is worshipped, and even sets himself up *in God's temple*, proclaiming himself to be God. (2 Thessalonians 2:4)

It may surprise us to read of the temple and the holy place, of offerings and sacrifices as part of the daily worship. It sounds more Jewish than Christian.

Who?

In Revelation 12:7-9 we read of a future great battle in heaven between the angels of Michael and Satan, with the former being victorious and the latter being cast to earth and pursuing a certain woman (12:13-17). This woman is clothed with the sun, the moon and twelve stars (12:1), which is a clear symbol of the nation of Israel with Abraham and Sarah at its head and with its twelve tribes (Genesis 37:9-10).

What follows in Revelation is a battle between Satan, his two beasts and certain nations which follow him, including Babylon, on one side and the people of Israel on the other. Neither Revelation nor such passages as Matthew 24 describe a battle between Satan and the Christian church. Rather it is conflict between Satan and the nation of Israel. This is emphasised by some of the details given in the text. For example, the second beast of Satan is able to bring fire down from heaven (Revelation 13:13). This sign was used in the Old Testament to confirm to Israel God's full support for a particular leader. We can think in this context of people like Abraham, Moses, Aaron, David and particularly Elijah. What they said and stood for was validated with fire from heaven. A similar phenomenon was experienced by those in the upper room on the Day of Pentecost (Acts 2).

Another example is the fact that the Israelites were expressly told not to make an idol of anything on earth and never to bow down to one (Exodus 20:4). In Revelation 13:15 they are being coerced into breaking that commandment by being forced to bow down and worship an image of a man.

Further, the Jews were told to tie symbols of the Law of Moses and what it stood for on their hands and on their foreheads (Deuteronomy 6:8). These are to be replaced by the mark of the beast. Following this, John writes about 144,000 (Revelation 14:1) which we have earlier been told is made up of 12,000 from each of the tribes of Israel (Revelation 7:5-8).

What?

If we can refrain from reading things into this passage and its surrounding chapters, then we are more likely to gain a better understanding of the subject matter. If we note exactly what is said, we will see clearly that this part of the Bible is dealing exclusively with the Jews, Jerusalem, and Judea. At the centre is the temple with its holy place. This may cause us problems, especially if we hold the view that there is no future for the nation of Israel in God's plan and purpose. If we do hold such a view then we may be tempted to read into certain parts of the Bible things which are not there. When the Bible speaks about Jews worshipping God in the temple some time in the future, we are tempted to *interpret* that as Christians worshipping God in churches. It would be better to avoid such an interpretation and allow the Bible to mean what it says. The Jews are to be in Judea, worshipping God in their temple in Jerusalem. Everything appears to be just right for them when suddenly, they become subject to this beast of a man, are made to worship his image in God's temple, and are forced to take his mark in order to obtain food and drink.

When?

The situation described in Revelation 14-18 lasts for about three and a half years. We read in Daniel 9:27 of one "seven", generally accepted as referring to seven years. In the middle of the seven-year agreement, the covenant which allowed the Jews to present morning and evening sacrifices and offerings in their temple in Jerusalem is to be broken.

In Revelation 11:1-3 we read that the holy city, Jerusalem, is to be trampled on for 42 months - three and a half years. However, God ensures that a testimony to Him continues by preserving two witnesses for 1,260 days - three and a half Jewish years.

In Revelation 13:5 the beast is to have authority for 42 months, during which time he pursues the woman (Israel) in the wilderness for a time (one year), times (two years) and half a time (half a year) - Revelation 12:14.

This three and a half year oppression of Israel is ended by the return of Christ.

Why?

I have already suggested that it would be impossible for many parents to watch their own flesh and blood starve to death. If faced with one of their own children having a skeletal body and bloated stomach, most parents would do anything to obtain food and drink for that child. Thankfully the Bible does not teach that the world is to be placed in such a situation. However, it does state that the inhabitants of Jerusalem and Judea will be, but if they do find themselves in that position it will be their own fault. They do not have to take the mark of the beast to obtain food for their family. There is to be another source.

In Matthew 24 we read that when the people of Israel see "the abomination that causes desolation" standing in the holy place, they are to flee to the mountains. If they are outside, either in the fields or on roof tops, they are not to go back to the house for anything, not even for a cloak. They are to flee with nothing, not even food and water (Matthew 24:15-18). To rush off to the mountains without taking any provisions may appear stupid, but it will not be then, at that time. Revelation 12:6 and 14 state that God has prepared a place for the woman (Israel) and that He is to care for her for 1,260 days. In the past God fed, watered, and clothed Israel during their forty years wandering in the wilderness. It will be a small matter for Him to do the same again for just three and a half years.

Thus no Jew need take the mark of the beast to obtain food and drink for his wife and children. He can, if he so wishes, bow down and worship the image and take the mark. In doing so he ensures that his name will not be written in the book of life. His end is destruction, not immortality.

Application

Revelation is a complicated book and it is impossible to sort out all the details at the moment. People living in those future days, when its predicted events unfold before their eyes, will understand it with far greater clarity than is possible today. However, a straightforward reading and interpretation of the book shows that it is dealing with Jews. Some of these are Christians, some worship God according to the Law of Moses, some forsake both Christ and the Law. The people addressed in Revelation were Christian Jews of the dispersion, those who had been scattered amongst the cities of the Roman Empire. The book tells them what is to happen to their fellow-Jews who live in Jerusalem and Judea.

The passage we have been considering talks about an image of a beast which is to be set up in the holy place of the temple in Jerusalem. This profanity will be worst for those Jews worshipping God according to the Law, but the situation could be even blacker. Those who do not flee to the mountains may get caught and dragged into the temple and forced to bow down and worship this image. Also, they will not be able to buy or sell unless they take the mark of this beast.

All this seems far removed from our current situation. This passage may have little application for Gentile Christians living today. However, as we gaze across the seas and see some of the present Arab-Israeli hostilities, we realise how easily and how speedily it could all come to pass.

In conclusion

One lesson we can learn from this chapter is that when we do approach the Bible we obtain a very different understanding of its contents when we let "Jew" mean "Jew", and *not* "Christian", and when we let "temple" mean "temple", and *not* "church".

Another lesson is that this chapter has shown us the truth of 1 Corinthians 10:13, that God will not let any be tempted beyond what they can bear, that He will, with the temptation, provide a way out so that all can stand up under it. He certainly will provide a way out for that future generation of Jews who will be faced by the beast, his image, and his mark. Yet they need not worry about their food, drink, and clothing. God will provide it.

We will never be subject to such great persecution as those Jews will be. However, when we are faced with trials and tribulation, tests and temptation, let us turn to God in prayer and look for *His* way out.

Part IV

Formalising the Approach

In this book we have suggested that in approaching the Bible we must note the people addressed and the people spoken of. But more than that, we need to pay attention to when something was spoken or written and to when it relates.

We have proposed that on certain occasions there were significant changes in God's dealings with mankind. Our thesis is that God has dealt with different people in different ways at different times. However, we are far from the first either to notice or to suggest this.

In this section we shall be dealing with the history of this approach and formalising it. As such the next few chapters are somewhat technical and some readers may care to turn to Part V, page 273, and chapters 26 to 30, before embarking upon chapters 19 to 25.

19. The History of the approach

Justin Martyr (110-165)

Justin was converted from paganism to Christianity. He became the most notable of the second century apologists: those writers who defended the Christian faith. He advanced the concept of differing programmes in the Bible. When discussing the question whether God always had the same requirements for righteousness, Justin wrote:

> For if one should wish to ask you why, since Enoch, Noah with his sons, and all others in similar circumstances, who neither were circumcised nor kept the Sabbath, pleased God, God demanded by other leaders and by the giving of the law after the lapse of so many generations, that those who lived between the times of Abraham and of Moses be justified by circumcision and other ordinances - to wit, the Sabbath, and sacrifices, and libations, and offerings. (*Dialogue with Trypho*; 92)

For Justin, then, there was a difference in what God wanted from different people. What was expected from Enoch and Noah was different from what was expected from Abraham and Isaac which, in turn, was different from what was expected of Moses. That, in its turn, would be different from what God expected from Christians in the present dispensation. Justin had earlier written about this present dispensation, with its gifts of power, (*Dialogue with Trypho*; 87).

Irenaeus (130-200)

Irenaeus was born in Asia Minor and studied under Polycarp, bishop of Smyrna. He went to Gaul and became bishop of Lyon in 177. His books and writings were intended to counteract Gnostic ideas present there. He wrote, giving reasons why there are only four Gospels.

> ... the Gospel is quadriform, as is also the course followed by the Lord. For this reason were four principal covenants given to the human race: one, prior to the deluge, under Adam; the second, that after the deluge, under Noah; the third, the giving of the law, under Moses; the fourth, that which renovates man, and sums up all things by means of the Gospel, raising and bearing men upon its wings into the heavenly kingdom. (*Against Heresies*; 3,9,8)

Here he does not use any term to describe these four divisions. However, like Justin Martyr, he uses the word dispensation in his writings. He often speaks of the dispensations of God and especially of the Christian dispensation. His four divisions are as follows:

1. Under Adam - prior to the flood
2. Under Noah - after the flood to Sinai
3. Under Moses - the giving of the law
4. Under Christ - the Gospel

Clement of Alexandria (150-220)

In about 185 Pantaenus, a converted Stoic philosopher, was teaching Christians in Alexandria. He was succeeded as leader of the school by Clement, whose great achievement was to put over the gospel in terms which could be understood by people of Greek culture. He held to four dispensations: three patriarchal ones (in Adam, Noah and Abraham) as well as the Mosaic. In *The Stromata, or Miscellanies*, book V, chapter VI, he writes:

> Again, there is the veil of the entrance into the holy of holies. Four pillars there are, the sign of the sacred tetrad of the ancient covenants.

In his *Elucidation on The Tetrad*, A. Cleveland Coxe states:

> It is important to observe that "the patriarchal dispensation", as we too carelessly speak, is pluralized by Clement. He clearly distinguishes *three* patriarchal dispensations, as given in Adam, Noah, and Abraham; and then comes the Mosaic. (*The Ante-Nicene Fathers,* II, 476.)

Augustine (354-430)

Augustine was born in Numidia, in modern day Algeria. He excelled in the literary education of his day and lectured in rhetoric at Carthage. After becoming a Christian in 387 he was sent to assist the Bishop of Hippo and in 395 was, himself, elected bishop there. He was the author of the often quoted "Distinguish the times, and the Scripture is in harmony with itself." He also wrote:

> The divine institution of sacrifice was suitable in the former dispensation, but is not suitable now. For the change suitable to the present age has been enjoined by God, who knows infinitely better than

man what is fitting for every age, and who is, whether He give or add, abolish or curtail, increase or diminish, the unchangeable Creator of mutable things, ordering all events in His providence until the beauty of the completed course of time, the component parts of which are the dispensations adapted to each successive age, shall be finished, like the grand melody of some ineffably wise master of song, and those pass into the eternal immediate contemplation of God who here, though it is a time of faith, not of sight, are acceptably worshipping Him ... There is no variableness with God, though in the former period of the world's history He enjoined one kind of offerings, and in the latter period another, therein ordering the symbolic actions pertaining to the blessed doctrine of true religion in harmony with the changes of successive epochs without any change in Himself ... if it is now established that that which was for one age rightly ordained may be in another age rightly changed - the alteration indicating a change in the work, not in the plan, of Him who makes the change, the plan being framed by His reasoning faculty, to which, unconditioned by succession in time, those things are simultaneously present which cannot be actually done at the same time because the ages succeed each other. (*To Marcellinus*, 138,5,7)

Augustine taught that "that which was for one age rightly ordained may in another age be rightly changed". This is illustrated, in the above paragraph, by noting that "the divine institution of sacrifice was suitable in the former dispensation, but is not suitable now".

A different approach

In Justin Martyr, Irenaeus, Clement, and Augustine we have examples of early Christians who saw changes in the way in which God dealt with mankind. They looked in the Bible and saw those changes. They noted that the later parts, or dispensations as they called them, were of more relevance to their time than the earlier ones. Perhaps the most popular division was the fourfold one of Adam to Noah; Noah to Moses; Moses to Christ; Christ onwards.

However, there were other Christians who took a different approach to the Bible. To answer the charge that the Old Testament was sub-Christian, Tertullian (155-222), the first major Christian author to write in Latin, did not take the approach of Justin, Iranaeus, Clement, and Augustine. Instead he mingled the Law and the Prophets with the Gospels and Letters. As a result his own Christianity has been called a "baptized Judaism". His follower Cyprian, who was Bishop of Carthage from 248-258, mingled Christian ministers with Old Testament priests, and Christian ordinances with Old Testament sacrifices.

Other Christians dealt with the problem of the differences between the Old and New Testaments by allegorising or spiritualising the Old. The anonymous *Letter of Barnabas* (70-120), which came from Alexandria, claimed that the law of Moses had never been meant to be taken literally.

> This then is why he (Moses) mentioned the swine; You shall not associate, he means, with men who are like swine ...
>
> Neither shall you eat the eagle or the hawk, or the kite, or the crow. You shall not, he means, associate with or come to resemble such men as do not know how to provide their food by toil and sweat, but lawlessly seize what belongs to others.
>
> You shall not eat, he goes on, sea eel or polyp or cuttlefish. You shall not, he means, associate with such men ... who are utterly ungodly and already condemned to death ...
>
> Moses received three decrees about food, and uttered them in the Spirit, but they (Israel) in their fleshly desire, received them as having to do with eating. (*Letter of Barnabas* 10:3-9)

The writer even saw the number of Abraham's servants, 318, as pointing to the cross of Christ.

Origen (185-254), the most prolific writer of the early church, was the most influential allegorizer of the Scriptures. He moulded church thinking for centuries afterwards, and we shall see why in a moment.

To sum up: during the early centuries of Christianity there seem to have been three different approaches to the Bible. Clearly, different things were recorded in different parts of the Bible and to explain this:

(1) Some Christians saw God as dealing with different people in different ways at different times. These different dealings they termed dispensations.
(2) Other Christians tried to keep a unity by mingling the Old Testament with the New.
(3) The third group spiritualised the Bible, treating it, and especially the Old Testament, allegorically.

In the course of time this first approach, the one we are particularly interested in, disappeared from the scene. After Augustine, we can find nothing written about the need to notice the dispensations in Scripture for well over 1000 years. Why should this have been so?

The loss of freedom

> Scholars of Church History have indicated that the concept of orthodoxy was introduced into Christendom, not in the 1st Century, but early in the 4th Century, under the leadership of the Roman emperor Constantine. He desired a unified Christianity as a state religion, in order to consolidate his own power. (See, for example, Martin A Larson's *The Religion of the Occident*, chapter 16.)
>
> It seems that in the earlier centuries of the Christian era, there was a fairly healthy and free enquiry among Christians with respect to the most profound Scriptural topics, including the nature of the God-head and the Person of Christ. Once orthodoxy was established this changed. To be orthodox was to be safe. What was orthodox was well defined by creeds and could be stated and applied with absolute dogmatism. Not to be orthodox could mean the loss of home, possessions and family, even life itself. Healthy enquiry was displaced by an unhealthy fear. (Daniel Andersen, *Bible Study - a personal quest*)

Constantine was emperor from 306 to 337 and the state religion he set up was a unified Christianity, based on a combination of the second and third approaches mentioned above. The church established a priesthood based on the Jewish priesthood; infant baptism was the spiritual equivalent of circumcision, and so on. This approach to the Bible became the orthodox approach and any other approach was not tolerated. The freedom of the first centuries was lost and was not restored for well over 1000 years. The approach of distinguishing the dispensations and of noting the different dealings God had with mankind was supressed and lost.

The return of freedom

The Renaissance started in Italy in the 14th Century and spread abroad during the next two hundred years. It opened men's minds. It gave them the thirst for knowledge. It encouraged a spirit of enquiry. What had been considered orthodox by the church for centuries was being challenged.

An Italian physician, Marsilius of Padua (1270-1342), protested against the power of the papacy and the priests. He maintained that the supreme standard was the Bible. The Englishman William of Occam (1280-1347) took a similar line.

In England John Wycliffe (1320-1384) denied the infallibility of the pope. He declared that Christ is the only head of the church. He, and others, went throughout the land preaching the Bible. However, probably his greatest achievement was to translate the Latin Bible into English. This was a tremendous step forward, for at that time people were completely ignorant of what the Bible said and were dependent upon the church for instruction. However, this new English Bible was not widely available as the printing press had not been invented. It was not until 1526 that William Tyndale, who was martyred in 1536, brought out the first printed New Testament. This was followed nine years later, in 1535, by Coverdale's first printed Bible in English. This formed the basis of *The Great Bible* of 1539.

Miles Coverdale (1488-1568)

Miles Coverdale was an English bishop and more information about him is given in Appendix 1. He translated the Bible into English from the Latin and German versions. He also superintended the printing of *The Great Bible* of 1539. He wrote:

> It shall greatly help you to understand the Scriptures, if you mark, not only what is spoken, or written, but of whom, and to whom, with what words, at what time, where, to what intent, with what circumstances, considering what goes before, and what comes afterwards.

These words have provided the framework of this book and we need make no further comment upon them.

Having started in Italy, the Renaissance spread abroad, continuing to open men's minds during the 15th and 16th Centuries. Wycliffe, Tyndale, and Coverdale all lived during this time. They helped to lay the ground for the Reformation. Indeed John Wycliffe has been called "the morning star of the English Reformation". These men did much to make the Bible easily accessible and to break the bonds of orthodoxy. Healthy and free enquiry amongst Christians was again possible.

After the important doctrinal issues of the Reformation had been settled people started to consider, once again, God's different dealings with mankind. It was not long before the type of approach favoured by Justin Martyr, Iranaeus, Clement of Alexandria, and Augustine was seen again. Within a few years of one another a Frenchman and an Englishman published two interesting books, each advocating this type of approach.

John Edwards (1639-1716)

In 1699 John Edwards published a two-volumed work of 790 pages. His purpose was:

> To display all the Transactions of Divine Providence relating to the Methods of Religion, from the Creation to the end of the World, from the first Chapter of Genesis to the last of Revelation. (*A Compleat History or Survey of All the Dispensations* 1, 5)

His dispensational scheme was as follows:

1. Innocency and Felicity - Adam created upright.
2. Sin and misery - Adam fallen.
3. Reconciliation - Adam recovered.

Edwards' third section covered the time from Adam's redemption to the end of the world. He subdivided it as follows:

A. Patriarchal economy.
    1. Adamic, antediluvian.
    2. Noahical.
    3. Abrahamic.
B. Mosaical.
C. Gentile (concurrent with A and B).
D. Christian or Evangelical.
    1. Infancy, primitive period, past.
    2. Childhood, present period.
    3. Manhood, future (millennium).
    4. Old age, from the loosing of Satan to the conflagration.

This scheme is quite different from and very much more developed than any of those proposed by the early Church Fathers.

Pierre Poiret (1646-1719)

Pierre Poiret was a French philosopher. His major work, *L'OEconomie Divine*, was published in Amsterdam in 1687. In 1713 it was translated into English and published in London in six volumes under the title *The Divine OEconomy: or An Universal System of the Works and Purposes of God Towards Men Demonstrated.* His scheme is as follows.

1. Infancy - to the Deluge.
2. Childhood - to Moses.
3. Adolescence - to the prophets (about the time of Solomon).
4. Youth - to the coming of Christ.
5. Manhood - "some time after that".
6. Old Age - "the time of man's decay".
7. Renovation of all things - the millennium.

Isaac Watts (1674-1748)

Isaac Watts is perhaps best known as a hymn-writer. He was also a theologian whose writings fill six large volumes: *Watts' Works*. His outline of the Bible is as follows:

1. The Dispensation of Innocence, or the Religion of Adam at first.
2. The Adamical Dispensation of the Covenant of Grace, or the Religion of Adam after his Fall.
3. The Noahical Dispensation, or the Religion of Noah.
4. The Abrahamical Dispensation, or the Religion of Abraham.
5. The Mosaical Dispensation, or the Jewish Religion.
6. The Christian Dispensation.

Dr. Samuel Farmer Jarvis (before 1850)

In *The Ante-Nicene Fathers*, II, 477, A. Cleveland Coxe referred to the book the *Church of the Redeemed* by Dr. S. F. Jarvis, a clergyman from Boston, Mass., U.S.A.. According to a footnote the following words were written in Boston in 1850, some time after the death of Dr. Jarvis.

> My venerated and most erudite instructor in theology, the late Dr. Jarvis, in his *Church of the Redeemed*, expounds a dispensation as identified by (1) a covenant, original or renewed, (2) a sign or sacrament, and (3) a closing judgment. (See pp. 4, 5, and elsewhere in the great work I have named.) Thus (1) the Tree of Life, (2) the institution of sacrifice, (3) the rainbow, (4) circumcision, (5) the ark, (6) the baptismal and eucharistic sacraments, and (7) the same renewed and glorified by the conversion of nations are the symbols. The covenants and judgments are easily identified, ending with the universal Judgment.
>
> Dr. Jarvis died, leaving his work unfinished; but the *Church of the Redeemed* is a book complete in itself, embodying the results of a vast erudition, and of a devout familiarity with Scripture. It begins with Adam, and ends with the downfall of Jerusalem (the typical judgment), which closed the Mosaic dispensation.

The most interesting feature of this scheme is that Jarvis closed the Mosaic dispensation neither with Christ, nor with the Cross, but with the downfall of Jerusalem in AD 70.

Samuel Hanson Coxe (1793-1880)

Coxe put forward a sevenfold dispensational scheme which he backed up with Clement of Alexandria's fourfold one. This has been recorded for us by his son.

> The editor begs to be pardoned for referring to his venerated father's division (sustained by Clement's authority), which he used to insist should be further enlarged so as to subdivide the first and last, making *seven* complete, and thus honouring the system of seven which runs through all Scripture. Thus *Adam* embraces *Paradise*, and the *first covenant* after the fall; and the *Christian covenant* embraces a *millennial period*. So we have (1) *Paradise*, (2) Adam, (3) Noah, (4) Abraham, (5) Moses, (6) CHRIST, (7) a *millennial period*, preluding the Judgment and the Everlasting Kingdom. (A. Cleveland Coxe, *The Ante-Nicene Fathers*, II, 477).

Throughout this period, from 1687 onwards, there was much consideration of how best to understand and represent God's dealings with mankind throughout the ages. The approach of recognising that God had different dealings with different people at different times, having been suppressed for centuries, was now the subject of a considerable amount of literature.

John Nelson Darby (1800-1882)

John Nelson Darby, a leader and founder of the Plymouth Brethren, had much to do with systematising and promoting this type of approach to the Bible. In *The Collected Writing of J N Darby 2, 568-73*, his scheme is as follows:

1. Paradisaical state to the Flood.
2. Noah.
3. Abraham.
4. Israel.
    - A. Under the law.
    - B. Under the priesthood.
    - C. Under the kings.
5. Gentiles.

6. The Spirit.
7. The Millennium.

Benjamin Wills Newton (1807-1889)

B. W. Newton was a fellow of Exeter College, Oxford. In his commentary on Romans 11, he writes:

> Circumstances however occurred, that led me to consider with care the eleventh chapter of Romans. I could not close my eyes to the fact that the future history of the *literal* Israel was there spoken of; and it was put in marked contrast with the history of those who are at present being gathered out from the Gentiles during the time of Israel's unbelief ... I saw also that Israel when nationally converted, are not to be merged with the present Gentile church, for then they would have been represented in this chapter as graffed in upon the Gentile branch.

Newton distinguished four dispensations from Noah's day to the return of Christ.

> We have thus from Noah to the second coming of the Lord, four periods of distinct dispensations, of which three are continuing to exist together, and one has entirely passed away.
>
> The first of these comprehends the whole period from Noah to the second coming of the Lord. The dispensational arrangements of the first six verses of the ninth chapter of Genesis, still continue.
>
> The second is the Sinai dispensation, which was the seeking of the Abrahamic blessings in the Hagar way. And this terminated when our Lord pronounced desolation on Jerusalem.
>
> The third is the committal of power to the Gentile image; it commenced with Nebuchadnezzar, continues still, and will be terminated by the ten kingdoms and Antichrist.
>
> The fourth is the New Covenant dispensation, which has begun to bring in the Abrahamic blessings in the Sarah way, for the Church as citizens of Jerusalem which is above, has even at present, the Sarah character of blessing, though not in earthly things. And this commenced with the preachings of the Apostles, after the Lord gave them the cup of the New Covenant or Testament (for the word is the same in the original) in His blood. (*The Christian Witness*, 1835, p 298)

James H Brookes (1830-1897) and James M Gray (1851-1935)

In his book *Dispensationalism Today*, Charles Ryrie mentions two schemes published at the turn of the twentieth century. The first, by James Brookes, was as follows:

1. Eden.
2. Antediluvian.
3. Patriarchal.
4. Mosaic.
5. Messianic.
6. Holy Ghost.
7. Millennium.

The second, by James Gray, is slightly different.

1. Edenic.
2. Antediluvian.
3. Patriarhcal.
4. Mosaic.
5. Church.
6. Millennial.
7. Fullness of times.
8. Eternal.

C I Scofield (1843-1921)

The *Scofield Reference Bible* has probably done more than any other book to bring to people's attention this type of approach to the Bible. However, although Scofield was greatly influenced by Darby, his overall scheme seems to have more in common with that put forward by Isaac Watts.

1. Innocency.
2. Conscience.
3. Human Government.
4. Promise.
5. Law.
6. Grace.
7. Kingdom.

Other writers

We have now entered the twentieth century and there have been many, many writers who have taken an approach along these lines. For instance: Stuart Allen, Sir Robert Anderson, David Baron, A. E. Bishop, James H. Brookes, E. W. Bullinger, John R. Caldwell, William Campbell, Lewis Sperry Chafer, George Douglas, E. Schuyler English, J. H. Evans, Charles L. Fienberg, Clifton L. Fowler, Arno C. Gaebelein, Robbert A. Hadden, I. M. Haldeman, C. F. Hogg, Richard Holden, Harry A. Ironside, William Kelly, G. H. Lang, Clarence Larkin, Stewart P. MacLennan, F. E. Marsh, C. H. Mackintosh, Alva J. McClain, C. E. McLain, J. Eustace Mills, Harold P. Morgan, George Morrish, Charles Ozanne, Rene Pache, J. Dwight Pentecost, William L. Pettingill, S. Ridout, Charles C. Ryrie, Erich Sauer, Joseph Smale, W. Graham Scroggie, Cornelius Stam, Ernest Streets, W. H. Griffith Thomas, Leon Tucker, Merril Unger, W. E. Vine, John F. Walvoord, Charles H. Welch, and George Williams.

Conclusion

We have seen that the type of approach we have been advocating in this book was not uncommon in the early centuries of Christianity. However, with Constantine making a unified Christianity a state religion, orthodoxy was forced upon Christians. The approach favoured by the state church was, by and large, an allegorical one. Other views were suppressed for centuries. It was not until after the Reformation that people started to think again along the lines which we have been advocating in this book.

20. A significant aspect of the approach

At the end of chapter 19 we listed some of the people in the twentieth century who have advocated a dispensational approach towards the Bible. However, it should be stressed that there was little coherence amongst them: some suggest four dispensations, some seven, and some eight. Some subdivided these dispensations.

Even amongst those who had the same number of dispensations there was disagreement about what constituted some of their dispensations, particularly with regard to when they began and ended. In subsequent chapters we shall deal with this more fully, demonstrating that one reason for such discrepancies is the lack of precision and objectivity in the traditional definitions of a dispensation.

Nevertheless, the majority of the writers quoted and mentioned in the previous chapter (but not all) advocated that the dispensation in which we live began with the Pentecost of Acts 2. For reasons stated earlier this has to be questioned, and one of the significant parts of the approach to the Bible put forward in this book is that the dispensation of today commenced at the end of Acts, when the people of Israel were relieved of their position as God's stewards (Acts 28:25-28). Only then was the salvation of God sent directly to the Gentiles. This, however, is not a new understanding of events. Many writers of the past have seen the events described at the end of Acts as being of major importance.

Dr. Samuel Farmer Jarvis (Before 1850)

Dr. Jarvis, a Boston clergyman, wrote in his book *Church of the Redeemed* that he does not see the Mosaic dispensation ending at the Cross or with the Pentecost of Acts 2. Rather he sees its conclusion a few years after the end of Acts, with the destruction of Jerusalem, an event which took place in AD 70. Commenting on the *Church of the Redeemed*, A. Cleveland Coxe states:

> It begins with Adam, and ends with the downfall of Jerusalem (the typical judgment), which closed the Mosaic dispensation. (*The Ante-Nicene Fathers*, volume II, p 477.)

John Nelson Darby (1800-1882)

J.N. Darby, a leader and founder of the Plymouth Brethren wrote the following when commenting upon the last verses of Acts:

> Individuals from amongt them (Israel) enter into another sphere on other grounds, but Israel disappears and is blotted out for a time from the sight of God. (Volume 4, Acts-Philippians, *Synopsis of the Books of the Bible*, p 99.)

Charles Henry Mackintosh (1820-1896)

C. H. Mackintosh was born in County Wicklow in Ireland and after spending some time in business opened a school in 1844. Later he gave that up to concentrate on his writing and preaching, being very active in the Irish revival of 1859-1860. For some forty years he edited the magazine *Things New and Old.* Speaking of the last chapter of Acts he wrote:

> Here we read that "after three days [from the time of his arrival at Rome] Paul called *the chief of the Jews* together; and when they were come together, he said unto them, 'Men and brethren, though I have committed nothing against the people or customs of our fathers, yet was I delivered prisoner from Jerusalem into the hands of the Romans .... For this cause therefore have I called for you, to see you, and to speak with you; because that for the hope of Israel I am bound with this chain ....' And when they had appointed him a day, there came many to him into his lodging; to whom he expounded and testified the kingdom of God, persuading them concerning Jesus, both out of the law of Moses, and out of the prophets from morning till evening" (Acts 28:17,20,23).
>
> Here, then, we have this blessed "ambassador in bonds" still seeking out "the lost sheep of the house of Israel", and offering them, in the first place, "the salvation of God". But "they agreed not among themselves", and at last Paul is constrained to say, "Well spake the Holy Ghost by Esaias the prophet unto our fathers, saying, Go unto this people and say, Hearing ye shall hear, and not understand; and seeing ye shall see, and not perceive; for the heart of this people is waxed gross, and their ears are dull of hearing, and their eyes have they closed, lest they should see with their eyes, and hear with their ears, and understand with their heart, and should be converted and I should heal them. *Be it known therefore unto you, that the salvation of God is sent unto the Gentiles and they will hear it".*
>
> There was now no more hope. Every effort that love could make had been made, but to no purpose; and our apostle, with a reluctant

heart, shuts them up under the power of that judicial blindness which was the natural result of their rejection of the salvation of God ...

Thus closes the Acts of the Apostles, which, like the Gospels, is more or less connected with the testimony to Israel. So long as Israel could be regarded as the object of testimony, so long the testimony continued; but when they were shut up to judicial blindness, they ceased to come within the range of testimony, wherefore the testimony ceased. (*The Life and Times of Elijah the Tishbite*, *The Mackintosh Treasury*, p 333; see also page 328.)

Sir Robert Anderson (1841-1918)

Robert Anderson was born in Dublin and moved to London in 1873. He became Assistant Commissioner of the Metropolitan Police and the Chief of the Criminal Investigation Department. He was widely recognised as a popular lay-preacher and one of the most capable "defenders of the faith" at a time when "higher criticism" was threatening the church. He wrote seventeen major books, which underscored the inspiration and dependable authority of the Bible, the deity of Jesus Christ, and the necessity of the new birth.

His *Silence of God* was described by the *New York Herald* as "A book which has astounded religious Europe". It had run to nine editions by 1911. In it he writes of the Apostle Paul:

> Having been carried a prisoner to Rome, his first care was to call together - not the Christians, much though he longed to see them (Romans 1:10-11), but - "the chief of the Jews," and to them to give the testimony which he had brought to his nation in every place to which his ministry had led him. In his introductory address to them he claimed the place of a Jew among Jews: "I have done nothing (he declared) against the people, or the customs of our fathers" (Acts 28:17); but when these, the Jews of Rome, refused the proffered mercy, his mission to his nation was at an end; and for the first time separating himself from them, he exclaimed, "well spake the Holy Ghost through Isaiah the prophet unto *your* fathers" - and he went on to repeat the words which our Lord Himself had used at that kindred crisis of his ministry when the nation had openly rejected Him (Acts 28:25 *RV*; Matthew 13:13, cf. 12:14-16).
>
> My contention is that the Acts, as a whole, is the record of a temporary and transitional dispensation in which blessing was again offered to the Jew and again rejected. (*The Silence of God*, p 175)
>
> The apostle to the circumcision (Peter) gives place to the apostle to the Gentiles (Paul) as the central figure in the narrative (Acts), but yet in every place the Jew is still accorded a priority in the offer of blessing,

and it is not until, in every place from Jerusalem round to Rome, that blessing has been despised, that the Pentecostal dispensation is brought to a close by the promulgation of the solemn decree, "The salvation of God is sent unto the Gentiles" (Acts 28:28). (*The Silence of God*, p 56)

"*It was necessary*" he (Paul) declared at Pisidian Antioch, "that the Word of God should first be spoken to you (Jews)" (Acts 13:46 *RV*; cf. 17:2,10; 18:1-4). Even at Rome, deeply though he longed to visit the Christians there, his first care was to summon "the chief of the Jews," and to them "he testified the kingdom of God." And not until the testimony had been rejected by the favoured people did the word go forth, "The salvation of God is sent unto the Gentiles, and they will hear it" (Acts 28:17,23, 28). (*The Silence of God*, p 50)

George Williams (1850-1928)

The family of George Williams lived in Stillorgan in Ireland. He went to work as one of the paymasters in Dublin Castle, then the centre of the British Government in Ireland. He became associated with the evangelical revivals of the nineteenth century (especially that associated with D. L. Moody) conducting open-air campaigns in the south and west of Ireland. In his commentary on Acts 28:25-28 he wrote:

Seven times the Holy Spirit records the Divine judgment of verses 26 and 27, thus emphasizing its extreme importance, for it signalises the closing doors of the Kingdom to Israel consequent to their rejection of it. See Isaiah 6:9, Matthew 13:14, Mark 4:12, Luke 8:10, John 12:40, Acts 28:26 and Romans 11:8. This last passage predicts Israel's future repentance and acceptance of the King and His Kingdom.

The language of verse 28 is clear. The "salvation of God" was to be "sent" to the Gentiles, but the "Kingdom of God" was not to be "given" to them, for it was promised to Israel.

Thus the command "to the Jew first" (Acts 3:26 and Romans 1:16) was obeyed and fulfilled, and so is not now obligatory; for all are now regarded as sinners without distinction, and the Gospel is to be preached to them as such.

So Israel's action occasioned the sending of the Gospel to the Gentiles, and that enriched them partially (Romans 11:11); but Israel's repentance will occasion the incorporation of all the Gentile nations within the Kingdom of God, and then will be manifest the true Catholic Church. (George Williams, *The Student's Commentary on the Holy Scriptures*, p 850)

Arno C. Gaebelein (1861-1945)

A. C. Gaebelein was the publisher of the New York based Bible Study magazine *Our Hope*. He was a member of the original board that assisted C. I. Scofield in the preparation of *The Scofield Reference Bible*. In 1910, in the two volume edition of *The Gospel of Matthew*, he wrote:

> The dispensationalist believes that throughout the ages God is pursuing two distinct purposes: one related to the earth with earthly people and earthly objectives which is Judaism; while the other is related to heaven with heavenly people and heavenly objectives involved, which is Christianity. (Volume I, p 4)

Referring to Isaiah chapter 6 he wrote:

> Once more do we read the same words brought to remembrance by the Holy Spirit. In the last chapter of Acts, when Israel's apostasy and unbelief is fully established, Paul speaks then to the assembled Jews and adds, "Be it known, therefore, unto you that the salvation of God is sent unto the Gentiles and they will hear". (Volume I, p 272)

> The testimony which was begun by the Apostles up to the time when Israel rejected once more the offers of mercy from the risen Lord, when He was still waiting for their repentance as a nation, is an unfinished testimony. After that offer was again rejected the great parenthesis, the church age, began, and during this age (which is not reckoned in the Old Testament) there is no more Jewish testimony of the kingdom of the heavens. Israel nationally is set aside. (Volume I, p 209-210)

Joseph Smale

In 1909 Joseph Smale delivered a sermon on *The Greatest Truth I know After Twenty-five Years' Ministry* which was later published.

> The book of the Acts is the subject of the Kingdom. In the second chapter of Acts, a new kingdom dispensation began, but in the 28th chapter of Acts, we find that new kingdom declared to be impossible of development. The sentence of judicial blindness is pronounced upon the Jewish nation with the result that the salvation of God is sent to the Gentiles as such. Israel as a nation is no longer to be favoured; all her favours wait until the coming great tribulation has passed.

In June 1932, Smale wrote the following in *The Christian Fundamentals Magazine*:

> Let us hear the conclusion of the whole matter. The Church of the Prison Epistles is a secret kept from ages "hid in God", unrevealed, until after the laying aside by God of national Israel.
>
> Paul claims for the Church of this age, that it is the Church of the mystery, that is to say it is the Church of the Secret - of the Secret because the calling of such a church was kept a secret - hidden in God - from the ages and not made known, until revealed through His lips and pen (Ephesians 3:5-9; Colossians 1:25-26), a revelation that was made subsequent to the laying aside of Israel as a nation. The claim is therefore made for the Church of the mystery, that it is a spiritual organism absolutely new without any racial distinction in the members thereof (Colossians 3:11), blessed not because of Abraham, nor in Abraham, but blessed in Christ and for Christ's sake.

W. Graham Scroggie

Graham Scroggie was a noted Scottish pastor and writer of several books. In his *Know your Bible*, Volume II page 75, he writes:

> And how immense is the *Dispensational* value of the Acts. It is the most important dispensational book in the Bible because it tells us how the great change-over from Judaism to Christianity was made. It enables us to see the distinction between the Messianic Kingdom and the Christian Church; between the earthly and the heavenly, between the temporal and the eternal. Here the ends of ages meet, the one terminal, and the other germinal. Two dispensations swing on these hinges, one door closing, and the other opening.

Then, commenting upon Acts 28:25-29 in his book *The Acts of the Apostles*, he writes that these verses:

> Mark a momentous crisis. Judaism has now fallen! A long dispensation here ends.

George Douglas

Dr. George Douglas was from Cardiff in Wales. In an article published in the *Moody Bible Institute Monthly* in 1936 he wrote:

It is a common error to assume that the rejection and crucifixion of Christ was the historical crisis at which Israel was set aside. Under the influence of this erroneous conception, people are apt to read the rest of the New Testament as though it had no more to say concerning the earthly people ..... We learn from Acts 15 that the position of the Gentiles in the Church was only authoritatively settled some twenty years after Pentecost, and it is interesting to observe that even that settlement was on the lines and in harmony with Old Testament prophecy (Acts 15:13-17) ..... And when the Apostle Paul arrived in Rome, although as we learn from the first chapter of his Epistle to the Romans, the church there occupied such a prominent place in his affections, his first care was to summon together "the chief of the Jews", and it was as a Jew he addressed them, for his words are "our fathers", "my nation", "the hope of Israel" (Acts 28:17-20). But when they rejected his testimony, he said "your fathers" (v 25 *RV*). He now severed himself from Israel, and pronounced the solemn words which sealed their doom (vs 25-31) .....

In this book (Acts) we have the divine record of the Pentecostal dispensation, and that transition period was now ended. And here we note a very significant fact, which surely cannot be said to be accidental, that in the New Testament books written after the date of Acts 28, there is not a word to be said about Spirit manifestation except as a warning, such as 1 Timothy 4:1-2 ..... The evidential value of miracles depended largely upon a preceding revelation. They were a sign for those who possessed the countersign, namely the Jews, for "unto them were committed the oracles of God," and when they were definitely set aside by the apostolic pronouncement of Act 28:25-27, the signs definitely ceased.

Leon Tucker

Dr. Leon Tucker, editor of *Wonderful Word* magazine, wrote in his book *His Son, or Studies in the Epistle to the Hebrews*:

> We must look beyond the Gospels and the Acts and to the writings beyond, to discover the purpose of God in the church of the dispensation now present.

Robert A. Hadden

Dr. Robert A. Hadden was president of The Christian Fundamentals League and of the Bible Institute of Los Angeles. In the April 1931 edition of *The Christian Fundamentals Magazine* he wrote:

The Gospel of the Grace of God and "the Church, which is the Body" of Christ are not found in Matthew. The Holy Spirit assures us of that fact in Ephesians 3:9 and Colossians 1:25-27. From the beginning of time to the prison days of Paul, the Church which is "His Body" was an undiscoverable secret "hid in God".

Paul's letters and Acts 28:28

It would be wrong to give the impression that all, or indeed any, of the above writers agreed with the detailed approach advocated in this book. They were all dispensationalists, but more than that, they all saw something of significance occurring at the end of Acts. However, some of them did not relate their views on Acts with their comments on the epistles or letters written *during* Acts. For example, they might state that Israel was set aside at Acts 28:25-27 and that the announcement that God's salvation was sent to the Gentiles in Acts 28:28 signified the close of one dispensation and the start of another. They might state that the letters of James, Peter, John and Jude, as well as the letter to the Hebrews, were for Israel. However, some continued to hold that *all* of Paul's letters concerned this present dispensation. They failed to see that his earlier ones, the ones he wrote during Acts - Galatians, 1 & 2 Thessalonians, 1 & 2 Corinthians and Romans - were for that time. They involved the central people of Acts, Israel. The churches of that time were mixtures of Jews and Gentiles, with those of Hebrew descent still, rightly, occupying the first place and observing the Law of Moses.

We can see tension between their comments on the Acts of the Apostles and their comments on the letters written during Acts with a number of writers. It is there in C. H. Mackintosh's *The Life and Times of Elijah the Tishbite* and in the writings of George Williams, Graham Scroggie and others.

We read earlier Graham Scroggie's comments on the closing verses of Acts. He said that they "Mark a momentous crisis. Judaism has now fallen! A long dispensation here ends.". However, he also wrote:

> The Acts is a Book of Origins. Here are the beginnings of the Christian Church ... Acts is a dawn, a glorious sunrise, a bursting forth in a dark world of eternal light. (*Know your Bible*, volume II, p 75-76)

We read also what Arno C. Gaebelein wrote about the end of Acts. In essence it was:

> After that offer was again rejected the great parenthesis, the church age, began, and during this age (which is not reckoned in the Old Testament) there is no more Jewish testimony of the kingdom of the heavens. Israel nationally is set aside ..... In the last chapter of Acts, when Israel's apostasy and unbelief is fully established, Paul speaks then to the assembled Jews and adds, "Be it known, therefore, unto you that the salvation of God is sent unto the Gentiles and they will hear".

However, in the same book he wrote:

> The Magna Charta of the church is in the Epistles of Paul to whom the full revelation of the church was given. (*Gospel of Matthew* volume I, p 142)

That was written in 1910 and he seems to be implying that the Magna Charta for the church of this dispensation can be found in *all* the epistles of Paul. However, in the January 1936 issue of *Our Hope* magazine he appears to have modified this view.

> Do not regard the church as a subject of Old Testament Prophecy. Her unique origin, heavenly character, and eternal destiny - all in closest association with Christ - is a New Testament mystery, alone revealed by Paul in two of his prison Epistles - Ephesians and Colossians. (p 458)

Ephesians and Colossians were two of the letters Paul wrote after the announcement of Israel's blindness and deafness. He may have written them when under house arrest in Rome (Act 28:30). He also wrote Philippians and Philemon from there and later wrote Titus and 1 & 2 Timothy. These are the seven letters written after Acts 28:28.

Paul's earlier and later letters

Many of the writers quoted above came from dispensational groups which hold that the present dispensation of grace commenced with the Pentecost of Acts 2. They saw Paul as the apostle to the Gentiles and held that *all* his letters were primarily for this dispensation. As some of them read through the Acts of the Apostles they saw that it was at the end, rather than at the beginning or middle of Acts, that Israel lost their privileged position. It was not until Acts 28:28 that the Gentiles had independence from Israel and God's salvation was sent to them directly. In spite of the fact that they saw this clearly in Acts, it was not carried over to their understanding of Paul's earlier writings, though it would appear that, with time, some did. See, for example, the two quotations from Arno C. Gaebelein.

We have written of the tension that exists in some writings between the author's understanding of the end of Acts and how they saw the earlier letters of Paul. Other writers have shown a similar tension when dealing with all of Paul's epistles. Was teaching concerning this dispensation to be found in all of Paul's letters, or just those written after Acts 28:28? Some writings show a marked ambiguity concerning this.

In his book *Will the Church or any part of it go through the Great Tribulation*, Dr. F. E. Marsh answers a number of questions. His answer to the first we quote seems to imply that all Paul's letters are directly for this dispensation. His answer to the second places considerable emphasis on Ephesians.

> Question: Please differentiate between "the Church" founded at Pentecost, and that Church which is His body, and the ministry of which the Apostle Paul says was particularly committed to him.
>
> Answer: The Church founded at Pentecost was what Christ referred to when He said "I will build my Church," and was constituted through the Apostle Peter, which had Israel for its centre. The Church mentioned in Paul's Epistles is constituted of believers, irrespective of race or people, for "Christ is All and in all". That is, He is in all believers, because all believers are in Him.

> Question: What is the "Mystery" hidden throughout the ages?
>
> Answer: "The Mystery" or secret, was not made known till the time of the Apostle Paul. He distinctly declares that it was by "revelation" God "made known unto me the mystery ... which was not made known unto the sons of men, as it is now revealed unto His holy apostles and prophets by the Spirit, that the Gentiles should be fellow heirs, and of the same body" (Ephesians 3:6).

It would appear that Marsh has two churches running together during the Acts of the Apostles. One constituted by Peter and the other by Paul. When asked "What is the church?" he answers:

> The Church is said to be "The Church which is His body" (Ephesians 1:22-23); that it is a peculiar and distinct selection from Jews and Gentiles who are united to Christ in a living oneness by the Holy Spirit (1 Corinthians 12:13).

However, 1 Corinthians was written during Acts. Marsh sees the church described there as being the same as the one in Ephesians, and associated with Paul, rather than seeing it as the Church founded at Pentecost, and associated with Peter. It does make more sense to view the Acts of the Apostles and *all* the letters written during that time as one, with Peter and Paul working together. Any difference does not emerge until the end of Acts. In Acts 21:21-25 Paul is very much one with James and the Jewish Christians in Jerusalem.

A. E. Bishop is another writer who saw something distinctive in the letters Paul wrote after Acts 28:28 but who, none the less, wants to read the revelations contained in them into Paul's earlier writings.

> A careful study of the epistles, especially the latest epistles of Paul, which give the normal course of the church during the present dispensation, would dismount all from their hobbies, eliminate the last vestige of Judaism from their lives. (*Tongues, Signs and Visions - Not God's Order for Today*, p 5)

> Then came the revelation of the Church of the Mystery, one of the sublimest of God's masterpieces, hid from prophet, sage, apostle and saint until that time, and a further unfolding of that precious form of the Gospel of God's grace which Paul terms, "My Gospel". The distinctive truth of Ephesians, Philippians, and Colossians, but prominent in all Paul's Epistles, which, if heeded, eliminates from Christian life and ministry the last vestige of Judaism so fatal to God's present plan and purpose ..... These are the high standards placed before us in the Pauline Epistles, which reveal God's thoughts and plans for His Church - the Church of the Mystery - the Body of Christ. In all of the "Prison Epistles" there is not one hint of Pentecost, not an indication of a sign gift. (*Armour of Light*, p 211-212)

Bishop talks about the distinctive truth of Ephesians, Philippians and Colossians, letters written by Paul in the two years of Acts 28:30. However, in the same sentence he robs them of that distinctiveness by stating that their distinctive truths are also prominent in *all* Paul's letters.

Again, he talks about the Pauline Epistles, but needs to separate out "the latest letters of Paul" and his "Prison Epistles". Here we can see someone grappling with a dichotomy.

In 1871 Richard Holden wrote *The Mystery: The Special Mission of the Apostle Paul, the Key to the Present Dispensation*. In that publication, Holden displays a similar ambiguity to Bishop concerning Paul's later writings and his earlier ones.

> Let the reader then observe, first of all, that Paul claims to have had the truth in question given to him "by revelation" (Ephesians 3:3). Now the

word "revelation" means unveiling or uncovering, and is used in Scripture to signify the communication, by God, of truth not previously known, or, up to that time shrouded under the veil of secrecy. The fact of "a revelation" that the apostle claims for the truth he speaks of in this chapter, ought in itself to prepare us for the discovery in his teaching, of somewhat not to be met with in any previous portions of the Word of God. (p 10)

With this we would wholeheartedly agree. The mystery of Ephesians may be found in later writings, for example Colossians, but it cannot be found in any portions of the Word of God previous to Ephesians. That statement means that it cannot be found even in the earlier letters of Paul. However, Holden does not really take this view. He would not limit it to the later letters only.

> Whatever "the mystery" may be, it is something quite unknown until *the day of Paul* ... The present dispensation is, then, an interregnum or parenthetic period, contemplated indeed in the counsels of God, but not revealed till "given" to Paul. (p 11-12)

Instead of limiting the revelation of this mystery and the start of this dispensation until after Acts 28:28 and the giving of Ephesians, Holden widens it to embrace Paul's day. That is, all Paul's letters are seen to be directly for this dispensation.

Another writer who sees the importance of Ephesians but who, none the less, holds to all of Paul's letters is Dr. I.M. Haldemann.

> Christianity did not begin with John the Baptist. Christianity before Christ would be an anachronism. Christ Himself was not a Christian, much less John the Baptist ..... Paul tells us in his epistle to the Ephesians that the Church was not revealed to the sons of men in other ages. The prophets knew nothing about it. Moses had no conception of the Church. The patriarchs never dreamed of it. It was a secret, "hidden in God from the beginning". It was made known to Paul and by him alone fully and doctrinally revealed. Of the Apostles, Paul alone writes to the Church doctrinally. (*Satan as an Angel of Light*, p 31)

J. Sidlow Baxter wrote *The Strategic Grasp of the Bible* - a series of studies in the structural and dispensational characteristics of the Bible. At the end of the chapter entitled *A re-survey of the Acts (Part two)*, he quotes Acts 28:28 in capitals. Then, when commenting upon it, he says, again in capitals:

> The Jews have said "No" to the renewed offer of Jesus as Israel's Christ and King and Saviour. The "Kingdom" is now to be withdrawn and held in abeyance. For the time being (i.e. for this present age) the nation Israel is to be set aside as God's representative people on earth, and a far surpassing gospel of world-embracing divine grace is to be made known among all the nations of the Gentiles. (p 333-4)

The next chapter is entitled *Re-thinking the issues - The Acts (3)*. This he ends by again quoting Acts 28:28 in capitals and comments:

> Our Lord's return is no longer in any way dependent on Israel's attitude. *That* contingency has passed for ever. (p 350)

However, in the next chapter, headed *The "Christian Church" Epistles*, he puts Paul's earlier letters (Romans, 1 & 2 Corinthians, Galatians,1 & 2 Thessalonians, and, possibly, Hebrews) alongside the later ones (Ephesians, Philippians and Colossians), before dealing with the Pastoral letters (1 & 2 Timothy and Titus) and finally Philemon. He fails to distinguish between those written before Acts 28:28 and those written after it.

Dispensational consistency

Another writer who saw that the dispensational boundary had to be drawn at Acts 28:28, but who, nevertheless, treated all of Paul's writings as if they had been written in this dispensation, was Dr. E.W. Bullinger (1837-1913), editor of *Things to Come*. He, however, was to undergo a change of view. On page 92 of his *Autobiography*, Charles H. Welch (1880-1967) records a meeting between the two of them in 1908.

> *Welch*: From your writings Doctor, I believe I am right in saying that you do not believe "The Church" began at Pentecost, but rather, that the Dispensational Boundary must be drawn at Acts 28.
> *Bullinger*: That is so. I have made that quite clear.
> *Welch*: Well, what seems to me to stultify the position you have taken regarding Acts 28, is, that you nevertheless treat the whole of Paul's epistles as one group, starting with Romans, ending with Thessalonians, with Ephesians somewhere in the centre.

Welch goes on to state that Bullinger looked at him for a moment, then slapped his thigh with his hand and said, "That scraps half the books I have written. But we want the Truth, and the Truth is there in what you have said." Apparently Welch and Bullinger continued their discussion, considering the implications that arose from observing the relation of Paul's epistles to the boundary line of Acts 28, which is as follows:

Epistles before Acts 28	*Epistles after Acts 28*
Galatians	Ephesians
1 Thessalonians	Philippians
2 Thessalonians	Colossians
Hebrews	Philemon
1 Corinthians	1 Timothy
2 Corinthians	Titus
Romans	2 Timothy

Although Bullinger had written many volumes before this interview, he was to write just two after it, neither of which he completed: *The Companion Bible* and *The Foundations of Dispensational Truth*. Welch, on the other hand, was a young man of 28. He was to go on to commence *The Berean Expositor* magazine in 1909 followed three years later by his first of many books, *Dispensational Truth*.

Welch has often been credited with the discovery of the dispensational change at Acts 28:28. However, many who lived and wrote before him had seen the significance of the last pronouncement in Acts 28:25-28 of Isaiah 6, including Anderson, Bullinger, Mackintosh and many others. Some have suggested that Welch's breakthrough was to recognise that if the dispensational change came at the end of Acts, it was inconsistent to treat the earlier letters of Paul as one with his later letters. To leave Paul's earlier letters in with the Acts dispensation and to consider his later ones as pertaining to the post-Acts dispensation is consistent and far more sensible. However, Welch may not have been the first to come to this conclusion. Both Mackintosh and Holden had written of the differences between Paul's earlier and later ministries, although from their writings it does not seem as if they had come to as clear-cut a view as Welch.

> Let the reader then observe, first of all, that Paul claims to have had the truth in question given to him "by revelation" (Ephesians 3:3) ... The fact of "a revelation" that the apostle cliams for the truth he speaks of in this chapter, ought in itself to prepare us for the discovery in his teaching, of somewhat *not to be met with in any previous portions of the Word of God*. (Richard Holden, *The Mystery*, p 10)

> The doctrine of the Church's heavenly character was developed in all its power and beauty by the Holy Ghost in the Apostle Paul. Up to his time

> and even during the early stages of his ministry, the divine purpose was to deal with Israel. (C.H. McIntosh, *The Life and Time of Elisha the Tishbite*, *The McIntosh Treasury*, p 328)

This division in Paul's letters is most helpful and it has given rise to a more consistent dispensationalism which many writers this century have found helpful. We quote but two.

> Before Acts 28:28, Israel were urged to "turn again" in order that God might "send the Christ" unto them "even Jesus" (Acts 3:12,21 *RV*). But at Acts 28:28 Israel's hope of the Lord's return was deferred, for Paul declared in the words of Isaiah, that they were too blind to fulfil the required condition "turn again" (Acts 28:25,27 *RV*)
>
> Before Acts 28:28, Paul was bound for the hope of Israel (Acts 28:20). But after Acts 28:28 he became a prisoner for the Gentiles, in connection with the revelation of the Mystery given to him for them (Ephesians 3:1-3).
>
> Before Acts 28:28, a calling was in view whose blessings are associated with a time "from" the foundation of the world (Matthew 25:34). But after Acts 28:28, a calling came in view whose blessings are associated with a time "before" the foundation of the world. (Ephesians 1:3-4). (J Eustace Mills, *Before Acts 28:28 and After*)

> The New Covenant has to do with Israel and the Kingdom. We, as members of the church which is Christ's Body, have been "blessed with all spiritual blessings in the heavenlies in Christ" (Ephesians 1:3). We are not partakers of Israel's spiritual things as were the Gentiles during the Acts period (Romans 15:27), neither have we been grafted in among Israel and made partakers of the root and fatness of the olive tree (Romans 11:17). The position of believers in the dispensation of the mystery is "seated together in the heavenlies in Christ" (Ephesians 2:6) (John H Kessler, *Forgotten Truths Reaffirmed*, p 52)

We could go on to produce dozens of pages of quotations from writers who have taken this approach; people such as Stuart Allen, Tom Ballinger, E. W. Bullinger, William Campbell, John H. Kessler, Clifford McLain, J. Eustace Mills, Charles Ozanne, Otis Q. Sellers, Charles Welch and others. However, readers will be convinced of the value of the approach put forward in this book by using it for themselves, rather than by reading pages of quotations from people who hold similar views to the author.

Conclusion

In this chapter we have tried to show that many have taught that the events described at the end of Acts signal the setting aside of the special covenant relationship God had with the nation of Israel. These writers have also appreciated that with the words "God's salvation has been sent unto the Gentiles and they will listen" (Acts 28:28), Paul announced a change in the people who managed God's affairs. New administrators were appointed. A new stewardship, or dispensation, had begun. Following this event Paul remained in Rome under house-arrest for two years, during which time he probably wrote Ephesians, Colossians, Philemon, and Philippians. In Ephesians and Colossians in particular he makes known a new mystery, writing of a secret which had previously been hidden. This had been made known to him and the other apostles and prophets by a revelation from God (Ephesians 3:2-6). It is this "administration of the mystery" which Paul, from then on, wishes to make known to all men (Ephesians 3:9).

21. Formalising the approach

Throughout this book we have been attempting to follow the advice of Miles Coverdale, summarised by the questions "Who?", "Where?", "When?", "What?" and "Why?". To these we have added the injunction "Apply!". We have demonstrated this approach by discussing numerous examples. The use of examples to explain a theory or a system, in any branch of knowledge, is often helpful and aids clarification. However, it is now time to move from the specific examples and start to formalise the approach, to generalise it.

Traditional dispensationalism

We have based our approach upon the words of Miles Coverdale, who lived from 1488 to 1568. He was an English Bishop and translated the Bible into English from the German and Latin versions. He superintended the printing of *The Great Bible* in 1539.

John Nelson Darby (1800-1882) had much to do with sytematising and promoting an approach to the Bible known as dispensationalism. C. I. Scofield (1843-1921) is probably better known, mainly because of his reference Bible. While there are some similarities between the approah we have advocated in this book and what is commonly called dispensationalism, there are significant differences. To explain these, and to show the power and advantage of the approach set out in this book, it will be necessary to look at how other people have defined such terms as *dispensation* and *dispensationalism* and to show how the approach we are advocating differs. While in this discussion we will be disagreeing with certain views, it should be clearly understood by the reader that in doing this, we are in no way casting doubt upon the integrity, devotion, faith, and love for the Lord of the writers in question.

What is a dispensation?

Some of the early church fathers - Justin Martyr, Irenaeus, Clement of Alexandria, and Augustine - used the term dispensation. At the same time, they do not appear to have defined precisely what they meant by it. We should also point out that these people did not use dispensation in the same way as those who came after the Reformation. Neither are they dispensationalists, in the modern sense of the word. However, some of the principles they put forward developed into the more sophisticated system known today as *dispensationalism*. Indeed, it has been suggested that the early fathers held to primitive or early dispensational concepts.

After the Reformation the first person to put forward a dispensational approach was Pierre Poiret. *L'OEconomie Divine* was published in 1687. His scheme was:

1. Infancy - to the deluge.
2. Childhood - to Moses.
3. Adolescence - to the prophets (about the time of Solomon).
4. Youth - to the coming of Christ.
5. Manhood - some time after that.
6. Old Age - the time of man's decay.
7. Renovation of all things - the millennium.

With respect to modern day dispensationalism, Poiret's work is of great importance. Assessing it, and the above scheme, one writer says:

> There is no question that we have here a genuine dispensational scheme. He uses the phrase "period or dispensation" and his seventh dispensation is a literal thousand-year millennium with Christ returned and reigning in bodily form upon the earth with His saints, and Israel regathered and converted. He sees the overthrow of corrupt Protestantism, the rise of Antichrist, the two resurrections, and many of the general run of end time events. (Arnold H. Ehlert, *A Bibliography of Dispensationalism*, *Bibliotheca Sacra* 101:449-50)

A number of people who have followed a dispensational approach to the Scriptures have defined what a dispensation is. One of the first to give such a definition was Isaac Watts.

> The public dispensations of God towards men, are those wise and holy constitutions of his will and government, revealed or some way manifested to them, in the several successive periods of ages of the world, wherein are contained the duties which he expects from men, and the blessings which he promises, or encourages them to expect from him, here and hereafter; together with the sins which he forbids, and the punishments which he threatens to inflict on such sinners, or the dispensations of God may be described more briefly, as the appointed moral rules of God's dealing with mankind, considered as reasonable creatures, and as accountable to him for their behaviour, both in this world and in that which is to come. Each of these dispensations of God, may be represented as different religions, or at least, as different forms of religion, appointed for men in several successive ages of the world. (*Watts' Works*, Volume II)

Such a definition is both long and lacking in clarity. More modern writers have sought to give a clearer and more succinct definition.

> A dispensation is a period of time during which man is tested in respect to some specific revelation of the will of God. Seven such dispensations are distinguished in Scripture. (C. I. Scofield, *The Scofield Reference Bible*)

> (A dispensation denotes) a period of time during which God deals with man in a certain way. (Daniel P. Fuller, *The Hermeneutics of Dispensationalism*)

Many, including a number of dispensationalists, have disagreed with such definitions.

The Greek word for dispensation is *oikonomia* and it occurs a number of times in the New Testament.

> Jesus told his disciples: "There was a rich man whose manager (*oikonomos*) was accused of wasting his possessions. So he called him in and asked him, 'What is this I hear about you? Give an account of your management (*oikonomia*), because you cannot be manager (*oikonomos*) any longer.' The manager (*oikonomos*) said to himself, 'What shall I do now? My master is taking away my job (*oikonomia*). I'm not strong enough to dig, and I'm ashamed to beg - I know what I'll do so that, when I lose my job (*oikonomia*) here, people will welcome me into their houses.'" (Luke 16:1-4)

> If I preach voluntarily, I have a reward; if not voluntarily, I am simply discharging the trust (*oikonomia*) committed to me. (1 Corinthians 9:17)

> ... to be put into effect (*oikonomia*) when the times will have reached their fulfilment. (Ephesians 1:10) (That in the dispensation of the fulness of times. *KJV*)

> Surely you have heard about the administration (*oikonomia*) of God's grace that was given to me for you. (Ephesians 3:2)

> I have become its servant by the commission (*oikonomia*) God gave me to present to you the word of God in its fulness. (Colossians 1:25)

We can see here the variety of ways in which *oikonomos* is translated: management, job, discharging the trust, put into effect, administration, commission.

The usual criticism levelled at such formalised definitions of dispensation, as given by Scofield and Fuller, is that they are not true reflections of the word *oikonomia* since they say nothing about service, stewardship or management. Rather they emphasise a period of time, something that seems to be lacking in the Greek. Subsequent definitions given by dispensationalists have sought to correct this. For example:

> The word *oikonomia* bears one significance, and means "an administration", whether of a house, or property, or a state, or a nation, or as in the present study, the administration of the human race or any part of it, at any given time. Just as a parent would govern his household in different ways, according to varying necessity, yet ever for one good end, so God has at different times dealt with men in different ways, according to the necessity of the case, but throughout for one great, great end. (W. Graham Scroggie, *Ruling Lines of Progressive Revelation*)

> An economy is an ordered condition of things ... There are various economies running through the Word of God. A dispensation, an economy, then, is that one particular order or condition of things prevailing in one special age which does not necessarily prevail in another. (H. A. Ironside, *In The Heavenlies*)

Scroggie manages to avoid any mention of time. Ironside commences by defining a dispensation as an economy, but ends by linking dispensation with a "special age". This also raises another point: what one person may consider a *special* age, another may not. Such a definition is open to subjectivity, as, too, is the following one.

> A dispensation is a distinguishable economy in the outworking of God's purposes. (Charles C. Ryrie, *Dispensationalism Today*)

What one person finds *distinguishable*, another may not. We shall return to this later.

Seven Dispensations

Earlier we quoted Scofield's definition of dispensation. In this he stated that there were seven dispensations. Darby, also, stated that there were seven - but they did not agree on what constituted each of the seven.

Darby	*Scofield*
1. Paradisaical State (to the Flood)	1. Innocency
	2. Conscience
2. Noah	3. Human Government
3. Abraham	4. Promise
4. Israel	5. Law
- under law	
- under priesthood	
- under kings	
5. Gentiles	6. Grace
6. Spirit	
7. Millennium	7. Kingdom

Where Darby has one dispensation from creation to Noah, Scofield has two. However, where Scofield has the dispensation of Grace, Darby has two. This shows us one of the problems of traditional dispensationalism. The other is highlighted by Darby's fourth dispensation. He sees the need to split it into three subdispensations.

However, the situation is far more diverse than that. James Gray (1851-1935) came up with eight dispensations. We shall add these to the above for easy comparison.

Darby	*Scofield*	*Gray*
1. Paradisaical State (to the flood)	1. Innocency	1. Edenic
	2. Conscience	2. Antediluvian
2. Noah	3. Human Government	3. Patriarchal
3. Abraham	4. Promise	
4. Israel	5. Law	4. Mosaic
- under law		
- under priesthood		
- under kings		
5. Gentiles	6. Grace	5. Church
6. Spirit		
7. Millennium	7. Kingdom	6. Millennial
		7. Fulness of times
		8. Eternal

Gray does not agree with either Darby or Scofield as to how many dispensations there are or which sections of the Bible constitute a dispensation.

Eighteen dispensations

So, how many dispensations are there? The early church fathers saw four. After the reformation some said seven, the most popular number, but, others said eight and some suggested six.

However, there is no agreement on what these seven (eight or six) were. This can be very confusing and it does show us how inept the definitions of dispensation have been.

> How many "dispensations" are indicated in the Scriptures? This is a question that is more easily asked than answered ... When we refer to the different "dispensations" we refer to those subdivisions of the ages, in which the revealed will of God, carrying differing obligations, had been made known, and put into force. (Charles H. Welch, *An Alphabetical Analysis*, Volume 1, 208)

Here we are faced with the dilemma. How many dispensations are there? Welch goes on to give a list of what he terms "Outstanding Dispensations", but before doing so states:

> The following subdivision of the Purpose of the Ages does not claim to be perfect or complete, but no real distinction in administration has been ignored, though some may have been merged (as for example the special stewardship of John the Baptist, the period under Saul before the accession of David, and others, which would swell the list unduly).
>
> *Outstanding Dispensations*
>
> (NB. Some may overlap, and more than one can run together at the same time.)
>
> 1 Innocence. Adam unfallen. Paradise enjoyed.
> 2. Adam to Noah. The Fall to the Flood.
> 3. Noah to Babel. NB. - Some features of Genesis 9 remain unchanged.
> 4. Babel to Abraham. The Nations and the Nation.
> 5. Abraham to Egypt. The Exodus marks a critical change.
> 6. Exodus to Sinai. The covenant 430 years after the promise.
> 7. Sinai to Jericho. The forty years wandering.
> 8. Jericho to Saul. The land entered.
> 9. David to Christ. Here there are subdivisions which we have not noted.
> 10. The Earthly Ministry of Christ, His Birth, Life, Death, Resurrection, Ascension.

11. Pentecost to Peter in Prison, Acts 2-11.
12. Paul's First Ministry. The Gentile a wild olive contrary to nature.
13. Paul's Prison Ministry. The dispensation of the Grace of God and the dispensation of the Mystery.
14. The Resumption of Pentecost. The seven churches of Rev. 2,3.
15. The Day of the Lord. The Apocalypse.
16. The Millennial Kingdom and Revelation 20.
17. The Period between the end of the Millennium and the Great White Throne.
18. The End. The goal reached. God all in all.

As stated above, Welch does not claim the above to be either "perfect or complete". After giving the list he writes:

> Anyone is at liberty to add further subdivisons as the study of the Word makes such dispensations, administrations, or stewardships clear.

Here, I think, Welch has faced the problem of trying to say what are the dispensations in the Bible. However, he does not seem to give a formal definition of the word. Rather he talks about the Greek word.

> The Greek *oikonomia* is made up of the word *oikos* "house" and *nemo* "to administer", "to deal out", "to distribute". The word *oikonomia* is employed by Plato for the management of a household. (Charles H Welch, *An Alphabetical Analysis*, Volume 1, p 207)

Distinguishable dispensations

It would seem that over the years traditional dispensationalists have tried to come up with a definition of dispensation which omits any reference to age or time. They have done this by talking about it in terms of an economy or an administration, and in this they would seem to be right.

However, it would appear that the greatest problem they have to overcome is subjectivity. They need a definition which is objective: i.e. one not open to personal interpretation. Definitions used so far have led people to say that there are six, seven or eight dispensations - or eighteen or as many as you like! Even amongst people who agree to there being the same number, e.g. seven, there is disagreement over what constitutes those seven.

Ironside wrote of a dispensation being a *special* age. But "special" is a subjective word. What may be *special* to one person, may not be *special* to another. Ryrie wrote that a dispensation is a *distinguishable* economy. But is "distinguishable" a subjective word? If we take Ryrie's definition at face value and *distinguish* everything then we end up with the eighteen, or more, dispensations of Welch. However, I do not think Ryrie would want us to take *distinguishable* at its face value. When describing, rather than defining, dispensations, he wrote:

> If one were describing a dispensation he would include other things, such as the ideas of distinctive revelation, testing, failure and judgment. (Charles C. Ryrie, *Dispensationalism Today*)

One way to tell what is *distinguishable* seems to be, amongst other things, to note *distinctive* revelation. But "distinctive" is a subjective word leading to differing views. To illustrate this further, we will discuss the seven dispensations set out by Charles C. Ryrie in *Dispensationalism Today*.

Traditional Dispensations

The seven dispensations set out by Ryrie are as follows:

1. The dispensation of Innocency or Freedom.
   Genesis 1:28-3:6
2. The dispensation of Conscience or Self-Determination.
   Genesis 4:1-8:14
3. The dispensation of Civil Government.
   Genesis 8:15-11:9
4. The dispensation of Promise or Patriarchal Rule.
   Genesis 11:10 - Exodus 18:27
5. The dispensation of the Mosaic Law.
   Exodus 19:1 - Acts 1:26
6. The dispensation of Grace.
   Acts 2:1 - Revelation 19:21
7. The dispensation of the Millennium
   Revelation 20:1-15

What we shall do is to compare and contrast some of the above dispensations. We may agree with some of the changes set out, but what it will demonstrate is the subjectivity of the above divisions.

The flood - a distinctive change?

Genesis 9:1-17 records the covenant God made with Noah after the flood. The essential elements seem to be as follows:

1) Be fruitful and increase in number and fill the earth. (vs 1,7)
2) The fear and dread of you will fall upon all beasts, birds, creatures and fish. (v 2)
3) Everything that lives and moves will be for food, plus green plants. (v 3)
4) Must not eat meat with blood still in it. (v 4)
5) Capital punishment for murder. (vs 5-6)
6) Earth never to be destroyed by water again. The rainbow. (vs 8-17)

However, not all of these are changes.

1) The injunction to be fruitful, increase and fill the earth had been given to Adam (Genesis 1:28).
2) After the fall the ground was cursed, animals were killed (Genesis 3:17-19; 3:21). How much rule over the animals did Adam, and subsequent generations, lose?
3) Before the flood people ate plants just as after (Genesis 1:29-30). However, there is the possibility that they also, on occasions, ate meat for, after being offered to God as sacrifices, animals were eaten (cf. Genesis 4:1-4; 31:54).
4) Animals which were sacrificed would probably have been killed in a similar way before and after the flood, ensuring there was no blood in the meat.
5) Capital punishment was a possibility before the flood. Hence Cain's concern in Genesis 4:13-14.
6) This promise is new.

Now, you may not agree with all of the above comments. Whether or not all of them are right does not matter. The point here is this: whether there was a *significant* difference in the way God dealt with man before and after the flood is open to question. It is a matter of opinion. One person may not see any *significant* differences, but another may.

There may have been a rainbow in the sky every now and then after the flood, but by and large, people went about their lives in much the same way as they did before. Murder was wrong and punishable, probably by death, before as well as after. Sacrificing animals to God was as desirable before as after. One would hardly call what changes there were *significant*.

But what about the flood? That was a truly spectacular event and was used to wipe out all those who had rebelled against God. That is true. However, spectacular events need not mark the end of a dispensation. There is nothing implicit in the word dispensation (*oikonomia*) which suggests that a dispensation should end with a bang, but this is what some dispensationalists have thought and taught.

One aspect of traditional dispensationalism is, as Ryrie puts it, "ideas of distinctive revelation, testing, failure and judgment". It is true that traditional dispensationalists have always tried to look for times of great judgment as marking the ends of dispensations. They see it as a judgment of God upon people who have been tested by him and who have failed. However, the ideas of testing and judgment are quite foreign to the word *oikonomia*. A stewardship, a management, an administration, need not end drastically. And neither does a great judgment necessarily signify the end of an administration or stewardship.

God may well assess a group of people as having failed and judge them at any time. However, He can continue with a subgroup along the same, or similar, lines. This is what seems to have happened at the flood. There were some changes, but was there a change in dispensation? Who can say - if we use the traditional definitions of dispensation?

Pentecost! Law to Grace - a distinctive change?

According to Ryrie the dispensation of the Mosaic Law operated from Exodus 19:1 to Acts 1:26. Then, at Acts 2:1, we enter a new dispensation, the dispensation of Grace. But is it as simple as that? It may not be so, for a number of reasons.

1) Law

As we saw in chapter 9, the people of Israel, both those who believed that Jesus was the Christ and those who did not, continued to observe the Mosaic Law long after Pentecost. It is clear from Acts 15 that Jewish Christians continued to keep the Law and practice circumcision, and they were so zealous of these that many of them wanted the Gentiles to observe them also.

> Some men came down from Judea to Antioch and were teaching the brothers: "Unless you are circumcised, according to the custom taught by Moses, you cannot be saved." ... Then some of the believers who belonged to the party of the Pharisees stood up and said, "The Gentiles must be circumcised and required to obey the law of Moses." (Acts 15:1,5)

> "You see, brother, how many thousands of Jews have believed, and all of them are zealous for the law." (Acts 21:20)

Paul, himself, was diligent in his observance of the Law. For example, consider the following:

> On the sabbath they (Paul and Barnabas) entered the synagogue. (Acts 13:14)
>
> He (Paul) circumcised him (Timothy) because of the Jews. (Acts 16:3)
>
> As his custom was, Paul went into the synagogue, and on three Sabbath days he reasoned with them from the Scriptures. (Acts 17:2)
>
> Every Sabbath he (Paul) reasoned in the synagogue. (Acts 18:4)
>
> Before he sailed, he (Paul) had his hair cut off at Cenchrea because of a vow he had taken. (Acts 18:18; see Numbers 6:1-21)
>
> We sailed from Phillipi after the feast of Unleavened Bread. (Acts 20:6)
>
> Paul ... was in a hurry to reach Jerusalem, if possible, by the day of Pentecost. (Acts 20:16)
>
> I did not realise that he was the high priest; for it is written: "Do not speak evil about the ruler of your people." (Acts 23:5; see Exodus 22:28)
>
> I was ceremonially clean when they found me in the temple courts. (Acts 24:18)

There can be no doubt that Paul was a Christian. Neither can there be any doubt that after his conversion he was just as zealous for the Law as he was before. Consider Acts 21. Here James, the leader of the Christian church in Jerusalem, addresses Paul.

> "Take these men, join in their purification rites and pay their expenses, so that they can have their heads shaved. Then everybody will know there is no truth in these reports about you, but that you yourself are living in obedience to the law ... " The next day Paul took the men and purified himself along with them. Then he went to the temple to give notice of the date when the days of purification would end and the offering would be made for each of them. (Acts 21:24-26; see also Numbers 6:1-21)

Here we see Paul observing the Sabbath, circumcising, making Nazarite vows, honouring the feasts, respecting the high priest, and being sure he was ceremonially clean. In his letters written during Acts he was careful to show that he upheld the Law (Romans 3:31). The Law did not bring righteousness, but the Law was the God-pleasing way to live.

Thus, if we are to have a dispensation of the Mosaic Law we cannot end it at the close of Acts 1, for the Christian Jews continued throughout Acts to be rightly zealous of the Law.

Also, to end the Mosaic Law dispensation at the close of Acts 1 seems rather incongruous as Acts 2 opens with the feast of Pentecost, one of the main feasts of the Law! (See Leviticus 23.)

2) Grace

But did the dispensation of grace start at Acts 2? We do not read very far before we come to Acts 5, where two Christian Jews, Ananaias and Sapphira, are struck dead (vs 1-11). Their sin was telling lies. This action has more in common with a dispensation of Law, with its judgments, than it does with a dispensation of grace. And it is not isolated.

y

> On the appointed day Herod, wearing his royal robes, sat on his throne and delivered a public address to the people. They shouted, "This is the voice of a god, not of a man." Immediately, because Herod did not give praise to God, an angel of the Lord struck him down, and he was eaten by worms and died. (Acts 12:21- 23)

> Then Saul ... filled with the Holy Spirit, looked straight at Elymas and said ... "Will you never stop perverting the right ways of the Lord? Now the hand of the Lord is against you. You are going to be blind, and for a time you will be unable to see the light of the sun." Immediately mist and darkness came over him, and he groped about, seeking someone to lead him by the hand. (Acts 13:9-11)

Immediate judgments such as these upon Herod and Elymas do not have a place in a dispensation of grace. They seem to have more in common with the Old Testament and should make us ask whether there was a change of dispensation at Acts 2. That there were judgments from God during Acts cannot be denied. Paul wrote about others in one of the letters he wrote at that time.

> In the following directives I have no praise for you, for your meetings do more harm than good ... When you come together, it is not the Lord's Supper you eat, for as you eat, each of you goes ahead without waiting for anybody else. One remains hungry, another gets drunk ...

> Therefore, whoever eats the bread or drinks the cup of the Lord in an unworthy manner will be guilty of sinning against the body and blood of the Lord. A man ought to examine himself before he eats of the bread and drinks of the cup. For anyone who eats and drinks without recognising the body of the Lord eats and drinks judgment on himself. That is why many among you are weak and sick, and a number of you have fallen asleep. (1 Corinthians 11:17-30)

Here Paul wrote about the Corinthian Christians bringing judgment upon themselves - see also 1 Corinthians 10:1-11. Paul went on to say that if each man judged himself with respect to his attitude and behaviour at the Lord's supper, then he would not come under judgment from God (1 Corinthians 11:31). The next verses contain the important principle as to why judgments fell upon those people and what they should do to avoid them.

> When we are judged by the Lord, we are being disciplined so that we will not be condemned with the world. So then, my brothers, when you come together to eat, wait for each other. If anyone is hungry, he should eat at home, so that when you meet together it may not result in judgment. (1 Corinthians 11:32-34).

So was there a change of dispensation at Acts 2? There may not have been, for the Mosaic Law continued. Judgments continued. But wasn't there grace? Yes! There was. But there was grace before. Christ's words to Nicodemus in John 3 are all to do with grace. See also John 1:17 where we are told that "grace and truth came through Jesus Christ". There is grace in the Old Testament also. At the giving of the replacement stone tablets on which the Law was written, we read:

> The Lord, the Lord, the compassionate and gracious God, slow to anger, abounding in love and faithfulness, maintaining love to thousands, and forgiving wickedness, rebellion and sin. (Exodus 34:6-7)

There is grace in the Law. There is grace in the Gospels. Thus there was grace before Pentecost as well as after. Whether there is more grace after Pentecost and less judgment is open to debate. Whether the increase in grace and decrease in judgment is distinguishable enough to warrant a change in dispensation, is a matter of opinion. We cannot be definite if we limit ourselves to the traditional definitions of dispensation.

The Millennium! The last dispensation?

The length of God's kingdom upon earth, 1000 years, is given in Revelation 20:6. At the end of this millennial kingdom there is to be a great battle, with fire from heaven destroying those who attack God's people (20:7-9).

After this comes a resurrection of the dead, their judgment, and then the creation of the new heavens, the new earth, and the new Jerusalem. Conditions in this new sphere are to be very different. It is to be "the home of righteousness" (2 Peter 3:13), so different from this present one. If we read Revelation 21 we find that there is to be "no more death or mourning or crying or pain" (v 4). We learn that the "old order of things has passed away" (v 4). Those who have a place in this new creation, either in the new heavens, the new Jerusalem or upon the new earth, will be resurrected and righteous, immortal and eternal. How different from the Millennium which proceeded it. Is the new creation a "distinguishable economy in the outworking of God's purposes"? Most would say so, but apparently Ryrie would not. He does not list it among his dispensations, yet the change from this old creation to the new would be far more *distinctive* than the change from before and after the flood or before and after the Pentecost of Acts 2.

Conclusion

In this section we have been discussing the definitions of dispensation given by a number of Christians whom the author greatly admires. We have tried to show that those definitions are lacking in precision and objectivity. They are subjective and open to a wide variety of interpretations. As such they are not particularly helpful.

We have looked at how some people, using these subjective definitions, have come up with differing numbers of dispensations. And even those who have come up with the same number do not agree on which they are. We have seen that the definitions could lead us to having almost as many dispensations as we like: four; seven; eight; eighteen; or perhaps more.

We have looked at one writer's dispensations and have queried whether some of the changes he has suggested are distinctive and whether the economies he sees are indeed distinguishable from one another. And we have suggested that one economy which he does not see as distinctive, the new creation, is very different and distinguishable.

We suggest, therefore, that the underlying problem is the fact that all the basic definitions of dispensation are lacking.

22. A new approach

We concluded the previous chapter by suggesting that the traditional definitions of dispensation are lacking in precision and objectivity. However, there may be more to the problem than just that. If it was simply a case of a wrong definition then it should not prove too difficult to construct a new one which was both objective and precise. Yet, in spite of all their attempts to do this, traditional dispensationalists have failed. It may be that their basic, underlying idea of what constitutes a dispensation is wrong.

People

It would seem that over the years dispensationalists of all descriptions have been starting in the wrong place. To help explain this we need to consider one more definition.

> The Greek word rendered dispensation is *oikonomia* and refers to the act of administering. By the figure Metonymy, the act of administering is transferred to the time during which that administering is carried on. (E. W. Bullinger, *How to Enjoy the Bible*)

This is a great improvement on the previous definitions we have considered, with the possible exception of Scroggie's. However, it still omits one essential.

There is a danger in dispensationalism that its adherents become more interested in the acts of God than in God Himself, or the people He is dealing with. They can know more about God's plans and purposes than they know about His person. They may understand more about His judgments than they do about His character. We are not saying that all or most dispensationalists are like this. We are saying that this is an incipient danger in dispensationalism. In looking for distinguishable economies, distinctive revelations, and differing actions, God himself, His character and person, can get a little blurred. His actions and revelations become more important than His person and character.

Bearing this in mind we should note that the word for dispensation, *oikonomia*, is related to the word *oikonomos*. Now *oikonomia* gives us dispensation, administration, management, stewardship. *Oikonomos* gives us administrator, manager, steward.

Over the years dispensationalists have been concerned primarily with the details of the administration when they should have considered first *who* was doing that administrating: i.e. *who God's administrators were.* Dispensationalists have been more intent in looking at the rules of management, rather than looking at who was doing the managing: i.e. who were the managers.

Also, dispensationalists have been more interested in looking for a change in the rules or orders, rather than in looking for a change in personnel. The fact that a manager has his orders changed is of far less significance for both him and his employer than his losing his job and a new manager being installed. A change in the details of how a household is to be administered is less significant than appointing a new manager to administer that household. This is especially so for the old manager. Let us return to Luke 16 for a moment.

> Jesus told his disciples: "There was a rich man whose manager (*oikonomos*) was accused of wasting his possessions. So he called him in and asked him, 'What is this I hear about you? Give an account of your management (*oikonomia*), because you cannot be manager (*oikonomos*) any longer.' The manager (*oikonomos*) said to himself, 'What shall I do now? My master is taking away my job (*oikonomia*). I'm not strong enough to dig, and I'm ashamed to beg - I know what I'll do so that, when I lose my job (*oikonomia*) here, people will welcome me into their houses.'" (Luke 16:1-4)

Here we see that there wasy to be a change of manager (*oikonomos*). This was far more drastic for him than if he had been given a change of job (*oikonomia*). If he had been given different work to do, even if he had had a demotion, he would still have had a job (*oikonomia*). Thus, a change in personnel (*oikonomos*) is of more significance than keeping the same personnel and changing their job description (*oikonomia*).

Just as the person and character of God is more important than His actions - for His actions flow from His being - so are the administrators more important than what they do. If, then, the administrators are more important, they should be of greater interest than any change in what they are expected to do.

All who have been involved in employing people know and appreciate this. If you appoint the right people to a job, you can modify the job afterwards with few, if any, problems. However, if you appoint the wrong people ....! Thus people are more important than the jobs they do. Similarly, the administrators God has chosen to use are of more importance than what He has required them to do. (Please note: We are not saying that what God has wanted is not important. All we are saying is that if we are looking for distinctive changes, then *the times when God changes personnel are more distinctive than the times when he changes the rules and regulations for the same personnel.*)

It is in this way that successive generations of dispensationalists have put the cart before the horse. They have been concentrating their efforts on trying to find out where there is a change in the orders, the rules, the regulations. Having found some changes, they then have to ascertain whether these are different enough to give rise to a change in dispensation. Do they warrant a distinguishable economy, a distinctive revelation? It is at this point that subjectivity raises its ugly head and differences of opinion come in.

So before looking at where the rules of the household are altered, let us look first at when the managers of that household are changed.

God's administrators

1) The first administrators

In the opening pages of the Bible it would appear that anyone could be a steward for God. All that was required was a good conscience towards God, faith, and the offering of the animal sacrifices that God had instituted (Genesis 3:21; 4:4). Only Abel, Enoch and Noah are cited in Hebrews 11 as the faithful from that time, but that does not preclude others from having shared with them in this administration, albeit to a lesser extent.

2) The second administrators

The call of Abraham heralded a change. There was to be an added qualification for a person to be one of God's stewards.

> "I will make you into a great nation and I will bless you; I will make your name great, and you will be a blessing. I will bless those who bless you, and whoever curses you I will curse; and all peoples on earth will be blessed through you." (Genesis 12:2-3)

Here God took one man, one family, one nation. This was the start of something new. Even Ryrie acknowledges the significance of this.

> Until this dispensation, all mankind had been directly related to God's governing principles. Now God marked out one family and one nation and in them made a representative test of all. (Charles C.Ryrie, *Dispensationalism Today*)

However, it is unlikely that God chose Abraham, his family, and his nation to undergo tests as representatives of mankind. He chose them to be His servants on earth, with the aim of serving the rest of mankind, for His goal for them was to be a kingdom of priests to the other nations (Exodus 19:6). Neither can we agree with Ryrie that this dispensation started at Genesis 11:10. Nor did it start with Abraham's birth. It was heralded with the promise that God gave to him in Genesis 12:1-3. Ryrie's desire to start it at Genesis 11:10 is because he wishes to finish his previous dispensation with a judgment, the tower of Babel (11:1-9). As shown in the previous chapter, such judgments may or may not mark the end of a dispensation. By and large, they do not.

So it was that Abraham's descendants - Isaac, Jacob, Joseph - became God's stewards upon earth. The nation of Israel were to be His administrators. This situation continued throughout the Old Testament. The fact that the Israelites had their orders changed at the Exodus, were given wide-ranging new commands at Sinai, lived very different lives in the wilderness and in the promised land, were ruled in a variety of ways by judges, kings and prophets, none of these really constitutes a major dispensational change. The administrators were the same. They were the people of Israel. Orders were changed. Rules were altered. However, the people who carried them out were the same. Part of the work was preparing them to go, at some time, to the Gentile nations. At times certain nations and individual Gentiles received great blessings from God, but those blessings always came through Israel.

This does not change when we get to the Gospels. Israel are still the administrators. The occasional Gentile who is blessed has again to acknowledge the primacy of Israel (Matthew 15:21-28 and note verse 27; Mark 7:24-30 and note verse 27). Neither is there a change in stewards when we come to Acts, as we have shown in chapters 4 & 5.

The first quarter of Acts is exclusively Jewish. In the second quarter the occasional Gentile appears on the scene. In the second half of the book further Gentiles are brought in, but they still take second place to Israel (Acts 13:46; Romans 1:16) and the message of Christ as Saviour is taken to them by Israelites. The Gentiles still continue to receive blessings from God through Israel, who are still God's stewards. There has been no change in the stewards, although there may have been a change in their orders.

Also during Acts a number of letters were written exclusively to Jewish Christians: Hebrews, James, 1 & 2 Peter, 1 & 2 & 3 John, Jude, and Revelation. Paul wrote letters to mixed churches of Jewish and Gentile Christians: Romans, 1 & 2 Corinthians, Galatians, 1 & 2

Thessalonians. However, he is at pains to show the precedence of Israel (e.g. Romans 1:16; 2:9-10; 3:1-2).

Some may argue that there was a change in that the Jews who were now God's administrators had to have faith in Jesus as the Messiah. This is, indeed, correct. However, from Genesis 12 onwards it had always been necessary for them to have faith in God, and to believe whatever it was He wanted them to believe. Moses did not have to believe the same things that Abraham did. David did not have to believe all that Moses and Abraham had. Faith was necessary and Jews in the Old Testament who did not exercise their faith automatically ruled themselves out as God's administrators. Similarly, during the Gospels and Acts, any Israelite who did not have faith in Christ automatically ruled himself out of being one of God's stewards.

The important thing to note from the Acts, and the letters written during that time, is that God's work was still being carried out by Jews and, in the main, was for Jews. Gentiles did come in and receive the blessings of forgiveness, salvation, and eternal life, but they did so from the hands of believing Israelites who were still God's stewards.

3) The third administrators

One does not require a great deal of knowledge to be aware that, by and large, the people of Israel rejected Jesus as their Messiah. They rejected Him when He came personally. They rejected Him when Peter, James, John, Paul, Barnabas, and company preached Him during Acts.

Neither does one require a great deal of knowledge to be aware that Christendom today, and throughout the past centuries, has been dominated and administered by Gentiles who have placed their faith in Christ. That being the case, when was there a change in God's managers?

We have already discussed the third and final pronouncement from Isaiah 6, the chapter which talks about Israel being cut down (Isaiah 6:9-13). This came at the end of the Acts of the Apostles.

> "'Go to this people and say, "You will be ever hearing but never understanding; you will be ever seeing but never perceiving." For this people's heart has become calloused; they hardly hear with their ears, and they have closed their eyes. Otherwise they might see with their eyes, hear with their ears, understand with their hearts and turn and I would heal them.'" (Acts 28:26-28)

Through a calloused heart, and with eyes closed to Christ and ears shut to His messengers, Israel, as a special nation before God, was placed on one side. They lost their stewardship. God changed His administrators.

> "Therefore I want you to know that God's salvation has been sent to the Gentiles, and they will listen." (Acts 28:28)

At this time Paul was under house arrest in Rome. He was there for two years (Acts 28:30), during which time he probabaly wrote Ephesians, Colossians, Philemon, and Philippians. Just after the announcement of God's salvation being sent to the Gentiles, we read of Christian Jews and Christian Gentiles being brought together, of their being made one. This was achieved by freeing Christian Jews from the Mosaic Law with its commandments and regulations.

> For he himself is our peace, who has made the two one and has destroyed the barrier, the dividing wall of hostility, by abolishing in his flesh the law with its commandments and regulations. His purpose was to create in himself one new man out of the two, thus making peace, and in this one body to reconcile both of them to God through the cross, by which he put to death their hostility ... This mystery is that through the gospel the Gentiles are heirs together with Israel, members together of one body, and sharers together in the promise in Christ Jesus. (Ephesians 2:14-16; 3:6)

From this time onwards, the sole qualification to be one of God's managers was faith in the Lord Jesus Christ. Nationality did not matter. One could be a Jew, a Roman, a Greek. It mattered not. What mattered was the need to come to God through the Lord Jesus.

4) Future administrators

Many Christians believe that for the unfulfilled prophecies of the Bible to come to fruition there needs to be a restored nation of Israel living in the land of Judea. That there is a nation of Israel today may be a preparation for such events. However, the present nation has not been restored to the position its ancestors held from the time of Abraham to the end of the Acts of the Apostles. When God will restore them, only He knows. How it will be done, only He knows. That He will do it, however, is most certain, and when He does so it will signify another change of administrators. To discuss the prophetic events surrounding such a change is beyond the scope of this book. It is sufficient for us to appreciate that such a change is to take place.

A future, restored nation of Israel is to be appointed as God's stewards and will administer His plans and purposes throughout the millennium. At the end of that time there is to be resurrection, judgment, and a new creation. It would appear that the centre of the new earth is the new Jerusalem, with its twelve apostles and twelve tribes (Revelation 21:12-14). It would seem that the new earth is to be administered by raised and redeemed Israelites, and the redeemed nations are to go up to the new Jerusalem (Revelation 21:24-27).

To sum up

At the start of the Bible anyone was eligible to be one of God's stewards. All that was required was faith, a good conscience, and a willingness to offer God sacrifices.

This began to change with Abraham. In time only Israelites were eligible to be stewards. However, they needed more than physical descent from Abraham. Like him, they, too, needed faith and were also expected to obey the Law. What, precisely, they needed to believe may have changed but faith was essential. This situation continued throughout the Old Testament and into the New, up to the end of Acts.

Following this, things reverted to the situation where anyone of any race or nationality could be one of God's stewards. Again faith was necessary. It had to be placed in the Lord Jesus Christ.

Finally, there is to come a time when the people of Israel will be restored by God to their former position. When this has been done they will once more be God's stewards upon earth and will administer His affairs throughout the Millennium and beyond to the new earth.

Conclusion

To define a change of dispensation as taking place when God changes His stewards removes subjectivity. In addition, a change of managers, or stewards, is of greater importance than a change in their rules and orders, or any alterations in the job they have to do.

To look through the Bible and to see when there is a change in the administrators is relatively easy to do. It is unambiguous. One is not playing with subjective words like "distinctive" or "distinguishable" or "special". One has no relative words, no qualifying adjectives. Either this group is administering God's affairs or it is not. Either these are the requirements to be a manager of God's affairs or they are not.

Thus a change in administrators is of far greater importance than a change in what they have to do. That is, a change in the people doing a job is of greater importance than a change in job of those already employed.

23. Administrators and administrations

We concluded the last chapter by stating that we should take greater note of changes in those who manage God's affairs than we do of changes in the orders or tasks those managers may be given. That does not mean to say that there are not some major alterations in the roles or messages or duties of those administrators, an aspect we shall consider in a moment.

Whether we call those responsible for God's affairs on earth managers, administrators, stewards, or something else, is of minor consequence. The important issue is to appreciate that, at times, God has appointed particular people with particular credentials to administer His affairs. We may find, occasionally, that others have a minor or temporary role. However, that does not detract from the fact that the members of the former group have been appointed the administrators.

For example, Egypt had a role in feeding and preserving Israel and his descendants. Although this was a very important work for Egypt, and vital in God's purposes, Egypt was in that position thanks to Joseph. Again, Nebuchadnezzar issued a proclamation to the peoples, nations and men of every language, praising and exalting God. However, it was Daniel who had been instrumental in bringing Nebuchadnezzar to that point. Similarly, the king of Nineveh issued his decree to call upon God following the preaching of Jonah. Then, lastly, in the second half of Acts, Gentiles believed in Christ. However, they heard of Him through Christian Jews who were being used, at that time, to provoke the rest of Israel into repenting and believing. They were being used as a wild olive stimulates a cultivated one to bear fruit (Romans 11:11-21).

Thus the managers of God's affairs in the Bible are:

1) Until the call of Abraham - anyone with faith in God and who would come to Him through the sacrifices He had stipulated.
2) From Abraham to the close of Acts - any descendant of Abraham, through Isaac and Jacob, who believed what God required them to believe, and who obeyed what laws He wanted them to obey.
3) From the close of Acts until some future time - anyone of any nation who comes to God through faith in the Lord Jesus Christ.
4) From that future time onwards - descendants of Abraham, through Isaac and Jacob, believing what God will require them to believe.

We have been rather vague with regard to precisely what certain people were required to believe. However, one cannot generalise in this matter. "Without faith it is impossible to please God" states Hebrews 11:6. Moses was not called to believe exactly the same things as Abraham was. David was not asked to believe exactly the same as either Abraham or Moses. Peter and the twelve had different goals for their faith from Abraham, Moses and David.

Now if we wish to chart this approach we can have four headings and draw three clear time-lines separating them. Two of these are easily noted from Scripture. The third is not, as we do not know when in the future the change of stewards will take place.

Anyone faith	Israelites faith	Any nationality faith	Israelites faith
Genesis 12:1-3	Acts 28:28	? Future	

These, then, are our primary divisions in the Scriptures. They show us when there was a change in those managing God's affairs. They give us what we will term the major dispensational changes. Naturally, we would expect when new managers are appointed that the task to be done might be changed, and this is the case. Not only do the above represent the changes in God's administrators, they also mark the the major changes in how God's work was to be organised on earth. There may well be other, minor, changes which are of less importance.

Major dispensational changes

It is interesting to note that under the traditional definitions of dispensation the first two major changes, at Genesis 12:1-3 and Acts 28:28, were not picked out. This is because of the writers' desire, consciously initially, but subconsciously laterly, for a dispensation to end with some overtly dramatic failure and a clearly seen judgment from God. Thus Babel (Genesis 11:1-9) was seen as the end of a dispensation. This means a new one starting at Genesis 11:10. However, we know little or nothing about the years between the confusion of tongues and the promise given to Abraham (Genesis 12:1-3). It is quite likely that the relationship between man and God which operated after there were many languages was conducted in exactly the same way as it had been when there was only one tongue. After all, language is not a barrier for God.

A major change was announced not by the fall of Babel and the confusion of tongues, but years later with the call of Abraham.

Similarly the cross, or Pentecost, is seen by traditional dispensationists to be the start of a new dispensation because of Israel's failure to believe in Jesus and because of their responsibility for His crucifixion. However, for a number of reasons, there is no major dispensational change at this point.

1) There is no change in God's stewards. The Gospels are dominated by Israel, and so are the Acts of the Apostles and the letters written during that time. Even Acts 2 is careful to state that all those present in Jerusalem were "God-fearing *Jews* from every nation under heaven ... *Jews* and converts to *Judaism*" (Acts 2:5,11). Peter addressed his speech to "Fellow *Jews* and all of you who live in *Jerusalem* ... *Men of Israel* ... let all *Israel* be assured" (Acts 2:14,22,36), and his next speech was to "Men of *Israel*" (Acts 3:12).
2) The people of Israel were forgiven their sin of crucifying the Christ. On the cross He prayed, "Father, forgive them, for they do not know what they are doing" (Luke 23:34). We might wonder how on earth it was that they did not know what they were doing. But our judgment is irrelevant. Christ's is the important one. Also, referring to their rejection and crucifixion of Christ, Peter states "I know that you acted in ignorance, as did your leaders" (Acts 3:17). Now, under the Law of Moses, a sin committed in ignorance could be forgiven (Leviticus 4:1-27; Numbers 15:22-29). At the request of the Son the nation was forgiven and freed to carry on as God's stewards.
3) Christ had to suffer, as He pointed out Himself both before and after His resurrection (Matthew 16:21; Luke 24:26,44,46), and as stated by the angels (Luke 24:7) and Peter.

> "This man was handed over to you by God's set purpose and foreknowledge; and you, with the help of wicked men, put him to death by nailing him to the cross ... Now, brothers, I know that you acted in ignorance, as did your leaders. But this is how God fulfilled what he had foretold through all the prophets, saying that his Christ (Messiah) would suffer." (Acts 2:23; 3:17-18)

Thus the suffering, death and resurrection of the Lord Jesus Christ was all part and parcel of God's purposes. The details of how it would happen may not have been known, but that He was to suffer and die was a fact, indeed a necessity since he was the Lamb of God who was to take away the sin of the world (John 1:29,36).

There is no doubt about the fact that what was achieved by Christ's death on the cross has many more far-reaching effects than anything else that has taken place on this earth before or since. It has redeemed the whole creation. It has defeated sin and death. It has gained for us forgiveness and eternal life. However, all this was known beforehand, prophesied, and spoken about. So at the cross there was no major dispensational change; no change in purpose, no change in managers. That came later when, after a further thirty or more years of hearing from the lips of His witnesses that Jesus was the Messiah, the nation of Israel, by and large, still rejected Him. Not only that, they tried to prevent the apostles from speaking of Christ to the Gentiles. In this they filled up their sins to the limit (1 Thessalonians 2:16). In that they were not forgiven. They hardened their hearts, shut their eyes and closed their ears. God's salvation was sent to the Gentiles (Acts 28:25-28). Then things began to change.

There was no overtly dramatic judgment from God at that time, just a quiet leaving of Israel in their state of blindness and deafness and a gentle moving towards the Gentiles who were open. Within a few short years after the end of Acts the Romans came, destroyed Jerusalem and the temple, and carried the Israelites into exile. By the time the dust settled we are into the second century and the writings of the early church fathers. These indicate clearly that Israel had, indeed, been removed as God's stewards. All those fathers were Gentiles and their writings deal with matters pertinent to Gentiles.

The only remaining major dispensational change is still future, when the people of Israel are to be restored to their position of stewards. When this will be done, only God knows. How it will be done, only He knows. There have been many schemes of the future and many publications on prophecy. However, it would take too much space to discuss adequately the possible ways in which God could reinstate Israel. It is sufficient for our present purpose simply to acknowledge that He will restore them.

Minor dispensational changes - Adam to Abraham

The whole of this period is covered in just eleven chapters. Some see three minor dispensational changes, namely, (1) the fall, (2) the flood, and, (3) Babel. How significant those changes are is open to dispute.

We also need to ask, how important are those chapters to our understanding of the rest of the Bible and in our daily Christian lives? They are certainly not unimportant, nor should we cast doubt upon their veracity. It is just that most of us are remote from the issues they deal with. These opening chapters have little relevance in our prayers and practice. To go into great debates and discussions over these eleven chapters, where so little information is given, may be unprofitable at this point in time.

We need to be aware that, in those eleven chapters after creation, we have three notable events: the fall, the flood and Babel. With respect to God's dealing with men, things certainly were very different before and after the fall, but God's administrators did not change. They were still Adam and Eve. Although the advent of sin changed their relationship with God, their task was more or less the same. None the less, the fall does constitute a minor dispensational change.

With respect to the flood, there do not appear to have been any major changes before and after it, the advent of the rainbow being the most significant. As for Babel, what changed other than language? Language may be very important in human relationships, but it is irrelevant with respect to God's dealings with man.

Minor dispensational changes - Abraham to Acts 28:25-28

Within this period most people see two changes which are of significance, namely the giving of the Law and the crucifixion of Christ. We could add a third: the entry of Gentiles in the middle of Acts. The reason for doing so is that their advent was linked to the secret of the partal blindness of Israel (Romans 11:25). At that point of time, God did something new. We also need to consider this change for another reason. As Christians, the New Testament is of great importance to us and our understanding of it profoundly affects what we do and believe. Thus we need to pay closer attention to changes in the New Testament. However, before we do so, let us return to the Old. Some writers have suggested the following are the dispensational changes from Genesis 12:1-3 to Acts 28:28.

Abraham to Egypt	:	Abraham, Isaac, Jacob, Joseph
Exodus to Sinai	:	Moses, the Passover, the Red Sea
Sinai to Jericho	:	The Law, forty years in the wilderness
Jericho to Saul	:	The Promised Land, the Judges
Saul to Exile	:	Kings and Prophets
Exile to Return	:	In Babylon and Medo-Persia
Return to John	:	Back in the Land, waiting
John to Pentecost	:	John, Jesus
Pentecost to Mid-Acts	:	The twelve to the Jews
Mid-Acts to Acts 28:28	:	Jews first and also Gentiles

How helpful are these divisions? How significant are they? Some of them are open to dispute. However, the giving of the Law did dramatically alter the house rules that the stewards had to follow. From then on, God's administrators, Israel, had many new and different things to do. But more than that, the Mosaic Law formed the ground rules not only for the rest of the Old Testament and for the whole of the Gospels, but also for Christian Jews during the whole of the time covered by the Acts of the Apostles. From Sinai to the end of Acts the law was observed by the people of Israel and their leaders in the following way:

1) The Law in the wilderness
   This was implemented by Moses with the help of others.
2) The Law in the land
   a) Initially implemented by Joshua.
   b) Then came the Judges, who ruled Israel according to the Law.
   c) Then came the Kings. According to the Law, each king had to make his own copy of the Law and he was to read from it each day. (Deuteronomy 17:14-20)
   d) As the kings deteriorated so God sent prophets, to call people to repent and to turn back to the Law.
3) The Law in exile
   In exile there were prophets and Jews in high places, like Daniel, who lived according to the Law, setting an example to the rest of the Israelites.
4) The Law back in the land
   a) Ezra and Nehemiah re-established the kingdom in accordance with the Law.
   b) By New Testament times the Sanhedrin, which consisted mainly of Pharisees, Sadducees, and Teachers of the Law debated, interpreted, and administered the Law for Israel. Even though some of their interpretations were far removed from the spirit of the commandments given by Moses, the Law was the basis of their society. Christ stated that he had not come to abolish the Law, but to fulfil it (Matthew 5:17)
   c) In the Acts of the Apostles, the Christian Jews were zealous of the Law and keen to live by it (Acts 15:1-5; 21:20-26).

Thus the Law, its rules and regulations, its implementation, dominates the Scriptures from Exodus 19 to the end of Acts. That being the case we must be careful not to read it back into the earlier parts of Scripture - Genesis, Exodus 1-18 and Job. Neither should we read it forward into the later parts - Ephesians, Philippians, Colossians, 1 & 2 Timothy, Titus and Philemon. The first of these mistakes is common. The second is rare. What tends to happen is that people read the Acts and earlier letters as if the Law was inoperative. Some do this even to the Gospels.

Few would deny that there were significant changes when the Law came in at Sinai. Thus the introduction of the Law marks a minor dispensational change.

The Law did not pass off the scene until the people of Israel lost their position at Acts 28:25-28. The abolition of the Law coincides with the dismissal of Israel as God's stewards, both of which occurred at the end of Acts.

The change from Judges to Kings, and the appearance on the scene of prophets, did not change the need for the Israelites to observe the Law in their lives, though if we were to make a major study of those parts of the Old Testament, we should have to take such changes into account. However, compared to the giving of the Law at Sinai these cannot be described as even minor changes. Whether a change is significant or not, depends to some extent on how much importance and how much attention are given to the particular part of Scripture in which it occurs. There were some changes in Christ's ministry which, in absolute terms, may have been less drastic than the change from Judges to Kings. However, because Christ's ministry is of far greater interest to us, and is of far more importance, such changes may be worth noting. For example: each Gospel commences with the proclamation of the kingdom followed by the announcement of Jesus as its King. The king is rejected and then, finally, the kingdom is rejected. This forms the central part of each Gospel, as the following extract from *The Companion Bible* indicates.

	Matthew	Mark	Luke	John
Pre-Ministerial	1:1 -2:23		1:1 -2:52	
The Forerunner	3:1 -4	1:1 -8	3:1 -20	1:1 -28
The Baptism: in water	3:5 -17	1:9 -11	3:21-38	1:29-34
The Temptations	4:1 -11	1:12-13	4:1 -14	
The Kingdom proclaimed	4:12-7:29	1:14-20	4:14-5:11	1:35-4:54
The King proclaimed	8:1 -16:20	1:21-8:30	5:12-9:21	5:1 -6:71
The King rejected	16:21-20:34	8:31-10:52	9:22-18:43	7:1 -11:54
The Kingdom rejected	21:1 -26:35	11:1-14:25	19:1-22:38	11:54-18:1
The Agony: garden	26:36-46	14:26-42	22:39-46	
The Baptism: in death	26:47-28:15	14:43-16:14	22:47-24:12	18:2 -20:31
The Successors	28:16-18	16:15-20	24:13-49	21:1 -25
Post-Ministerial	28:19-20		24:50-53	

Such changes in Christ's ministry may explain the differences in the instructions He gave to His disciples (compare Matthew 10:9-10 and

Luke 22:35-38) though whether we would want to describe these as dispensational changes is another matter. They are worthy of note and are helpful in a detailed study of one of the Gospels.

As indicated before, there is a significant change in the middle of Acts. This was brought about by a hardening in part by Israel (Romans 11:25), which was countered by bringing in a number of Gentiles. Such a situation and such an action is described as a mystery (secret), presumably because nothing had been said about such a turn of events in the Law, the Prophets, and the Psalms. Neither had Christ referred to it. These Gentiles were to act like a wild olive grafted into the cultivated olive tree of Israel. This was an attempt to stimulate God's stewards into action (Romans 11:11-21). To bring about this situation required:

1) A vision to be given to Cornelius (Acts 10:1-8);
2) A vision to be given to Peter (Acts 10:9-19);
3) The Holy Spirit speaking to Peter (Acts 10:19-20);
4) Peter giving an explanation to Christian Jews as to why he visited Gentiles (Acts 11:1-18);
5) A ministry to the Gentiles being given to Paul (Acts 9:15);
6) Barnabas being sent to Antioch to see Gentile Christians (Acts 11:19-26);
7) A special council of Jewish Christians in Jerusalem being convened at which the Gentiles were asked to obey four rules which would allow the Jewish Christians to have fellowship with them without becoming unclean (Acts 15:1-29).

This does not constitute a major dispensational change as there had been no change in God's stewards. The people of Israel were still His administrators. However, the situation of partial hardness in Israel and the use of Gentiles to try to soften the hearts of the nation was very new. Both this situation and how God was to act in it were described by Paul as a secret - (see Romans 11:25; mystery = secret).

We have only to read the second half of Acts to see what effect these Gentiles had upon the Christian Jews and the non-Christian Jews. It may not have had a major effect in terms of world history, but it was a dramatic one for those concerned (e.g. Acts 13:45-50; 14:2; 17:5,13). Thus *the introduction of Gentiles in Acts, to provoke Israel to bear fruit, is a minor dispensational change.*

It is interesting to note that Paul also describes as a mystery (secret) the change at the end of Acts, when Israel had become blind and deaf and useless. God then sent His salvation to the Gentiles (see Ephesians 3:1-10; Colossians 1:25-27). We may read in the Old Testament about partial hardness in Israel and how God would treat such a situation (e.g.

Deuteronomy 28:15-44). But nowhere do we read that He would bring in Gentiles to provoke Israel, as He did mid-way through Acts. Again we may read in the Old Testament of what would happen should Israel become totally hard (e.g. Deuteronomy 28:49-68; Isaiah 6:9-13). But nowhere do we read that God would turn and use Gentiles as His administrators instead of Israel, as He did at the end of Acts. That had also been kept a secret.

Minor dispensational changes from Acts 28:28 to the restoration of Israel

This is the age in which we live. The books of the Bible written after Acts 28:28, excluding Acts itself which deals with earlier events, are but seven in number, and none have more than six chapters. If we wish to study events at the start of this dispensation then we will need to take into account the destruction of Jerusalem and the temple and the removal of Israel from their land. The effect this must have had upon the Jewish Christians who were enjoying their new-found freedom from the Law must have been traumatic. However, it seems to be of little consequence to our Christian lives and understanding - and the destruction of the temple is not even recorded in the Bible.

Again if we wish to make a study of the close of this dispensation we may wish to distinguish between the "later times" of 1 Timothy 4:1 and the "last days" of 2 Timothy 3:1. However, as these expressions occur but once in these last seven letters of Paul and as so little is said about them, we may be in danger of splitting hairs. That being the case, there are no minor dispensational changes within this period which are of help to us in our prayers, practice and understanding.

Minor dispensational changes after the restoration of Israel

There would seem to be two: the return of Christ and the creation of the new heavens, new earth, and new Jerusalem.

Some would divide the period from the restoration of Israel to the return of Christ into a number of subgroups. For example:

1) From the restoration to the making of the seven year covenant with the Antichrist.
2) The first three and a half years of that covenant.

3) The Great Tribulation of Israel: the last three and half years of that covenant, which ends with Christ's return.

Those who wish to make a study of the years leading up to Christ's return need a framework in which to set forth their views, and the one above has much merit. However, its value comes when we try to understand such books as Revelation and the various other prophetic passages.

In contrast to these, Christ's return saves His stewards, Israel, from extinction, converts them to Christianity, and brings in the Millennial Kingdom by equipping them as a kingdom of priests and sending them out to evangelise the nations of the world. The Kingdom, once set up, lasts for 1,000 years, at the end of which there is a rebellion which is put down by direct action from heaven. This is followed by a resurrection of the dead, their judgment, and the new heaven and earth (Revelation 20).

Again, those who wish to study the details of the beginning or the end of the Millennium may find it helpful to note that it takes time to equip Israel and that once they see that Jesus is their Messiah they enter a period of mourning, being grieved by their, and their forefathers', rejection of Him (Zechariah 12:10-14). Also, at the end, some would wish to separate off the time of the rebellion from the 1,000 year kingdom. However, none of these would seem to be even a minor dispensational change.

There is a view that the raising of the dead and their judgment constitute a minor dispensation. Certainly things will be very different when this is going on, but for how long does it last? We have but four verses describing these events (Revelation 20:11-15). One almost gets the impression that this is to be very rapidly carried out, that at the end of the Millennium God's time for this creation has expired and He wants to quickly reveal His new one and people it with His redeemed. Without underestimating how great and magnificent will be the raising of the dead and their judgment, it must be noted that it occupies, seemingly, very little time and takes but four verses to record.

However, the arrival of the new heaven and earth does bring in a new state of affairs, "the old order of things has passed away" (Revelation 21:4). It is populated with redeemed, raised, and righteous people. Sin, death, and Satan, the three great enemies, are not present. There is no pain, no crying, no mourning. The New Jerusalem, with its twelve tribes and twelve apostles (21:12-14), is at the centre of the new earth which is peopled by the redeemed nations (21:24-27). The new heavens are peopled by Christians of this present dispensation, enjoying their spiritual blessings in the heavenly places (Ephesians 1:3; 2:6-7).

What a lovely picture with which to end the future as far ahead as God reveals it to us.

But some think that this situation will one day end; that in the dispensation of the fulness of times God is "to bring all things in heaven and on earth together under one head, even Christ" (Ephesians 1:10). For me, that describes the situation in the new creation. Others think that this comes about by the new heavens, new earth and new Jerusalem being done away with so that all God's redeemed will be together in one place. If that is the case, it seems strange that nowhere does God make that clear.

To sum up

We believe it right to look first, not at when minor dispensations (orders and rules) change, but when the administrators change. By applying this principle, we see the following clearly defined divisions within the Scriptures:

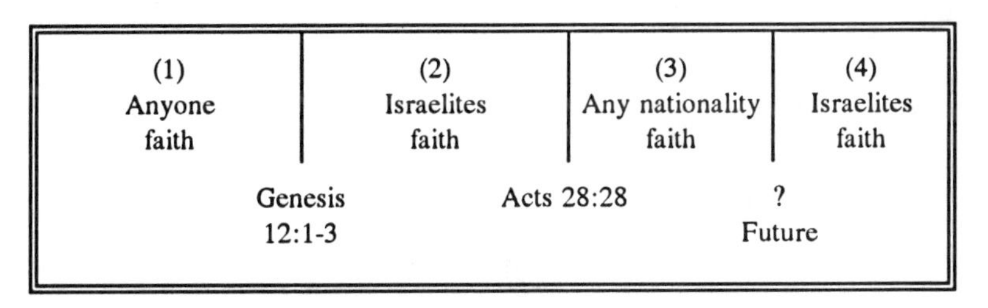

These, we suggest, are the *major dispensational changes*. Within each of the above administrations, orders may have been changed a number of times, but it only complicates and confuses things to have too many subdivisions. Also, as such subdivisions may be made on subjective grounds, having lots of them is likely to open up more and more areas of disagreement and dispute. However the following subdivisions for each of the above dispensations are likely to be the most helpful:

(1) Anyone	:	No minor dispensations.
(2) Israelites	:	The Law (Exodus 19); The grafting in of Gentiles (Acts 10).
(3) Any nationality	:	No minor dispensations.
(4) Israelites	:	The return of Christ; The new creation.

That being the case our diagram would be modified as follows:

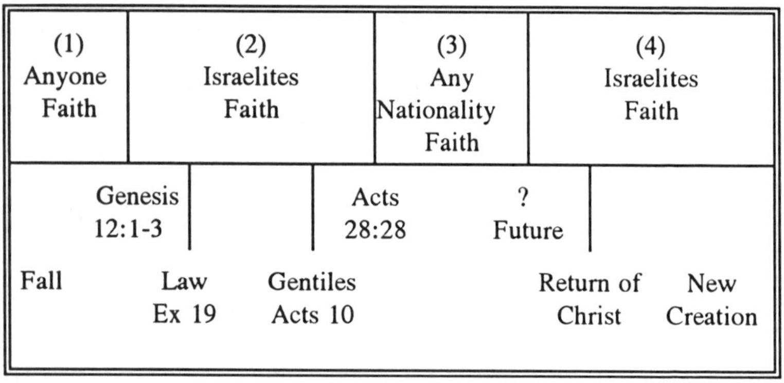

(1) Anyone Faith	(2) Israelites Faith	(3) Any Nationality Faith	(4) Israelites Faith
Genesis 12:1-3		Acts 28:28	? Future
Fall	Law Ex 19; Gentiles Acts 10		Return of Christ; New Creation

Or to put it in a table of major and minor changes.

Major dispensational changes	*Minor dispensational changes*
Changes of administrators with accompanying change in orders	Changes in orders but no change in the administrators
(1) Adam to Abraham	
	The Fall (Genesis 3)
(2) Abraham to Acts 28:25-27	
	The Law (Exodus 19);
	The grafting in of Gentiles (Acts 10; cf. Romans 11:11-25).
(3) Acts 28:28 to restoration of Israel	
(4) Restoration of Israel	
	The return of Christ; The new creation

We could add to the above the various other changes, too small even to be termed minor. However, that would only over-complicate the picture. What may be helpful is to have on the diagram the various books of the Bible relating to each part.

Major dispensational changes	*Minor dispensational changes*	*Relevant parts of the Bible*
Changes of administrators with accompanying change in orders	Changes in orders but no change in the administrators	
(1) Adam to Abraham	Before the Fall	Genesis 1-2
	The Fall	Genesis 3-11
(2) Abraham to Acts 28:25-29	Before the Law	Genesis 12 - Exodus 18, Job
	The Law	Exodus 19 & rest of Old Testament, the Gospels, and Acts 1-9
	The introduction of Gentiles	Acts 10-28:28 plus letters of James, John, Peter, Jude, and Paul's earlier letters: Galatians, 1&2 Thessalonians, 1&2 Corinthians, Romans. Hebrews.
(3) Acts 28:28 to restoration of Israel		Paul's later letters Ephesians, Colossians, Philemon, Philippians, Titus, 1&2 Timothy.
(4) Restoration of Israel onwards	The return of Christ The new creation	Prophetic parts of all Scriptures

Conclusion

It is right, therefore, to look first, not at when dispensations (orders and rules) change, but when the administrators change. It is these which give us the major dispensational changes. It is these which are unambiguous and objective. Only after we have settled when these changes occurred can we look to see if any alterations in the orders given to those administrators are of significance.

We need to appreciate that dispensations (administrations) are linked with people. We do this in politics by speaking of the Bush

Administration or the Reagan years, or of the Thatcher or Conservative Administration. This shows us that the people doing the administration are of primary importance. If this is the case in the politics of this world, it is even more so with God's dealing with mankind. Thus we may term the period from Genesis 12 to Acts 28:28 as the Jewish administration and the one since Acts 28:28 as the Gentile administration. If we added the administrator's names to the description of the dispensation then we would all have a better understanding of what God has been doing.

24. Changing administrators and their orders

We have mentioned previously that traditional dispensationalists have looked for great events, or judgments, in the Bible to mark the end of dispensations. As one of their writers has put it:

> A concise definition of a dispensation is this: A dispensation is a distinguishable economy in the outworking of God's purpose. If one were describing a dispensation he would include other things, such as the ideas of distinctive revelation, testing, failure and judgment. (Charles C. Ryrie, *Dispensationalism Today*)

However, we have already shown that we find both this definition and description lacking on a number of counts. First, the idea of testing and judgment is foreign to *oikonomia*, the Greek word for dispensation. Second, when God has changed His stewards He has not done so ostentatiously and suddenly, with a great show of power. Rather it has been done quietly, over a period of time - as we shall now show.

The change at Genesis 12

To end a dispensation with the confusion of tongues following the Tower of Babel leaves much to be desired. After this event God dealt with people as previously, the only change being the different languages upon earth. This may have had drastic effects upon people's ability to communicate with each other, but it had no effect whatsoever upon how humans communicated with God or He with them. Anyone who had faith in God, who believed what He wanted them to, and who would come to God through the sacrifices He had instituted, could be one of God's stewards.

If there is a change, it is not at the Tower of Babel, but with the call of Abraham or the promise God gave him. In Genesis 12:1-3 we read that:

> The Lord had said to Abram, "Leave your country, your people and your father's household and go to the land I will show you. I will make you into a great nation and I will bless you; I will make your name great, and you will be a blessing. I will bless those who bless you, and whoever curses you I will curse; and all peoples on earth will be blessed through you."

We must ask whether the situation completely changed from the moment those words were spoken? Or did it change slowly over a period of years, with God gradually changing His stewards from one group to another? Was everyone, from that instant onwards, to be blessed through Abraham and his descendants, or had God declared His intentions and from then on was going to work towards them? We may be tempted to go for the instant and immediate, but if we do so, we will be disappointed.

Following these words from the Lord, Abraham set out from Haran and went to Canaan. Then he went towards the hills east of Bethel and onto the Negev (12:4-9). A famine caused Abraham to live in Egypt for a while (12:10), but he eventually returned to the Negev and Bethel (13:1-4). After this Lot and Abraham parted, with Lot going to live near Sodom and Abraham living in the land of Canaan before moving his tents to the great trees of Mamre at Hebron (13:12-18).

It was while Abraham was there that a great battle took place at Sodom in which Lot was captured. Abraham left Hebron to pursue Lot as far as Dan. He recovered his nephew, his family and possessions, and returned. When they got to the Valley of Shaveh not only did the King of Sodom meet him, but so did someone else. However, before discussing this other person we must ask ourselves how long a period of time elapsed between Genesis 12:1-3 and Genesis 14:17. Thomson's *New Chain Reference Bible* suggests it is eight years. The Scofield *Reference Bible* note is similar.

Eight years after the promise made to Abraham in Genesis 12 we come across a person who is not a descendant of Abraham, who has not been blessed through Abraham, but who is a steward of God. He blesses Abraham, and others, for he is a priest of God in the city of Salem.

> Then Melchizedek king of Salem brought out bread and wine. He was priest of God Most High, and he blessed Abram, saying, "Blessed be Abram by God Most High, Creator of heaven and earth. And blessed be God Most High, who delivered your enemies into your hand." Then Abram gave him a tenth of everything. (Genesis 14:18-20)

This person, Melchizedek, in some ways belongs to, or is left over from, the era before God made the promise of Genesis 12:1-3. This incident shows that God did not suddenly drop all His previous stewards, but continued to work with them and through them. As His new purpose through Abraham grew, His previous purpose dwindled until, in time, only those who were descended through Abraham, Isaac, and Jacob could be His stewards. How long it took for the previous purpose to fade away totally, and to be completely replaced by the new one, we cannot say.

However, the lapse of time may have been quite lengthy because in Exodus 2:16-3:1 we read of Jethro, or Reuel, who was "a priest of Midian". He brought burnt offerings and sacrifices to God (Exodus 18:12; note the whole chapter). Although the Midianites were descended from Abraham (Genesis 25:1-6), they were not from Isaac. The promise given to Abraham in Genesis 12:1-3, that all peoples on the earth were to be blessed through him, was explained to mean through his offspring (22:17) and this was subsequently clarified to mean through Isaac (26:3-5) and ultimately through Jacob (28:14-15). Thus the Midianites did not qualify, yet some 400 years later we find Jethro was a priest of God in Midian. An even later example of God using a non-Israelite is Balaam (Numbers 22-24).

Another possible person in this transition period is Job. He was the priest for his family (Job 1:5). The book of Job, apart from the introduction and conclusion, fits into a time before the people of Israel went down to Egypt. Job may or may not have been a descendant of Abraham. If he wasn't, then he is another example showing how those not descended through Abraham, Isaac and Jacob could be stewards for God after the promise of Genesis 12.

The promise of Genesis 12 eventually became the dominant purpose of God. However, as just stated, it is impossible to say how long it took for that promise to become the sole purpose of God. Certainly it was God's declared intention that the people of Israel were to be "a kingdom of priests and a holy nation" (Exodus 19:6). The promise given to Abraham, Isaac and Jacob was repeated by Moses as part of the Law and after this we do not read of people from other nations being priests of God. So we see that at Genesis 12 there was not a sudden change to the people of Israel. The promise of God to Abraham was a herald, announcing what was to come.

The change at Exodus 20

After the Exodus the people of Israel eventually came to Sinai, where Moses went up to God (Exodus 19:1-3) and returned to the people with the words the Lord had commanded him to speak (19:7). Some time later, Moses went back up the mountain and returned to the people with more instructions (19:9-15). This happened a third time (19:20-25). How long did it all take?

Exodus chapters 20-23 contain the words that God spoke directly to the Israelites. Then Moses was called again to the mountain (24:12) and was away for forty six days (24:15-18). Chapters 25-31 record what the Lord said to Moses and end with the Lord giving him the two tablets containing the Law. In chapter 32 the people of Israel made a golden calf to worship, but when Moses saw it, he broke the two tablets (verse 19). Eventually two new tablets were made (34:1) and in the course of time more and more rules and regulations were added to the Law of Moses. However, this was not an overnight process, it took time. The events of Deuteronomy occurred nearly 40 years after Exodus.

When the people of Israel, God's stewards at the time, had a significant change in their instructions, their stewardship, their house-rules, God took care to see that this was done slowly and thoroughly. There was no quick and drastic change. For example, they were first told to keep the Sabbath in Exodus 16 when they received manna on six days but not on the seventh (verses 22-29). They were encouraged, if not forced, to keep the Sabbath in this way for nearly forty years until they entered the promised land, when the manna ceased (Joshua 5:12). God's desire for them to rest and worship Him on the seventh day was not merely announced, and left at that. The teaching is repeated several times in the Law of Moses and on subsequent occasions new rules pertaining to the seventh day, and new sabbaths other than the weekly one, were slowly introduced.

Again we can see that although the introduction of the Law was a significant change for God's stewards it was not sudden and dramatic. It took time for the people to be instructed and it took time for them to imbibe what was expected of them, respond and obey. Thus, again, a change is seen to occur slowly. The words from Sinai in Exodus 20, like those in Genesis 12, heralded a change, but the new era that came in took time to develop fully.

The change at Acts 10

Acts 10 records how Peter had first a vision from God (10:11-16) and then the Holy Spirit spoke to him (10:19-20), telling him to visit a Gentile, Cornelius. This he did, but we read of no further activity amongst the Gentiles by Peter. Indeed, not only was Peter seemingly inactive amongst the Gentiles, but so, too, were most of the Christian Israelites.

> Now those (Christian Israelites) who had been scattered by the persecution in connection with Stephen travelled as far as Phoenicia,

> Cyprus and Antioch, telling the message only to Jews. Some of them, however, men from Cyprus and Cyrene, went to Antioch and began to speak to Greeks also, telling them the good news about the Lord Jesus. The Lord's hand was with them, and a great number of people believed and turned to the Lord. (Acts 11:19-21)

It is evident that this had not happened before, in spite of Peter's visit to Cornelius. The Christians in Jerusalem were so concerned that they sent Barnabas to investigate.

> News of this reached the ears of the church at Jerusalem, and they sent Barnabas to Antioch. When he arrived and saw the evidence of the grace of God, he was glad and encouraged them all to remain true to the Lord with all their hearts. (Acts 11:22-23)

Barnabas then went to Tarsus to look for Saul, found him and brought him to Antioch. There they spent a whole year teaching a great number of people (11:25-26), before going up to Jerusalem (11:29-30).

At Jerusalem, Paul and Barnabas met Peter, James and John and came to an agreement.

> They saw I (Paul) had been entrusted with the task of preaching the gospel to the Gentiles, just as Peter had been given the task of preaching the gospel to the Jews. For God, who was at work in the ministry of Peter as an apostle to the Jews, was also at work in my ministry as an apostle to the Gentiles. James, Peter and John, those reputed to be pillars, gave me and Barnabas the right hand of fellowship when they recognised the grace given to me. They agreed that we should go to the Gentiles, and they to the Jews. (Galatians 2:7-9)

Paul and Barnabas returned from Jerusalem to Antioch (Acts 12:25). There they were set apart for the work to which God had called them and they sailed for Cyprus (Acts 13:2-4). Eventually they arrived in Antioch in Pisidia, where many Jews and Gentiles came to believe in the Lord Jesus Christ (13:14,26,43).

However, it was some time previously, in Acts 9:15, that God had announced to Ananias that Paul was to carry His "name before the Gentiles and their kings". How slowly this came about. It was not until three years after Damascus that Paul first visited Jerusalem (Acts 9:26; Galatians 1:18). Following this he went to Tarsus, in the region of Syria and Cilicia (Acts 9:30; Galatians 1:21). Some time after this Peter visited Cornelius. Some ten years or more after Paul's conversion, Barnabas collected Paul and took him to Antioch where they stayed for a year.

They then went to Jerusalem, returned to Antioch and embarked on the first missionary journey. From the announcement to Ananias to Paul's first speaking to Gentiles in Antioch was at least ten years. From that announcement to the commencement of his first missionary journey was at least twelve.

Gentile Christians of the Acts period had a special role, they were to share in the blessings of Israel and so provoke them, hopefully, to repentance (Romans 11:11-25). This was a new and significant change in the relationship between Jews and Gentiles in God's purposes. However, it was not brought in overnight. First there was Cornelius, followed by the Gentiles in Antioch. After this came Paul's agreement with Peter, James and John which preceded his first missionary journey. That work had "opened the door of faith to the Gentiles" (Acts 14:27), but the terms on which those Gentiles were fully accepted were not settled until the Jerusalem Council in Acts 15. Thus this change did not come in quickly and suddenly. It came about slowly over a period of years.

The change at the end of Acts

In Acts 28:25-27 we have the final pronouncement of Isaiah's prophecy foretelling deafness and blindness upon the nation of Israel, resulting from a hardened heart. This is followed by the words:

> "Therefore I want you to know that God's salvation has been sent to the Gentiles, and they will listen!" (Acts 28:28)

However, Gentiles had been saved previously under the ministry of such people as Peter and Paul. They had been saved to arouse Israel (Romans 11:11,14). Here, at the end of Acts, we have something different. Previously, in harmony with God's purposes of that time, the Gentiles had received the blessing of salvation through the ministries of certain Israelites. They had also shared in other blessings of Israel (Romans 15:27), thus provoking Israel (Romans 11:11-25). Neither of these is the case today. Things have changed. Acts 28:28 heralds that change, but when, exactly, did Israel finally and completely lose their privileged position?

Following the announcement in Acts 28:28 we read:

> For two whole years Paul stayed there in his own rented house and welcomed all who came to see him. Boldly and without hindrance he

preached the kingdom of God and taught about the Lord Jesus Christ. (Acts 28:30-31)

During those two years Paul probably wrote Ephesians, Colossians and Philemon and, towards the end of that time, near to his release, Philippians. It is generally accepted that Ephesians was a circular letter. It is impersonal, which is uncharacteristic of Paul's letters to specific churches. Copies of it were made and sent to the different churches. It is this letter, more than any other, which speaks of the changed relationship between Jewish and Gentile Christians. No longer is the Gentile second to the Jew. God made the two of them one by abolishing the Law for the Jewish Christians, destroying its commandments and regulations (Ephesians 2:11-18; see also Colossians 2:13-17). Jewish Christians were now heirs together, sharers together, and members together in one body with the Gentiles (Ephesians 3:6).

This new relationship was a secret, a mystery which had been unknown to previous generations in earlier ages for it had been hidden in God (Ephesians 3:5,9; Colossians 1:26). However, God revealed this change to Paul and to the apostles and prophets at that time (Ephesians 3:1-5). But when did this happen, and over how long a period? How soon after the conference in Rome between Paul and the Jewish leadership did all this take place? We do not know. It would have taken time to copy letters, dispatch them, and deliver them by hand to distant churches. Paul's words in Acts 28:28 heralded a change, but it may have taken a little while for God to finish totally with Israel. However, it is not likely to have taken much more than seven years.

Most commentators date Paul's arrival in Rome in Acts 28:16 between AD 62 and 64. He was there only three days before he called together the leaders of the Jews. They arranged to meet Paul on a certain day and it was on that day that Paul uttered the judgmental words upon Israel (Acts 28:26-27).

In AD 70 the Romans destroyed Jerusalem, razed the temple to the ground, and carried the Israelites into exile, scattering them throughout the lands of their empire. By that time, at the very latest, there could be no doubt that Israel were no longer the central nation in God's purposes. He was now working through anyone of any nation and a Gentile could be a steward as much as any Jew, provided he had faith in the Lord Jesus Christ.

Again, it would seem that there was no overnight, drastic action. The change was heralded by Paul's pronouncement and over the next few years God began to work through His new stewards. By the time AD 70 arrived Israel's hardness, deafness and blindness was complete. With

Rome's annihilation of Judea and Jerusalem, we are past the New Testament era and into the realm of church history. The earliest leaders and writers were all Gentiles, showing us that God's salvation had been sent to the Gentiles and that they had, indeed, listened.

Change in the future

As Israel is once again a nation occupying its own land, one of the questions that people naturally want answered is, "When will Israel become, again, the centre of God's attention?" The traditional dispensationalist usually answers by saying that this will happen when the church of this dispensation is raptured, an event, according to them, which takes place seven years before Christ returns. This view is based upon their interpretation of 1 Thessalonians 4:13-17, Daniel 9:24-27 and their concept of a dispensation.

We have mentioned previously that traditional dispensationalists have looked for great events, or judgments, in the Bible to mark the end of dispensations. There can be little doubt that if such a rapture of the Christian church took place then that would be a great event. However, there are a number of problems with this view.

First, as has been suggested in this chapter, changes in dispensations have not been accompanied by spectacular judgments and events. Rather, God has announced a change and then started to work towards it. His previous purpose slowly fades away as His new one gains ascendancy.

Second, the subject of 1 Thessalonians 4 is the coming, *parousia*, of Christ. In all other places in the New Testament *parousia* refers to His *return* to the Mount of Olives, His *presence* upon the earth. To make special exception for this verse to refer to His coming in the air only, as Vine does in his *Expository Dictionary of New Testament Words*, is unsatisfactory. 1 Thessalonians 4:13-17 must refer to Christ's return to the earth and to Israel. This is further demonstrated with references to the archangel, who is Michael and Israel's prince (Daniel 10:21; Jude 9), and a trumpet call, which takes place when Christ returns to Israel (Matthew 24:31). Trumpets are linked with Israel (Leviticus 23:23-25; Numbers 29:1-6) and are the subject of Revelation 8 and 9, a very Jewish book. It is at the last trumpet that the dead are raised (1 Corinthians 15:52), an event linked to Christ's return (Revelation 20:4-6).

Third, it is impossible to fit all the unfulfilled prophecy relating to Israel into seven years. For example, the king of the north is to make a seven-year covenant with Israel to allow them to offer their evening and morning sacrifices in the temple. However, much has to happen to this king, some of which involves Israel, before that seven-year agreement is made.

Fourth, the subject of 2 Thessalonians, which is obviously the same as the subject of 1 Thessalonians, is clearly Christ's return to earth (2 Thessalonians 2:8).

Because of the above, and other similar objections, certain traditional dispensationalists no longer advocate that 1 Thessalonians is the hope of the church. They see that passage, rightly, as dealing with Christ's return to Israel. However, they would still advocate that the church will be raptured, stating that a rapture of the church is a natural consequence of a dispensational theology which distinguishes Israel and the church.

> The distinction between Israel and the Church leads to the belief that the Church will be taken from the earth before the beginning of the tribulation (which in one major sense concerns Israel). Pretribulationalism has become a major part of dispensational eschatology. Originally this was due to the emphasis of the early writers and teachers on the imminent return of the Lord; more lately it has been connected with the dispensational conception of the distinctiveness of the Church. (Charles C. Ryrie, *Dispensationalism Today*.)

The pretribulation rapture of the Church seven years before Christ's return may be a natural consequence of the traditional understanding of dispensationalism, but it is not a natural consequence of dispensationalism at all.

If the view is that things suddenly change, that dramatic events herald in change, then that conclusion may be correct. The traditional view sees this dispensation ending suddenly, and Israel restored as a nation before God overnight. Something like the rapture of the church might fit into their idea of a dispensation. However, a rapture of the church is not a logical consequence of a dispensational approach to the Bible. Neither is it the result of making a distinction between Israel and the Church. Another scenario is possible, and indeed more likely, one which we shall consider in a moment.

Another objection to 1 Thessalonians being the hope of the church of this dispensation is that Thessalonians was written during the Acts period, before Acts 28:28. It is thus the hope of the church of the Acts period, a church in which Israel has precedence. That being the case, its subject must be the return of Christ to Israel and to the earth. Seeing this, and other objections similar to those above, Charles H. Welch, in *That Blessed Hope* and elsewhere, advocated that the hope of the church should be found in the letters written after Acts 28:28. He stated that the hope of the church was Christ's appearing in glory, which he dated 21 years before Christ's return based on an explanation of Daniel 9:24-27 different from that held by most traditional dispensationalists, and which we will examine shortly. For Welch the hope of the church can be summed up in two verses.

> When Christ, who is your life, appears (*phaneroo*), then you also will appear with him in glory. (Colossians 3:4)

> We wait for the blessed hope - the glorious appearing (*epiphaniea*) of our great God and Saviour, Jesus Christ. (Titus 2:13)

But both *phaneroo* and *epiphaniea* are intimately linked with His *parousia*, His second coming.

> And now, dear children, continue in him, so that when he appears (*phaneroo*) we may be confident and unashamed before him at his coming (*parousia*) ... But we know that when he appears (*phaneroo*), we shall be like him, for we shall see him as he is. (1 John 2:28; 3:2)

> And then the lawless one will be revealed, whom the Lord Jesus will overthrow with the breath of his mouth and destroy by the splendour (*epiphaniea*) of his coming (*parousia*). (2 Thessalonians 2:8)

Welch may well be correct in stating that Colossians 3:4 and Titus 2:13 give the hope of the church. However, he may well be wrong in stating that this takes place 21 years before Christ's second coming (*parousia*). Both *phaneroo* and *epiphaniea* are closely linked to His *parousia*. It is true that in 2 Thessalonians 2:8 *epiphaniea* is used adjectivally, rather than as a noun, but it would seem that there is a close connection between the two.

Nevertheless, Welch's interpretation of Daniel 9:24-28, allowing something like 21 years for the unfulfilled prophecies relating to Israel, is different from that of traditional dispensationalists. We will quote the passage and deal first with their understanding.

> Seventy 'sevens' (490 years) are decreed for your people and your holy city to finish transgression, to put an end to sin, to atone for wickedness, to bring in everlasting righteousness, to seal up vision and prophecy and to anoint the most holy.
>
> Know and understand this: From the issuing of the decree to restore and rebuild Jerusalem until the Anointed One, the ruler, comes, there

> will be seven 'sevens' (49 years), and sixty-two 'sevens' (434 years). It will be rebuilt with streets and a trench, but in times of trouble. After the sixty-two 'sevens', the Anointed One will be cut off and will have nothing. The people of the ruler who will come will destroy the city and the sanctuary. The end will come like a flood: War will continue until the end, and desolations have been decreed. He will confirm a covenant with many for one 'seven' (7 years). In the middle of that 'seven' (after 3 1/2 years) he will put an end to sacrifice and offering. And on a wing of the temple he will set up an abomination that causes desolation, until the end that is decreed is poured out on him. (Daniel 9:24-27)

The view of the traditional dispensationalist is that the 490 years starts with the issuing of the decree to rebuild the temple. From the issuing of the decree to the completion of the temple took 49 years. From the time when the temple was completed until Christ was crucified was 434 years. 434 + 49 = 483. They claim that the dispensation changed at the Cross, or at Pentecost, and at that time Israel lost its central role in God's plan. Thus only seven years of the 490 are left for the future fulfilment of unfulfilled prophecy relating to Israel. However, there are a number of problems with this explanation.

First, unfulfilled prophecy requires more than seven years. Second, the prophecy of Daniel 9 relates to Israel and Jerusalem (verse 24) and neither Israel nor Jerusalem were finished with at the cross. Israel did not lose its premier position before Acts 28:25-28 and Jerusalem was not destroyed until A.D. 70. We have been at pains in this book to demonstrate just how much the nation of Israel dominates the Acts of the Apostles, the letters of Peter, James, John, and Jude, and occupies first place in Paul's earlier letters, the ones he wrote during Acts.

That being the case, Welch suggested that the 49 years, from the issuing of the decree to rebuild the temple to its completion, should not be taken out of the 490 years. In other words the 490 years started when the temple was completed, not with the issuing of the decree to rebuild it. With the crucifixion coming 434 years after the completion of the temple, there were 490 - 434 = 56 years left for Israel after the cross. Welch argued that the Acts of the Apostles occupied 35 years, at the end of which Israel's blindness and deafness was complete. Thus there are 56 - 35 = 21 years left of Daniel's 490 years. In other words, Israel would become God's special nation 21 years before Christ returned. This may or may not be correct. However, to have the church removed from earth at the same point of time seems most unlikely.

In his book *Elijah's Coming and other Unfulfilled Prophecies*, C. E. McLain argues that John the Baptist did not fulfil all the prophecies relating to Elijah. He goes on to advocate that the commencement of the next dispensation will start with the coming of Elijah. This may not be anything grand or glorious in the scale of human events. John the Baptist ended four hundred years of God's silence by preaching in the Desert of Judea "Repent, for the kingdom of heaven is near" (Matthew 3:1). It is doubtful if his first efforts even reached the ears of the leaders in Jerusalem, let alone the world leaders in Rome. Similarly, Elijah's future call to Israel for them to repent may be equally small, going unnoticed not only by the United Nations and the European Parliament, but also by the Knesset in Israel.

However, as with other dispensations, once the message of change has been heralded, then God starts to work His new purpose. His previous purpose is allowed to run its natural course and for a while the two will run side by side, the new growing and the old shrinking. It is possible that this present dispensation will last for a few years, running alongside the new one before it slowly dies out. Alternatively it could run for a much longer period, the church's manifestation with Christ in glory taking place just prior to, or at the same time as, His return - *phaneroo* and *epiphaniea* being closely linked with *parousia*. However, according to Revelation 12:5-6 a section of Israel is snatched up to heaven and to God's throne three and a half years before Christ returns. It may be that this is the point in time when Christ appears in glory in heaven, for we do know that at that time Satan is cast out (Revelation 12:7-9).

When we read of the start of this present dispensation in Ephesians we see that God described it as a mystery, a secret that had not previously been revealed to mankind. However, it was made known at that time and is now clear for anyone to read and understand. The destiny of the church of this dispensation is to be manifest in glory with Christ in the heavenly realms (Ephesians 2:6-7; Colossians 3:4). It seems highly unlikely that all Christians will disappear off the face of this earth when God heralds His return to the people of Israel. Like the start of other dispensations, a new work in Israel is more likely to begin in a small way, but it will build up and just prior to the last 3 1/2 years we learn that Israel is to preach the gospel of the kingdom to all nations (Matthew 24:14). So, again, we see that a new dispensation comes in not suddenly, with great drama, but quietly, with a voice calling Israel to repent.

The change at the return of Christ

It is most certainly true that the return of Christ will be dramatic and quick, the most overtly spectacular event ever to happen on this earth. Yet its results are not immediate.

Israel are gathered from one end of the heaven to the other (Matthew 24:31), after which they will look on Him whom they have pierced and mourn for a period of time (Zechariah 12:10-14; Revelation 1:7).

Joel has the destruction of the northerner in 2:20, an event which takes place at Christ's return. Following this the land is restored (v 21), the animals are restored (v 22) and the people of Israel are restored (v 23). Only after all this is the Spirit poured out (v 28), equipping Israel to fulfil their role as a kingdom of priests to the other nations of the world and enabling them to bring in God's kingdom upon this earth. Their preaching of the gospel of the kingdom to all nations before Christ returns (Matthew 24:14) appears to fall largely upon deaf ears. However, afterwards, that saved and restored nation, indwelt and empowered by His Spirit, see very different results as His kingdom fills the whole earth (Daniel 2:35,44), but this takes time.

In the wildnerness it took time to introduce Israel to the old covenant and to teach them the Law. It would seem that after Christ's return, it will take time to introduce Israel to the blessings and glories of the new covenant and to prepare them for their new role on the millennial earth.

A new heaven and earth

Peter tells us about the end of this world and the creation of a new one, which takes place after the millennium.

> The heavens will disappear with a roar; the elements will be destroyed by fire, and the earth and everything in it will be laid bare. (2 Peter 3:10)

He goes on to say:

> That day will bring about the destruction of the heavens by fire, and the elements will melt in the heat. But in keeping with his promise we are looking forward to a new heaven and a new earth, the home of righteousness. (2 Peter 3:12-13)

He says nothing about how long the destruction of the old or how long the creation of the new will take.

John ends Revelation 20 with the raising of the dead and the destruction, in the lake of fire, of both death and Hades. He opens chapter 21 with:

> Then I saw a new heaven and a new earth, for the first heaven and the first earth had passed away, and there was no longer any sea. I saw the Holy City, the new Jerusalem, coming down out of heaven from God, prepared as a bride beautifully dressed for her husband. (Revelation 21:1-2)

It is tempting, at this point, to argue that all this takes time, just as the original creation did. However, it is more correct for us to acknowledge that nothing is said about how long God takes to judge the dead, to destroy the present creation, and to make a new one. Of course He could do all these things instantly, but will He? We are told so little.

Conclusion

In this chapter we have tried to show that the traditional view that dispensations end suddenly and new ones then burst forth onto the stage is not borne out by Scripture. What is true is that at some specific point God says or does something which heralds a new purpose, a change in His plans. From then on the previous purpose begins to fade. Over a period of time the old and the new may run together. However, the new gains ascendancy and eventually the old disappears. This was true with the promise given in Genesis 12, the Law given in Exodus 20, the Gentiles being grafted in to Israel in Acts 9-15, the end of Israel announced at Acts 28:25-28, and the restoration of Israel sometime in the future. This view of gradual ascendancy of one purpose, and the slow decline of another, may not fit totally the changes surrounding the return of Christ. However, it is clear that it will take time to restore and equip Israel before they are sent out as a kingdom of priests. Neither does it fit the creation of the new heavens and new earth, it being impossible for the old to carry on as it is destroyed before the creation of the new. However, the first creation took place in stages over a period of time (see Genesis 1 and 2) and it may be that in creating new heavens and a new earth God will do so in stages over a period of time.

The phasing-out of one purpose and a phasing-in of the new is therefore more Scripturally correct at Genesis 12, Exodus 20, Acts 9-15, Acts 28:28, and with the future restoration of Israel than the sudden, dramatic, instant changes suggested by the traditional view.

25. What is this approach?

We feel a need as human beings to give things names. That being the case, what name can we give this approach? It has much in common with traditional dispensationalism, but there are differences. In traditional dispensationalism the approach seems to be:

1) God
2) What is God doing?

In our approach, the order seems to be:

1) God
2) Who is God working with?
3) Where is God working?
4) When is He working there with those people?
5) What is God doing?
6) Why is God doing it?
7) What can we learn from this to apply to our situation today?

We do not intend to imply, by the above listing, that traditional dispensationalists do not consider the people God is working with, or that they do not take into account where He is working, or why He is working in a particular way. It does suggest that they rightly start off with God, but go straight to His actions, making differences in His actions the boundaries of major dispensations. In this, we are suggesting, they are wrong. It is best to go from God, first to the people with whom He is working. Changes in the administrators, rather than changes in any orders and rules, mark the major changes.

Is this approach dispensational?

The Greek word translated dispensation, *oikonomia*, has been defined as follows in Bullinger's *Critical Lexicon and Concordance* of the New Testament:

> Stewardship, management of a household or of household affairs; stewardship, administration.
>
> Administration of a household, actively the administrative activity of the owner or the steward; passively, that which is administered (English economy), i.e. disposition of things, scheme or dispensation.

Here we can see that the emphasis is upon managing and administering. Dispensationalism, therefore, is to do with action, what is done. Thus traditional dispensationalists have been true to their name by concentrating on God's actions.

However, intimately linked with *oikonomia* is the word *oikonomos*, defined as follows by Bullinger:

> Steward, *oikonomos*, a house-manager, one who had authority over the servants of a family, assigning their tasks etc., and generally managing all the affairs and accounts. These persons were generally slaves, but also freemen. They also had charge of the pecuniary affairs of the sons.

Stewards and their stewardships, administrators and their administration, are intimately linked. They should not be, and perhaps cannot be, separated. Although traditional dispensationalists in their definition of a dispensation have tried to get away from the idea of time being an integral part of a dispensation, no doubt to satisfy some of their critics, it is impossible to do so. Stewards are appointed and may, after a period of time, be changed. An administration runs for a period of time and is then changed. Orders are given and after a period are altered. Perhaps the only definition of dispensation which correctly links these two together is the following:

> The Greek word rendered dispensation is *oikonomia* and refers to the act of administering. By the figure of Metonymy, the act of administering is transferred to the time during which that administering is carried on. (E. W. Bullinger, *How to Enjoy the Bible*)

Metonymy, or change of noun, is the figure of speech where one name or noun is used instead of another to which it stands in a certain relation. Hence the above definition is saying that acts of administering and the times during which the affairs are being administered are so intimately linked that they cannot be separated. A dispensation may not be a period of time, but it lasts for a period of time. Thus if traditional dispensationalists use a reference to time in their definitions or explanations of what is a dispensation, it is churlish for people to object.

Consider Bullinger's definition of dispensation given above. Not only should the word *oikonomia*, by the figure Metonymy, be transferred to the time during which the administering is being carried on, perhaps it should also be transferred to those *people performing the administering*. If that be the case, then what is being suggested in this book is dispensationalism, hopefully a more consistent dispensationalism. It is one that considers God first, but which looks at the people with whom He is working before considering what He wants them to do.

All of us are most concerned about who is dealing with our affairs. If we have confidence in them, then we may allow them to deal with more and more. If we are not too happy, we may not put any new business their way. If we are displeased then we may remove what business we have with them.

It is the same in politics. If Americans have been happy with the Republican administration, then they will vote for it a second term. If the British have been unhappy with the Conservative administration, then they will not vote for another term. **The administration is defined by the people running it.**

Thus it is right to consider God's administrators before we consider His administrations. Traditionally, dispensationalists have not done this, which has resulted in their seeing major dispensational changes where none exist and in their missing some which do exist.

Why this approach?

There are a number of advantages in this approach. As we have argued above, it does provide us with a better means of studying the Bible. But there are other reasons, some of which are hinted at in the following definition of dispensation.

> The word *oikonomia* bears one significance, and means an administration, whether of a house, or property, of a state or a nation, or as in the present study, the administration of the human race or any part of it, at any given time. Just as a parent would govern his household in different ways, according to varying necessities, yet ever for one good end, so God has at different times dealt with men in different ways, according to the necessity of the case, but throughout for one great, grand end. (W. Graham Scroggie, *Ruling Lines of Progressive Revelation*)

We need to recognise that "according to varying necessities, yet ever for one good end, so God has at different times dealt with men *in different ways*, according to the necessity of the case". However, before that, we would put that "God has at different times dealt with *different* men in different ways". If we are to make sense of God's actions as recorded in the Bible then we must take note of:

(1) the different people with whom He has worked;
(2) the different places;
(3) the different times;
(4) the different orders, rules, administrations.

We must recognise that God may have one overall purpose "to bring all things in heaven and earth under one head, even Christ" (Ephesians 1:10). However, in order to bring that about He has had different administrators and has given them different duties. If we do not recognise these changes then we may not have a coherent or consistent overview of the Bible. Also we are likely to run into a number of problem passages.

It is true that not all things change. Certain teachings run throughout the Scriptures. For example: all are sinners, none are righteous, all need faith, sin needs a sacrifice, God desires a right morality. No matter which part of the Bible we turn to, we will read of these. However, over and above such fundamentals, if we have no coherent overview and no systematic approach we may find other passages abstruse and difficult .

The practical consequences of this approach

This approach brings before us the people with whom God has worked and the people to whom He has spoken. As Gentile Christians, this approach makes us see the place of Gentiles in various parts of God's plan.

1) From Abraham to halfway through Acts, Gentiles had but the crumbs from Israel's table; they were very much second in every way and any blessings they did have came through Israel.
2) In the second half of Acts the Gentiles were still second to Israel. However, they shared in Israel's blessings and their salvation was intended to arouse Israel.
3) After Acts, God's salvation was sent to the Gentiles. They became God's stewards, and there was no distinction between Jewish and Gentile Christians.

What, then, are the most important parts of the Bible for us? Please note, this is *not* to say that the rest is unimportant. All is essential and necessary and one cannot understand the later parts without the earlier ones. We are simply asking, "Which are the most important parts for people alive today?" We would suggest it is those last letters of Paul. However, to fully understand and appreciate them we need his earlier letters as well as the letters of Peter, James, John, and Jude, the Acts of the Apostles, the Gospels, and the Old Testament.

The approach advocated in this book highlights for us those parts of the Bible which contain the most relevant truth from God for Christians today. That being the case we should base our doctrine and practice, our prayers and praise, upon those, rather than upon other parts which may have been written for Jewish Christians at a very specific point in time, or for Gentile Christians when they were second to and dependent upon Israel. For example, it may be better for us to base our prayers upon those Paul wrote in Ephesians, rather than upon those James wrote to the twelve tribes scattered abroad (James 1:1). It may be best for us to base our practice upon what is required in Ephesians and Colossians, rather than trying to emulate the Jewish apostles in the Acts period. In doing this, we will meet with God's approval for we will be nearer to correctly handling the word of truth.

> Do your best to present yourself to God as one approved, a workman who does not need to be ashamed and who correctly handles the word of truth. (2 Timothy 2:15)

Conclusion

We do not want to give the impression that we should not and need not study the earlier writings. We need to if we are to understand the later ones. In his last letter Paul wrote concerning the Old Testament:

> All Scripture is God-breathed and is useful for teaching, rebuking, correcting and training in righteousness, so that the man of God may be thoroughly equipped for every good work. (2 Timothy 3:16)

However, to get the maximum benefit from those Scriptures we need to correctly handle them. We are suggesting that this is just what we are trying to do with this approach. We ask first "Who?", "Where?", "When?", "What?", "Why?". Only after answering these can we accurately "Apply!"

Part V

Teachings of the Approach

If we accept that the Bible is God-breathed then it contains no contradictions. However, that does not mean to say that God has always wanted the same thing from the same people throughout all ages. Neither does it imply that God has always promised the same things to all people. Indeed if we read through the Bible chronologically we will note that revelation is progressive, that His wishes do change with time. We also note that even at one particular period of time He has wanted different things from different people. This does not imply that God is a God of disorder. Rather it is a measure of His infinite wisdom, recognising the differing needs of different sections of mankind, and the changing needs of people with the passage of time.

In one sense no part of the Bible is about us. All of it was written nearly two thousand or more years ago. It was addressed to peoples very different from ourselves. Any attempt to apply all of its teachings to ourselves is doomed to failure. There is a tendency for us to embark on a "picking and choosing" theology. That is, we apply to ourselves certain parts, those we like, and ignore others, the ones we do not like. However, this is not a sensible method of approaching the Bible. Although no part of the Bible is about us, *all* of it is *for us*. Paul wrote to Timothy, stating not only that "All Scripture is God-breathed", but also that:

> All Scripture ... *is useful.*(2 Timothy 3:16)

And it is useful for:

> ... teaching, rebuking, correcting and training in righteousness, so that the man of God may be thoroughly equipped for every good work. (2 Timothy 3:16-17)

We are not only told that the Bible is useful, but we are told also that one of its purposes is "so that the man of God may be thoroughly equipped for every good work". Thus our approach to it is important if we are not to be ill-prepared workmen of God.

It has been suggested in this book that Christians today should put greater emphasis on what is said to and of Gentiles. It has also been advocated that greater importance should be given to the later, rather than the earlier, parts of the Bible. If what is said of Jews differs from what is said of Gentiles, then for us the conflict should be resolved by giving greater weight to what is said of Gentiles. Similarly, if what is said of Gentiles at an earlier time is different from what is said at a later time, the conflict is best resolved by paying more attention to God's later revelation.

That being the case, what are some of the major teachings in the most recent instruction God has given man in the Bible? This is the subject we shall address in this final section. We shall see that some of these teachings are no different from what had been revealed earlier. However, there are differences, but we shall not deal with them all. What we present here are examples and readers are encouraged to compare scripture with scripture for themselves and to search and study other subjects. If they do choose to take this approach further they will be embarking upon a most exciting and stimulating voyage.

26. The Godhead

What picture of the Godhead is painted in these last letters of the Bible? Is it any different from Paul's earlier epistles? Or from the general epistles or the Gospels or the rest of Scripture?

The Father

All of these later letters open by referring to "the God and Father of our Lord Jesus Christ" (Ephesians 1:2,3 and see also v 17; Philippians 1:2; 4:20; Colossians 1:2,3; 1 Timothy 1:2; 2 Timothy 1:2; Titus 1:4; Philemon 3).

He is both God and Father, and father-like He extends grace, mercy, peace, and love to all His children (Ephesians 1:2; 6:23; Philippians 1:7; Colossians 1:2; 1 Timothy 1:2; 2 Timothy 1:2; Titus 1:4; Philemon 3).

Different letters say different things about what the Father has done for the believer. For instance we read that He has blessed believers in the heavenly realms with every spiritual blessing, chosen them to be holy and blameless in His sight, predestined them to be adopted sons, redeemed them and forgiven them. All this, and more, is in harmony with the riches of His grace (Ephesians 1:3-7).

Paul addressed his prayers and praise to God the Father. For examples of prayers see Ephesians 1:17; 3:14; Philippians 1:3; Colossians 1:3. For praise and thanks see Ephesians 1:3,6; 5:19-20; Colossians 1:12; 3:17. He asked that God the Father might give believers the Spirit of wisdom and revelation, and that He might enlighten the eyes of their heart (Ephesians 1:17-18). Paul also prayed that believers would have a greater knowledge of the love of God and display it (Ephesians 3:17-19; Philippians 1:9). He asked that they might know His will (Colossians 1:9).

Paul emphasised that there is only one God and Father, Who is over all and through all and in all (Ephesians 4:6; 1 Timothy 2:5). This One is able to do immeasurably more than all we ask or imagine (Ephesians 3:20). He is the blessed and only Ruler, the King of kings and Lord of lords. He alone has immortality and lives in unapproachable light. No-one has seen Him or can see Him (1 Timothy 6:15-16). Yet He works in believers (Ephesians 1:19; Philippians 1:6; 2:13), meeting all their needs (Philippians 4:19).

Much more is said in these letters concerning God the Father, but what we find is an all-powerful God, Whose power is guided by His love. He extends grace and love, peace and mercy, to His people. He is a God Who wants to see His people grow in wisdom and enlightenment, and Who wants them to have a greater knowledge of Him. He desires them to acknowledge both His love and His will more fully in their lives.

The Son

Paul sees himself as an apostle, servant, and prisoner of Jesus Christ (Ephesians 1:1; 3:1; Philippians 1:1,13-14; Colossians 1:1; 4:7; 1 Timothy 1:1; 2 Timothy 1:1; Titus 1:1; Philemon 1:1). Christ is the One in Whom we have redemption and forgiveness, reconciliation and peace, salvation and eternal life. All this, and more, is a result of His shed blood on the cross (Ephesians 1:7; Colossians 1:20,22; 1 Timothy 2:6; 2 Timothy 3:15).

Jesus Christ is the One Who loved us and gave Himself for us, a fragrant sacrifice (Ephesians 5:2; Philippians 2:8; 1 Timothy 1:15). He is the one mediator between God and man (1 Timothy 2:5), the One Who destroyed death and brought life and immortality to light (2 Timothy 1:10).

Christ is the One Who was raised from the dead, ascended from the earth and is now seated at the Father's right hand in the heavenly realms (Ephesians 1:20; 2:6; 1 Timothy 3:16; 2 Timothy 2:8). As such, all God's purposes are centred in Him (Ephesians 1:10,22; Philippians 2:10-11; Colossians 1:17-20). He is the chief corner stone of all that the Father is building (Ephesians 2:20).

Christ is the One Who may dwell in our hearts by faith (Ephesians 3:17). He apportioned grace and gave gifts (Ephesians 4:7,8,11).

He is the image of the invisible God Whom no-one has seen or can see (1 Timothy 6:16). All things were created by Christ and for Christ (Colossians 1:15-16), and in Him all the fulness of the Deity lives in a bodily form (Colossians 1:19, 2:9). He is, indeed, our great God and Saviour, Jesus Christ (Titus 2:13). He is in very nature God (Philippians 2:6).

In these later letters we have some of the most Christ-exalting passages in the whole of the Scriptures. Consider, for instance, the following four passages:

> That power is like the working of his mighty strength, which he exerted in Christ when he raised him from the dead and seated him at his right hand in the heavenly realms, far above all rule and authority, power and dominion, and every title that can be given, not only in the present age but also in the one to come. And God placed all things under his feet and appointed him to be head over everything for the church, which is

> his body, the fulness of him who fills everything in every way. (Ephesians 1:19-23)
>
> He is the image of the invisible God, the firstborn over all creation. For by him all things were created: things in heaven and on earth, visible and invisible, whether thrones or powers or rulers or authorities; all things were created by him and for him. He is before all things, and in him all things hold together. And he is the head of the body, the church; he is the beginning and the firstborn from among the dead, so that in everything he might have the supremacy. For God was pleased to have all his fulness dwell in him, and through him to reconcile to himself all things, whether things on earth or things in heaven, by making peace through his blood, shed on the cross. (Colossians 1:15-20)
>
> Christ Jesus:
> Who, being in very nature God,
> did not consider equality with God
> something to be grasped,
> but made himself nothing,
> taking the very nature of a servant,
> being made in human likeness.
> And being found in appearance as a man,
> he humbled himself
> and became obedient to death -
> even death on a cross!
> Therefore God exalted him to the highest place
> and gave him the name that is above every name,
> that at the name of Jesus every knee should bow,
> in heaven and on earth and under the earth,
> and every tongue confess that Jesus Christ is Lord,
> to the glory of God the Father. (Philippians 2:5-11)
>
> Beyond all question, the mystery of godliness is great:
> He appeared in a body,
> was vindicated by the Spirit,
> was seen by angels,
> was preached among the nations,
> was believed on in the world,
> was taken up in glory. (1 Timothy 3:16)

Also, in these later letters, we learn something new of Christ. Not only that He ascended to the *heavenly realms*, a term unique to Ephesians, but that He was made head of the church which is His body (Ephesians 1:22-23; 4:15; 5:23; Colossians 1:18; 2:19). Although the figure of a body was used of groups of believers during the time of Acts (see 1

Corinthians 12:12-27; Romans 12:4-5) Christ was never said to be the head. Indeed, in 1 Corinthians 12:16-17 Christians are likened to parts of the head.

In Ephesians 3 Paul writes about a mystery (a secret) concerning Christ, stating that something new about Him had then been revealed which, previously, had not been known.

> Surely you have heard about the administration of God's grace that was given to me for you, that is, the mystery made known to me by revelation, as I have already written briefly. In reading this, then, you will be able to understand my insight into the mystery of Christ, which was not made known to men in other generations *as it has now been revealed* by the Spirit to God's holy apostles and prophets. (Ephesians 3:2-5)

Further comments upon this passage come in a later chapter. For now it is sufficient to ask what is this mystery (secret) concerning Christ which Paul had already written about briefly in Ephesians? What new insight had he had into the Saviour which had not previously been revealed in the way it was then? Part of the answer is that Christ is portrayed as the head of the church which is His body. Throughout the Scriptures the Lord is spoken of as being near to His people. To Israel He was as close as a husband to a wife. However, it is not until these later letters that we learn of such oneness between Christ and Christians, a oneness so close as to be portrayed in a head to body relationship.

The Spirit

The work of the Holy Spirit varies considerably throughout the Scriptures. In these later letters people are sealed with the Spirit upon believing the gospel of salvation, and are sealed with Him until the day of redemption. The indwelling Spirit guarantees believers their future inheritance in the heavenly realms (Ephesians 1:13-14; 4:30).

It was through the Spirit that God revealed His truth to the holy apostles and prophets (Ephesians 3:5; 1 Timothy 4:1) and He is the One through Whom God strengthens believers in their inner being, enabling Christ to dwell in their hearts by faith (Ephesians 3:16-17). It is by the Spirit that God helps believers (Philippians 1:19).

There is one Spirit and it is by that one Spirit that we have access to the Father, through Christ. It is by the Spirit that we worship Him (Ephesians 2:18; 4:4; Philippians 3:3). The word of God is the sword of the Spirit and believers should pray in the Spirit (Ephesians 6:17-18).

He is described as the Spirit of wisdom (Ephesians 1:17) and we are encouraged to be filled by Him (Ephesians 5:18). There is a unity and fellowship of the Spirit which believers are exhorted to keep through the bond of peace (Ephesians 4:3; Philippians 2:2) and failure to do so can grieve Him (Ephesians 4:30).

27. Salvation

God, Who is our Saviour, desires all men to be saved and come to a knowledge of the truth (1 Timothy 2:3-4). Twice in Ephesians chapter 2 it is emphasised that this salvation is by grace through faith. It is not by works, preventing anyone from boasting (verses 5-9). However, God, Who has saved us through rebirth and renewal by the Spirit, calls us to a holy life, for we are created in Christ Jesus to do good works (2 Timothy 1:9; Titus 3:5; Ephesians 2:10).

Four gifts

Christ Jesus came into the world to save sinners (1 Timothy 1:15). He did this by shedding His blood on Calvary's cross. As a result, we have been redeemed from all wickedness (Titus 2:14). Now in Christ we have redemption and the forgiveness of sins. We have been brought near to God, reconciled to Him and are at peace with Him (Ephesians 1:7,14; 2:13; Colossians 1:14,20).

As a result of this we should forgive one another, just as in Christ God has forgiven us (Ephesians 4:32; Colossians 3:13). Indeed, God has forgiven us *all* of our sins (Colossians 2:13). Eternal life and righteousness are ours through faith, for we have been justified (1 Timothy 6:12,19; Titus 1:2; 3:7; Philippians 3:9).

All of this is in accordance with the riches of God's grace which He lavished upon us (Ephesians 1:8). Freely we have been saved from the consequences of sin and death, having been given eternal life. We have been redeemed. All our sins have been forgiven and we have been given a gift, God's righteousness. The fruits of His righteousness we should display in our lives, but its totality we shall not possess until the next (Philippians 1:11; 3:9). All that is required from us to obtain this, and so much more, is faith in Christ our Saviour.

In Christ

But there is more for the believer than the four gifts mentioned above: forgiveness, redemption, eternal life, and righteousness. If we consider just Ephesians we shall read much more of what Christians receive from God because they are "in Christ". Any who put their faith in Christ are considered by God to be "in Christ". As such, many spiritual blessings follow. Ephesians lists some of them.

God has blessed us in the heavenly realms with every spiritual blessing *in Christ* (1:3).

God chose us *in Him* before the foundation of the world to be holy and blameless in His sight (1:4).

In love He predestined us to be adopted as His sons *through Jesus Christ* (1:5).

He has freely given us of His glorious grace *in the One He loves* (1:6).

In Him we have redemption through His blood, the forgiveness of sins (1:7).

God has made known to us the mystery of His will according to His good pleasure, which He purposed *in Christ* (1:9).

In Christ we were also chosen, in order that we might be to the praise of His glory (1:11-12).

And we were included *in Christ* when we heard the word of truth, the gospel of our salvation (1:13).

Having believed the gospel, we were marked *in Him* with a seal, the promised Holy Spirit (1:13).

Previously we were dead in our transgressions and sin and as such were by nature objects of wrath. But because of His great love for us God, Who is rich in mercy, made us alive *with Christ*, even when we were dead in transgressions (2:1-5).

Not only are we saved by grace, but also God raised us up *with Christ* and seated us *with Him* in the heavenly realms *in Christ*, in order that in the coming ages He might show the incomparable riches of His grace expressed in His kindness to us *in Christ Jesus* (2:6-7).

Believers are God's workmanship, created *in Christ Jesus* to do good works (2:10).

Gentiles in other ages were further from God than the people of Israel. They were excluded from citizenship in Israel and were foreigners to the covenants of promise. As such they were without hope and without God in the world. But now *in Christ Jesus* Gentile believers have been brought near *through the blood of Christ* (2:12-13).

Christ has made Jewish Christians and Gentile Christians one. He destroyed the barrier between them, the dividing wall of hostility, by abolishing *in His flesh* the law with its commandments and regulations. His purpose was to create *in Himself* one new man out of the two (2:14-15).

Through Christ both Jewish and Gentile Christian have access to the Father by one Spirit (2:18).

As a consequence, Gentile believers are no longer foreigners and aliens. Rather they are fellow-citizens and members of God's household. *In Christ* the whole building is joined together and rises to become a holy temple *in the Lord*. And *in Christ* we are being built together to become a dwelling place in which God lives by His Spirit (2:19-22).

All believers now, whether Jew or Gentile, are heirs together, members together of one body, and sharers together in the promise *in Christ Jesus* (3:6).

In Christ, and through faith *in Him*, we may approach God with freedom and confidence (3:12).

Here are just some of the marvellous blessings believers have *in Christ*. We have considered just the first half of Ephesians. More is told us in the second half, and in the other letters. No wonder Paul pauses to write "to the praise of his glorious grace" (Ephesians 1:6). He is, indeed, a God of grace.

Identification

We read in Romans 6:5 that believers are identified with Christ in His death. As such they shall be united with Him in resurrection. However, when we come to Ephesians we learn that believers are not only identified with Christ in death, burial and resurrection. There is much more.

We are told that God not only sees us as raised from the dead, but raised up to the heavenly realms and seated there in Christ (Ephesians 2:6). His purpose in doing this is that in the coming ages He is to show us the incomparable riches of His grace (Ephesians 2:7).

For believers in previous dispensations eternal life is to be spent upon the earth. This is the hope expressed in the Lord's prayer (Matthew 6:10; see also 5:5) and this was the expectation of John when he saw the holy city, the heavenly Jerusalem, coming down out of heaven from God (Revelation 21:1-2; Hebrews 12:22). To be identified with Christ in His death, burial and resurrection was sufficient for those people, their final destiny being upon the new earth.

By contrast, if we are to spend eternity in heaven, we must also be identified with Christ in His ascension to the heavenly realms, and this is just what Ephesians teaches. In fact it says more. For just as Christ is seated there, having completed His work of redemption, so, too, are we seen to be seated there, having been redeemed.

However, there is one more aspect of identification which we read of only in these later letters, God's final written revelation to mankind.

> Since, then, you have been raised with Christ, set your hearts on things above, where Christ is seated at the right hand of God. Set your minds on things above, not on earthly things. For you died, and your life is now hidden with Christ in God. When Christ, who is your life, appears, then you also will appear with him in glory. (Colossians 3:1-4)

Colossians also records believers' identification with Christ in His ascension. However, it goes further, stating that we are to be identified with Christ in His appearing. Indeed, we are to be identified with Him *in glory*. Here, again, we see further truth revealed in these last letters of Paul and it helps us in our understanding of the Bible if we recognise when God did reveal such teaching. We cannot properly understand the Gospels, Acts, and earlier epistles if we read back into them something which we have learned from Paul's last letters: that is, teachings of which at the time of writing none of the authors, let alone their readers, had any idea.

28. Practical teaching

In the previous two chapters we have learnt that God is a God of love and grace, freely forgiving those who have faith in Christ Jesus. We find that we have been redeemed and have the promise of God-given righteousness and eternal life. All this is by grace. It is not of works, ensuring that no-one can boast (Ephesians 2:9; 2 Timothy 1:9; Titus 3:5). However, in these later letters we find that our works are of the utmost importance to the Lord.

Works

We are His workmanship, and we have been created in Christ Jesus to do good works (Ephesians 2:10). On a number of occasions Paul stressed to both Timothy and Titus the need for good deeds (1 Timothy 2:9-10; 5:10,25; 6:18; 2 Timothy 3:17; Titus 2:7,14; 3:8,14).

However, he also warned believers against wicked works, or the deeds of darkness (Ephesians 5:11; Colossians 1:21; Titus 1:16). But what constitutes good works? And what are the works of darkness?

These last seven letters are full of good advice about what makes up the Christian life. The letters to the Ephesians and Colossians are each in two distinct halves, the first half dealing mainly with doctrine and the second primarily with practice. When reading each we learn first what the Lord has done for us. Only afterwards do we read what He would like us to do in return. What follows is a brief synopsis of what the Lord would like believers to do and what He wants them not to do or to remove from their lives.

Ephesians makes several references to "living the life" ("walking worthy" *KJV*). See Ephesians 4:1,17; 5:2,8,15. We are exhorted to live a life worthy of our calling, to live a life of love and to live as children of light. We are told to be careful how we live, not as unwise, but as wise, and not as unbelievers. However, we shall concentrate upon Colossians because there Paul aptly condenses what is taught elsewhere.

Practical Christianity in Colossians

Colossians 3:5-9 exhorts believers to put to death whatever belongs to their earthly nature and lists these as:

sexual immorality,
impurity,

lust,
evil desires,
greed.

After describing greed as idolatry, the passage goes on to say that we must rid ourselves of even more. Such things as:

anger,
rage,
malice,
slander,
filthy language.

Colossians 3:12-15 tells us that instead of these, we must clothe ourselves with:

compassion,
kindness,
humility,
gentleness,
patience,
forgiveness,
love,
peace,
thankfulness.

Then come special instructions for wives and husbands, children and parents, workers and masters (3:18-4:1).

All these come under the headings of morals and graces, and we shall find similar teachings in Ephesians and the other later letters. Indeed, we shall find very little difference throughout Scripture in the morals God expects from His people and in the loving and forgiving graces He wishes them to exhibit, but how can we acquire them? Ridding ourselves of what belongs to our earthly natures, and putting on what goes with the new, is helped by setting our minds on things above, not on earthly things. We need to set our hearts on things above where Christ is seated at the right hand of God (Colossians 3:1-2). If we do that, what belongs to our earthly nature will die (Colossians 3:5). To help us in this we have the Holy Spirit to strengthen us with power in our inner being (Ephesians 3:16). That power is God's resurrection power. It is His mighty strength which He exerted when He raised Christ from the dead and seated Him at His right hand in the heavenly realms (Ephesians 1:19-20).

Religious practices

There are other aspects to the Christian life which do not come under the umbrella of morals and graces. These are to do with certain religious practices like the eating of certain meats, circumcision, fasting, obeying Sabbath Law, and many more.

Under the Mosaic Law the Jews had to abstain from eating certain meats and the ones they could eat had to be killed in a certain way. They had to circumcise their male children on the eighth day, fast on certain occasions, observe the Sabbath Law, and much else. However, under the terms of the Mosaic Law Gentiles were never told to abstain from certain meats, or to eat meat killed in a certain way. Neither were they to circumcise their children, fast or to observe the Sabbath ceremonies. However, Gentiles who lived in Israel were told not to work on the Sabbath.

This was still the situation during the time covered by the Gospels and by the period covered by the Acts of the apostles, with one small exception which we shall come to. Certainly, if we read through Acts we shall see the Christian Jews still observing the Law of Moses (e.g. Acts 21:20). In this they were right. If their witness to their fellow Jews was not to be impaired it was necessary for them to continue obeying the Law. They were not under the Law. That is, they did not have to keep the Law to obtain righteousness, rather it was their right and proper Christian duty to keep it. Doing so enabled them to continue in fellowship with those Jews who had not yet come to believe that Jesus was the Christ (Messiah).

As we progress through Acts we find Gentiles being saved and, naturally, wanting fellowship with the Jewish Christians. How could these Jewish Christians have fellowship with Gentiles without rendering themselves unclean according to the Mosaic Law, and unclean in the eyes of the Jews who did not yet believe? The solution came at the council of Jerusalem where Gentiles were asked to "abstain from food polluted by idols, from sexual immorality, from the meat of strangled animals and from blood" (Acts 15:20).

However, when we read these later letters we find the situation in Acts to be no longer the case. Jewish Christians were not expected to observe the Mosaic Law and Gentiles did not have to worry about what they ate.

> For he himself is our peace, who has made the two (Jew and Gentile) one and has destroyed the barrier, the dividing wall of hostility, by

abolishing in his flesh the law with its commandments and regulations. (Ephesians 2:14-15)

He forgave us all our sins, having cancelled the written code, with its regulations, that was against us and that stood opposed to us ; he took it away, nailing it to the cross. And having disarmed the powers and authorities, he made a public spectacle of them, triumphing over them by the cross. Therefore do not let anyone judge you by what you eat or drink, or with regard to a religious festival, a New Moon celebration or a Sabbath day. These are a shadow of the things that were to come; the reality, however, is found in Christ. (Colossians 2:13-17)

Here we need to point out one common misunderstanding. It states that the Law, the written code, with its commandments and regulations, was abolished *by* the cross. Note, it does not say *at* the cross, as some read. Much was achieved *by* the cross which did not come about *at* the cross. We read that Jesus Christ "has destroyed death and has brought life and immortality to life through the gospel" (2 Timothy 1:10), yet people continue to die. Sin, Satan, and death were all defeated *by* the cross, yet all are still very much with us, but only for a limited time. There is to come a day when all three will be no more (2 Peter 3:13; Revelation 20:10; 21:4).

By the cross the Law was taken away, yet it continued for a number of years afterwards. Throughout the whole of Acts Jewish Christians rightly continued their observance of it. When their nation rendered itself blind and deaf to God through hardening its heart against Jesus Christ (Acts 28:25-27), then the need of Christian Jews to witness to their fellow countrymen became of secondary importance to witnessing to the world in general. As such they were freed from the need to keep the Law. No one should any longer judge them by what they ate or drank, or what they did on special religious festivals, New Moons or Sabbath days. Even circumcision, one of the big issues of Acts 15, became irrelevant for the Jews.

In him (Christ) you were also circumcised, in the putting off of the sinful nature, not with a circumcision done by the hands of men but with the circumcision done by Christ. (Colossians 2:11)

Watch out for those dogs, those men who do evil, those mutilators of the flesh. For it is we who are the circumcision, we who worship by the Spirit of God, who glory in Christ Jesus, and who put no confidence in the flesh. (Philippians 3:2-3)

Paul would not have written such statements during the Acts period and we find no such things in his earlier letters. At that time he did not circumcise Titus, who was a Greek, but he did circumcise Timothy whose mother was a Jewess (Galatians 2:3; Acts 16:1-3). The difference in Paul's actions during the time covered by Acts is explained by taking note of whether he is dealing with Jews or Gentiles.

However, we find altogether different teaching in the later letters. Gentiles are certainly not expected to circumcise their children for religious reasons today. Neither are they commanded to keep the Sabbath Law, fast, or observe any other details of the religious Mosaic Law. In this dispensation, however, this is also true for the Jewish Christians. None the less we recognise that "the law is good if a man uses it properly" for "All Scripture ... is profitable" (1 Timothy 1:8; 2 Timothy 3:16-17) and there is much we can learn from it, especially with respect to practical teaching as well as types and shadows, i.e. teaching typifying aspects of our Saviour's work.

Again there is a danger here that we can read back into the Gospels, Acts, and earlier letters a situation which did not arise until much later. We need to recognise that the people to whom Christ spoke when on earth were Jewish people under the Law of Moses. We must also appreciate that during Acts the Christian Jews continued, rightly, to observe that Law, not for righteousness, but as their right and proper duty to God. To read freedom from the Law back into the Gospels and Acts can only result in misunderstanding.

Equality

From Genesis 12:1-3 onwards and throughout the Old Testament it is taught that Gentiles were to be blessed through the descendants of Abraham. As a result we see them occupying second place to the Jew.

In the Gospels the Saviour sent out the twelve with express orders *not* to go into the way of the Gentiles and told a Canaanite woman that He had been sent only to the lost sheep of Israel (Matthew 10:5-6; 15:24). Only when she acknowledged her subordinate place did He grant her what she had asked for. Only at the end of the Gospels do we read of the disciples being told to go to all the nations (Matthew 28:19; Mark 16:15; Luke 24:47; see also Acts 1:8).

Yet during the period covered by the Acts of the Apostles, the Jews continued to have first place in God's purposes, as well as many advantages (Romans 1:16; 2:9-10; 3:1-2; 9:4-5). Indeed, the gospel had to be preached to them first, and Paul did this wherever he went (see Acts 13:46 and note, for example, Acts 14:1; 17:1,10; 18:4).

However, this situation, which had commenced at Genesis 12 and continued through the Old Testament, Gospels, and Acts, changes totally with a new secret (mystery) revealed by God in Ephesians. Paul first wrote of the previous position of Gentiles.

> Therefore, remember that formerly you who are Gentiles by birth and called "uncircumcised" by those who call themselves "the circumcision" (that done in the body by the hands of men) - remember that at that time you were separate from Christ, excluded from citizenship in Israel and foreigners to the covenants of the promise, without hope and without God in the world. (Ephesians 2:11-12)

However, he went on to tell them of their new position.

> But now in Christ Jesus you who once were far away have been brought near through the blood of Christ. (Ephesians 2:13)

Paul then explained to them how this had been achieved.

> For he himself is our peace, who has made the two (Jewish and Gentile Christians) one and has *destroyed the barrier*, the dividing wall of hostility, by *abolishing in his flesh the law with its commandments and regulations*. His purpose was to create in himself one new man out of the two, thus making peace, and in this one body to reconcile both of them to God through the cross, by which he put to death their hostility. He came and preached peace to you who were far away (Gentiles) and peace to those who were near (Jews). For through him we both have access to the Father by one Spirit. (Ephesians 2:14-18)

Finally, he dealt with the consequences of this change.

> Consequently, you are no longer foreigners and aliens, but fellow-citizens with God's people and members of God's household. (Ephesians 2:19)

Paul went on, in the next chapter, to refer to this - "as I have already written briefly" (3:3). He describes it as "the mystery (secret) made known to me by revelation" (3:3). Certainly, nowhere earlier in Scripture do we read of this change in relationship between Israel and the Gentiles. In fact, Paul states that it "was not made known to men in other generations as it has now been revealed" (3:5).

Later Paul stated that his aim was "to make plain to everyone the administration of this mystery, which for ages past was kept hidden in God" (3:9). And in Colossians 1:26 he wrote of "the mystery that has been kept hidden for ages and generations, but is now disclosed to the saints". All this shows the newness of this new revelation from God, this mystery (secret).

> This mystery is that through the gospel the Gentiles are heirs together with Israel, members together of one body, and sharers together in the promise in Christ Jesus. (Ephesians 3:6)

Now all nations are on the same footing before God. There is no favoured place for just one of them. All believers of whatever race or nationality are equal heirs, equal sharers, and equal members in the church which is His body. They are now the stewards or administrators of this new dispensation.

29. Other teaching

The work of the Spirit

In chapter 26 we considered what the later letters teach concerning the Godhead - Father, Son, and Spirit. It is certainly true that the ministry of the Holy Spirit changes considerably as we peruse the pages of Scripture. Consider, for example, some of the things we learn of Him and His work.

In the Old Testament the Holy Spirit came upon certain of the people of Israel to strengthen them physically (Judges 14:5-6) and to enable them to do all manner of skilful and artistic work (Exodus 28:1-5; 31:1-5). He enabled them to prophesy (Numbers 11:24-30), to administer and judge with wisdom (Judges 3:10; 6:34; 11:29; 13:24-25), and to exhibit many other talents and skills that they needed to enable them to do what God wanted. However, the Spirit did not abide with them continually. Neither did He indwell them permanently. When the task was over, when the work was completed, He departed and they lost those special skills and abilities. He would also leave if there was extreme disobedience, as in the case of King Saul (1 Samuel 16:14).

Furthermore not every Israelite experienced the enabling of the Holy Spirit. Joel did testify of a time coming when the Spirit would be poured out upon all flesh (Joel 2:28), but nowhere in that passage is it ever suggested that the Holy Spirit was to indwell continually and remain permanently with the people.

This situation changed after the cross, when those who placed their faith in Christ were sealed with the Spirit until the day of redemption (2 Corinthians 1:22; Ephesians 1:13; 4:30).

However, the New Testament distinguishes between *having* the Spirit, which is true of all believers today and being *filled* with the Spirit, which is the believer's privilege and duty. Having the Spirit guarantees us our inheritance (Ephesians 1:13-14). He marks us off as Christians. Being filled with the Spirit is another matter, however, for it is the filling of the Spirit which empowers people to do certain things.

As stated above, in Old Testament times people were empowered to have greater physical strength, better artistic ability, more administrative skills. They were wiser and could prophesy.

During Christ's time on earth little is said of the Holy Spirit. It is not until Pentecost, and afterwards, that we read of the gifts of the Spirit where people were empowered to perform all sorts of miraculous acts including healing and raising the dead, and to have greater knowledge and wisdom, as well as the ability to speak in tongues and interpret them (1 Corinthians 12:7-11). When we read through the Acts of the Apostles, and some of the earlier letters, we see many references to these particular signs and wonders. However, when we read the last seven letters of Paul *there is a complete absence of them.*

From James 5:13-16 we learn that a believer could become ill because of sin in his life, but if he confessed it to the elders and they prayed over him and anointed him, he would be cured. Yet Timothy was a man of God, called by Paul "my true son in the faith" (1 Timothy 1:2). None the less he had "frequent illnesses", presumably from some stomach complaint (1 Timothy 5:23). During Acts Paul healed such people at a distance by sending a handkerchief (Acts 19:12). After Acts all he could send was good advice. Yet both Paul and Timothy were good and active Christians. Paul was equally filled with the Spirit. It would seem that the Spirit no longer empowered him to heal.

This is not an isolated case in these last seven letters. In his last letter, Paul informs Timothy that he has "left Trophimus sick at Miletus" (2 Timothy 4:20). During Acts, when on Malta, Paul left no-one sick. He healed them all (Acts 28:7-9).

Lastly, there is the case of Epaphroditus, who was so ill that he nearly died. Not only did this upset the Philippians, it upset Paul, who was with him. However, Epaphroditus did not die. He recovered and Paul, rightly, thanked and praised God for restoring Ephaproditus. However, it is clear from the passage (Philippians 2:25-27) that Paul himself could do nothing to heal Epaphroditus and spare everyone great worry and anxiety.

As we have already said, there is a complete absence from these later epistles of the miracles associated with being filled with the Spirit in Acts. None the less believers are exhorted to be filled with the Spirit (Ephesians 5:18), but with what does He fill people nowadays? The following are extracts from Paul's prayers.

> I pray ... that you may be filled to the measure of all the fulness of God. (Ephesians 3:19)

> And this is my prayer ... that you may be filled ... with the fruit of righteousness that comes through Jesus Christ. (Philippians 1:9-11)

> We have not stopped praying for you and asking God to fill you with the knowledge of his will through all spiritual wisdom and understanding. (Colossians 1:9)

In addition Epaphras prayed for the Colossians that they might stand firm in the will of God, mature and fully assured - filled full with assurance (Colossians 4:12).

Clearly the work of the Spirit has changed, just as it had done on a number of occasions in the past. But that is not the only change that we note.

The return of Christ

In some of the earlier letters of Paul it is clear that he is expecting Christ to return soon. For example, in 1 Corinthians he advises against marriage - advice he reverses in 1 Timothy 5:14.

> Because of the present crisis, I think it is good for you to remain as you are. Are you married? Do not seek a divorce. Are you unmarried? Do not look for a wife. But if you do marry, you have not sinned; and if a virgin marries, she has not sinned. But those who marry will face many troubles in this life, and I want to spare you this. What I mean, brothers, is that the time is short. From now on those who have wives should live as if they had none ... For this world in its present form is passing away. (1 Corinthians 7:26-29,31)

Paul's point here is that Christ was *soon* to return, but before He did so, Israel was to undergo the great tribulation. This was the reason why Paul thought it unwise to bring children into the world, an inevitable result of marriage in those days, and why he suggested married men should live as if they did not have a wife. In this he said no more than Christ, Who also warned of the great distress in the days leading up to His return; "How dreadful it will be in those days for pregnant women and nursing mothers!" (Matthew 24:19-21).

This is not the only reference Paul makes to an imminent return of Christ. Again he tells the Corinthians that their generation was the one "on whom the fulfilment of the ages has come" (1 Corinthians 10:11). Then, when writing to the Thessalonians, he shows that he expected to be alive at the second coming.

> *We* who are left till the coming of the Lord, will certainly not precede those who have fallen asleep. (1 Thessalonians 4:15)

Romans 13:12 records that:

> The night is nearly over; the day is almost here.

And Hebrews 10:37 has:

> For in just a very little while, He who is coming will come and will not delay. (See also 10:35.)

But Paul is not the only writer who expected Christ to return soon. John states:

> This is the last hour. (1 John 2:18)

> The time is near ... Look, he is coming with the clouds ... "Here I am! I stand at the door and knock ... Behold, I am coming soon! ... Do not seal up the words of the prophecy of this book, because the time is near ... Behold, I am coming soon! ... Yes, I am coming soon." ... Come, Lord Jesus. (Revelation 1:3,7; 3:20; 22:7,10,12,20)

And James has:

> Be patient, then, brothers, until the Lord's coming ... You, too, be patient and stand firm, because the Lord's coming is near ... The Judge is standing at the door! (James 5:7-9)

Peter describes the days in which he lives as the "last times" (1 Peter 1:20) and goes on to say:

> The end of all things is near. (1 Peter 4:7)

This is an echo of what he said in Acts when addressing the people of Israel.

> Repent, then, and turn to God, so that your sins may be wiped out, that times of refreshing may come from the Lord, and that he may send the Christ, who has been appointed for you - even Jesus. He must remain in heaven until the time comes for God to restore everything, as he promised long ago through his holy prophets. (Acts 3:19-21)

From this passage it would appear that the order of events was that Israel was required first to repent. This would enable their sins to be wiped out and the times of refreshing would then come from the presence of the Lord following Christ's return. However, as we have seen before, Israel did not repent. Rather they hardened their hearts against Jesus. This rendered them spiritually blind and deaf. After that, God's salvation was sent to the Gentiles (Acts 28:25-28).

From this time on, there is no mention of Christ's near return. In fact His coming (*parousia*) is not even mentioned in any of Paul's last letters. He talks of Christ's appearing and manifestation, but never once of His coming. This does not mean to say that Christ will not return, He most certainly will. But the nearness of it was no longer a possibility during Paul's later life and so he wrote:

> So I counsel younger widows to marry, to have children, to manage their homes and to give the enemy no opportunity for slander. (1 Timothy 5:14).

Here is a further example of how things changed at the end of Acts.

Prayer

There are various parts to the Christian life, some of them overlapping. They may be termed:

> worship, praise and fellowship;
> prayer - private and corporate;
> Bible reading and study;
> service and good works.

In this book none of the above, with the exception of Bible study, has been considered in depth. However, let us now look at the contents of the prayers in these last letters.

In Ephesians there are two major prayers. In the first (1:16-23) Paul emphasises that he has not stopped giving thanks for the believers to whom he is writing. He has not stopped remembering them in his prayers.

He keeps asking that the God and Father of our Lord Jesus Christ may give them the spirit of wisdom and revelation and he gives the reason for his prayer - so that they may know Him better.

He prays that the eyes of their heart may be enlightened and, again, he gives the reason for his prayer in Ephesians 1:18-19. It is in order that they may know three things:

(1) The hope to which the Father has called them.
(2) The riches of His glorious inheritance in the saints.
(3) His incomparably great power for believers.

The second prayer is in Ephesians 3:14-21. Here Paul's prayer is that first the Father will strengthen believers in their inner being with power through His Spirit, and again he gives his reason. It is in order that Christ way dwell in their hearts by faith.

Then he prays that, once they have been rooted and established in love, they may have power, and again he gives his reasons for his request. There are three:

(1) For believers to be able to grasp how wide and long and high and deep is the love of Christ.
(2) For them to know this love which surpasses knowledge.
(3) That they may be filled with the fulness of God.

The first prayer ends with the exaltation of Christ and the second with a doxology of praise.

The other references to prayer are in 5:20, where believers are urged to thank the Father for everything; 6:18, where they are told to pray in the Spirit on all occasions; and 6:19, where Paul asks them to pray for him.

Philippians opens with thanksgiving, asserting that God will complete His good work in believers (1:3-6). Then Paul prays that their love may abound more and more in knowledge and depth of insight. Again Paul gives his reasons, and again there are three (1:9-11):

(1) That they may be able to discern what is best.
(2) That they may be pure and blameless until the day of Christ.
(3) That they may be filled with the fruit of righteousness that come through Jesus Christ.

Paul also thanks the Philippians for their prayers (1:19) before telling them not to be anxious about anything. Instead, in everything, by prayer and petition *with thanksgiving*, they are to present their requests to God. If they do this, he does not say their prayers will be answered. However, he does state that the peace of God, which transcends all understanding, will guard their hearts and minds in Christ Jesus (4:6-7).

Paul tells the Colossians that he always thanks God for them in his prayers (1:3). He repeats this later in the chapter (v 9) before telling them that he has not stopped asking God to fill them with the knowledge of His will through all spiritual understanding. He again gives his reasons (1:10-12). They are in order that believers may:

(1) Live a life worthy of the Lord;
(2) Please the Lord in every way;
(3) Bear fruit in every good work;
(4) Grow in the knowledge of God.

Paul also asks that they may be strengthened with all power according to God's glorious might. The reasons for this request are in verses 11 and 12 and are:

(1) That they may have great endurance and patience;
(2) That they may joyfully give thanks to the Lord.

Paul instructs the Colossians to do everything in the name of Christ, giving thanks to the Father (3:17) and to devote themselves to prayer (4:2). He asks them to pray for him so that he may proclaim the mystery of Christ, and do so clearly (4:3-4). He closes by mentioning that Epaphras was always wrestling in prayer for them (4:12).

1 Timothy contains the injunction that requests, prayers and intercession, and thanksgiving should be made for everyone, and Paul draws attention to two particular groups: kings and all those in authority (2:1-2). The reason for this is simply in order that we may live peaceful and quiet lives in all godliness and holiness (2:2). This is good and pleasing to our Saviour, Who desires all men to be saved and to come to a knowledge of the truth (2:3-4).

Paul wants people to pray everywhere, but when they do so it should be without anger or disputing (2:8). The widow is encouraged to pray day and night, asking God for help (5:5). And Timothy is told that all foods can be eaten (a significant statement for the Jewish Christians of that time, which included Timothy who had been circumcised in Acts 16:1-3). Nothing is to be rejected provided it is received with thanksgiving, for it is consecrated by the word of God and prayer (1 Timothy 4:3-4).

In 2 Timothy the only mention of prayer is in the opening verses where Paul states that he prays constantly for Timothy (1:3). There are no references in Titus.

In the remaining post-Acts letter Paul tells Philemon that he thanks God for him (v 4). He then goes on to pray that Philemon's love may be active in sharing his faith (v 5). This is so that Philemon will have a full understanding of every good thing we have in Christ (v 6). Paul ends by stating that because of Philemon's prayers Paul hopes to be released soon and restored to them (v 22)

It is interesting to read Paul's reasons for what he asks for, and we may learn much from them. Also, we need to note that the petitions in these prayers are very different from the contents of most Christian intercession nowadays, and this may be one reason why so many prayers go unanswered. Some prayers today are not the least bit Bible-based. Others are, but their contents have more in common with the prayers of the Gospels or of the general epistles of Peter, James, and John. These do differ in a number of respects from those of Paul. One important difference is that in those former times there was a definiteness in the prayers, an assertion that they would receive what they asked for. What we need to note about these prayers of Paul is that there is a lack of such assertion. The requests were couched in more moderate language, with Paul asking that God *might* do this or *might* give that.

For the Ephesians, Paul prayed that they *might* receive the spirit of wisdom and revelation, in order that they *might* have a better knowledge of God; that the eyes of their heart *might* be enlightened in order that they *might* know the hope of their calling, the riches of God's inheritance, and His great power (Ephesians 1:17-19). His request for the Philippians was that their love *might* abound more and more, in order that they *might* be able to discern what is best and right and *might* be pure and blameless (Philippians 1:9-10). For the Colossians it was that they *might* live a life worthy of the Lord and that they *might* please Him in every way (Colossians 1:10). These stand in stark contrast to the assertive requests of James and John with their assertion of definitely obtaining what was requested (e.g. James 1:5-7; 1 John 3:21-22).

30. Summary and Conclusion

It has not been our intention in this book to set out an exhaustive theology resulting from this approach to the Bible. Rather we have tried to make readers think about the approaches they and others use.

We opened by asking two questions.

What is your approach?
Which approach should we take?

There we discussed four different approaches: a literal one, a figurative one, a critical one, and a dispensational one.

Next we endeavoured to develop the dispensational approach, the one advocated in this book. We did so by considering:

The people in the Old Testament;
The people in the New Testament;
The places written about;
The time when things were written and the time written about;
What was said;
The reason for what was written;
A possible application to our situation.

We then used this approach to look at certain subjects and passages. The subjects considered were:

The Sabbath;
Circumcision;
Fasting;
Tithing
Healing.

The passages covered dealt with:

Jesus Christ is the same yesterday, today and forever;
The unforgiveable sin;
The sin and unto death;
I will do whatever you ask in My name;
The mark of the beast.

Having used this approach, we then formalised it by considering:

The history of the appraoch;
One significant aspect of the approach;
Formalising the approach;
A new approach;
Administrators and administration;
Changing administrators and their orders;
What is this approach?

Then, in the last four chapters, we looked at how some doctrines are treated in the last seven letters of Paul. These were:

The Godhead - Father, Son and Holy Spirit;
Salvation - forgiveness and eternal life, redemption, righteousness and identification;
Practical teaching - works, religious practices, and equality;
Other teachings - the work of the Spirit, the return of Christ, and prayer.

With some of these subjects, we saw that significant new truth was revealed in the later letters, Ephesians and Colossians in particular. With other subjects, particularly those dealing with sin, salvation, and the Christian life, we found that there was little or no difference from what we find in the earlier parts of the Bible. Thus in considering any subject we have to follow the teaching through the whole of the Bible, or the whole of the New Testament in some cases, noting if there are any changes. A verse or two quoted out of context cannot be used to justify any position.

Conclusion

Our sincere prayer is that this book will have helped the reader come to a better understanding of the Bible and a deeper appreciation of the plans and purposes of our God. In 1870 Richard Holden, a leader of the Brethren Movement, wrote:

> To make all men see what is the dispensation, or in other words, to be the divinely appointed instructor in the character and order of the present time, as Moses was in the dispensation of the law, is that special feature in the commission of Paul in which it was distinct from that of the other Apostles ... If then it shall appear that, far from seeing "what is the dispensation of the Mystery" (Ephesians 3:9, *RV*) *the mass of Christians have entirely missed it*, and, as a natural consequence, have almost completely misunderstood Christianity, importing into it the

> things proper to another dispensation, and so confounding Judaism and Christianity in an inexpressible jumble; surely it is a matter of deep humiliation before God, and for earnest prayerful effort to retrieve, with God's help, this important and neglected teaching. (*The Mystery: The Special Mission of the Apostle Paul, The Key to the Present Dispensation*)

In this book we have attempted to do just that.

God is not a God of disorder, although it may appear from a cursory reading of the Scriptures that He is. Different things are said at different times to different people. Different actions have been undertaken by God and different acts have been required of His people.

It has been my aim to advance principles which will help us deal objectively with such differences. By *distinguishing particularly between Jews and Gentiles* and by *giving greater emphasis to later revelation*, we will have a better understanding of what God is doing now and a clearer idea of what He wants *us* to do. We may then be better servants of our Saviour and clearer witnesses to the great plan of salvation He has for the inhabitants of this world.

Soli Deo gloria

Appendix 1

Miles Coverdale

There can be little doubt that Miles Coverdale has been a great inspiration to the author, and to many others. But what do we know of him? I am greatly indebted to an article by David Osgood, published in the November 1990 edition of *Grace and Truth*, for much of what follows.

Miles Coverdale was born in the North Riding of Yorkshire in 1488. He was educated at Cambridge and was ordained a priest in Norwich at the age of 30. He joined the Augustine friars at Cambridge, where he came into contact with the reformers, including Robert Barnes who, as his prior, greatly influenced him. As a result of Barnes' encouragement and his own studies, Coverdale began openly preaching against the mass.

It is generally accepted that Coverdale worked with Tyndale in Hamburg in 1529. He also assisted Tyndale in his translation of the Pentateuch into English. He worked extremely hard and began his own translation of the Bible into English, a work he completed in 1535 when aged 47. In the preface of that Bible he wrote:

> It shall greatly helpe ye to understande Scripture, if thou mark not only what is spoken and written, but to whom, and of whom, with what words, at what time, with what intent, what circumstances, considering what goeth before and what followeth.

This version was the first complete Bible to be published in English. It was printed in Southwark and a second edition, which received royal licence and commissioning, appeared in 1537.

Coverdale's Bible may have had its limitations. This was largely due to his limited mastery of Latin and Greek, and to his having at his disposal only the Greek text collated by Erasmus, which had been published earlier that century. He also relied upon other versions to determine the meaning of some passages of which he was unsure. These included both Luther's and Tyndale's translations.

Although we have used Coverdale's quotation as the basis of the approach advocated in this book, we do not wish to give the impression that this is what Coverdale, himself, did. Although completely earnest in his intention, it seems that Coverdale did not understand, completely, God's change from a dispensation dominated by Law to one in which the inherent feature was grace. Indeed, what came out of the Reformation was not a gospel of full and free grace, as preached by Paul. Rather it was a gospel of grace and forgiveness, but one to which works and Law were attached. None the less, Coverdale's achievement of being the first to have the Bible printed in English should never be underestimated.

It was about this time that he was befriended by Thomas Cromwell, whom he had met at the home of Sir Thomas More. Cromwell had Coverdale travel to Paris to superintend the production of another English version of the Bible. However, before it was completed the Inquisition broke out in Europe. The printing presses and types and some of the French workers were brought to England. This was how *The Great Bible*, or *Cromwell's Bible*, was completed. It was presented to King Henry VIII in 1539, when Coverdale was 51. This one-volume Bible was to be used in every church in the land.

However, the freedom of the Renaissance and Reformation was short-lived. The Inquisition had begun on the Continent and changes at the Royal Court in England caused Coverdale problems. His friend, Thomas Cromwell, who had been a close confidant of Henry VIII, fell out of favour.

Cromwell was the son of a Putney blacksmith and innkeeper. After military service he became known and favoured by Cardinal Wolsey and was appointed his collector of revenues. Cromwell's considerable abilities brought him to the notice of the King and he soon gained influence with Henry. In 1533 Cromwell became Chancellor of the Exchequer and the following year he became Vicar General with a commission to hold a visitation of all churches. This enabled him to enhance his plans to abolish papal authority and to propose church reform. The King agreed to his plan, which was to sell off cheaply the land owned by the monasteries.

Cromwell was present when Ann Boleyn was escorted to the Tower of London and later he witnessed her execution. He was influential in negotiating the King's marriage to Anne of Cleves, for which he was made Earl of Essex. However, the marriage soon turned sour and Cromwell bore the brunt of Henry's dissatisfaction. He was arrested on 10th June 1540 and was, himself, sent to the Tower of London.

Even in prison, however, he was still useful to Henry and gave vital evidence to support the King's divorce from Anne. But even this did not regain him favour and, although subservient to Henry to the last, he was beheaded at the Tower of London on July 28th 1540. So, the year after his *Great Bible* had been produced with the help of Coverdale, Cromwell was executed.

This brought changes in Coverdale's fortunes for he had lost an influential friend and a great supporter. Whether Cromwell had earlier been a moderating influence on Henry or not, we cannot tell. However, the King's policies changed after Cromwell's execution and Coverdale had to flee from England for safety, landing in Holland and finally settling in Strasbourg.

After Henry's death in 1547 the reformers began to gain more influence and Coverdale, then nearly 60, was able to return to England. Edward VI was on the throne and Coverdale, who was back in favour, became Bishop of Exeter. He preached many notable sermons there and continued to promote the teaching of the Reformation.

Unfortunately for the reformers, Edward died and Mary Tudor acceded to the throne. Being a devout Catholic by upbringing she opposed the reformers and Coverdale had to flee once again, with the added threat of being burnt to death if he was caught. He appealed to Denmark for refuge and spent the next six years in exile. It was probably during this time that Coverdale assisted with the publication of the *Geneva Bible* in 1557, when he was 69. He also translated the works of various continental reformers into English.

He was able to return to England two years later, when he was 71. He assisted in the consecration of Matthew Parker as Queen Elizabeth's new archbishop. However, owing to his deep convictions on many matters, and to strict puritanical views which had been strengthened while abroad, Coverdale was not reappointed to his former bishopric in Exeter. He never left England again and lived the life of a partial recluse until his death in London in January 1569. He was 81.

In his last years he did see the calvinistic *Geneva Bible*, which he worked upon during his exile, become the most widely used version in England. It continued to be used until it was gradually displaced by the *King James Authorised Version* which appeared in 1611.

Appendix 2

The dating of John's writings

It is right that Christians who hold a minority view on a particular subject should openly state that they do so and give their reasons. The commonly held view is that John's writings belong to the closing years of the first century, and the author readily admits that he does not concur with this. However, as this is not a book dealing with the chronology of New Testament writings it would be inappropriate to give a detailed explanation of this position. None the less, it is incumbent upon the author to give at least an outline of his reasons.

The Synoptic Gospels and Acts

The generally accepted view is that Mark was the first of the synoptic Gospels to be published, followed by Matthew and then Luke. Acts was published after these and ends with Paul spending two years in his own hired house in Rome (Acts 28:30). As Luke does not say what happened to Paul after this, the conclusion drawn is that it was at this time, two years after the final pronouncement of Isaiah 6 in Acts 28:25-27, that the Acts of the Apostles was published.

In that case, Luke's Gospel was published some time before, which places the date of its publication in the Acts period: i.e. before Acts 28:28. This would also be true of both Mark and Matthew.

In this brief synopsis we shall not be considering detailed dates. Rather we shall examine whether books and letters were written during the time covered by the Acts of the Apostles or later: i.e. before or after the events described in Acts 28:17-28. That being the case, it would seem that Matthew, Mark, and Luke were published sometime during the Acts period, and the Acts of the Apostles shortly afterwards.

The letters of Paul

There has been much agreement over many years amongst conservative scholars as to when Paul wrote his letters. As an example we give the order advocated by the following writers, spanning over 100 years. However, some of these do not give an exact order, prefering to group some of the letters together, and suggesting that they were all written at practically the same time: e.g. Ephesians, Colossians and Philemon.

A) *The Life and Epistles of St. Paul*, W.J. Conneybeare and J.S. Howson, 1862.
B) *The Life and Work of St. Paul*, F.W. Farrar, 1879.
C) *The Companion Bible*, E.W.Bullinger, 1914.
D) *The Scofield Reference Bible*, C.I. Scofield, 1917.
E) *In the Steps of St. Paul*, H.V. Morton, 1936.
F) *Know your Bible*, Graham Scroggie, 1940.
G) *The Apostle of the Free Spirit*, F.F.Bruce, 1977.

	A	B	C	D	E	F	G
Written *before* the events of Acts 28:17-28	1Th	1Th	Gal	1Th	Gal	1Th	Gal
	2Th	2Th	1Th	2Th	1Th	2Th	1Th
	1Co	1 Co	2Th	Gal	2Th	1Co	2Th
	2Co	2Co	1Co	1Co	1Co	2Co	1Co
	Gal	Gal	2Co	2Co	2Co	Gal	2Co
	Rom	Rom	Rom	Rom	Rom	Rom	Rom
Written *after* the events of Acts 28:17-28	Phm	Php	Eph	Eph	Php	Eph	Eph
	Col	Col	Php	Php	Col	Col	Php
	Eph	Eph	Col	Col	Phm	Phm	Col
	Php	Phm	Phl	Phm	Eph	Php	Phm
	1Ti	1Ti	1Ti	1Ti	1Ti	1Ti	1Ti
	Tit	Tit	Tit	Tit	Tit	Tit	Tit
	2Ti	2Ti	2Ti	2Ti	2Ti	2Ti	2Ti

From the above it can be seen that during the Acts period it is considered that Paul wrote Galatians, 1 and 2 Thessalonians, 1 & 2 Corinthians, and Romans - in that order. However, some would place Galatians after Thessalonians. Some, who uphold the Pauline authorship of Hebrews, place that letter in this period also; see *Perfection or Perdition?* by Stuart Allen and Charles Welch for the authorship and dating of Hebrews.

After the events described in Acts 28:17-28 Paul wrote Ephesians, Colossians, Philemon, Philippians, 1 Timothy, Titus, and 2 Timothy, again in that order. Some would place Colossians before Ephesians, whereas others would place it last. The reasons for such differences do not concern us here. It is sufficient for our purposes to recognise the unanimity of agreement over the dating of Paul's letters. This is possible because the Acts of the Apostles contains so much about Paul's life and because we have so many of his letters. All this information enables us to ascertain where and when Paul wrote.

That being the case, it would seem sensible if we attempted to tie in the rest of the New Testament letters with those written by Paul and, wherever possible, to give priority to internal evidence when it comes to dating any New Testament document.

The General Epistles of James, Peter, and Jude

The writings of these three men were directed to Christians who were very much part of the nation of Israel. James addressed his letter "To the twelve tribes scattered among the nations" (James 1:1) and Peter wrote to the same people: "To God's elect, strangers in the world, scattered throughout Pontus, Galatia, Cappadocia, Asia and Bithynia" (1 Peter 1:1; 2 Peter 3:1).

It is a commonly held view that the letter of James was written early in the book of Acts, and Josephus records that James was stoned to death in Jerusalem at about the time Paul arrived in Rome (Acts 28:14-16).

However, some would place Peter after the end of Acts. This seems unlikely for he was writing to the same people as James: Christians who were distinctly Jews. This distinction became irrelevant after Acts 28:25-28 and so it makes more sense to place his writings earlier, during the Acts of the Apostles.

This view is supported by Galatians 2:7-9 where Peter, together with James and John, agreed that they would minister to the Jews and Paul and Barnabas would go to the Gentile nations. As such distinctions ceased at the end of Acts (cf. Ephesians 2:14-22), then it seems likely that Peter wrote before this time.

In addition Peter described his days as the "last times" and stated that "the end of all things is near" (1 Peter 1:20; 4:7). Such a view has more in common with the situation when James wrote (cf. James 5:7-9), and with the earlier letters of Paul. At that time he, too, wrote that "The night is nearly over; the day is almost here" (Romans 13:12), and that "the fulfilment of the ages has come" (1 Corinthians 10:11). Such expressions, and the expectation of the imminent return of Christ, are absent from Paul's later letters. It seems more sensible, then, to date Peter's writings in line with that of James and with Paul's earlier letters, rather than along with his later ones.

The letter of Jude, the brother of James, is also very Jewish, demanding not only a knowledge of the Old Testament, but also of Hebrew apocryphal writings: the *Book of Enoch* and the *Assumption of Moses*. Again, with a reference to the return of Christ with thousands of his holy ones to judge the world (Jude 14-15), it has more in common with the works of Peter and James than with the later writings of Paul.

Hebrews, as its name implies, was written specifically to Hebrews who were still under the old covenant (Hebrews 8:13) and who expected Christ to return soon (Hebrews 10:25,37). As the Law, including the old covenant, had been abolished at the end of Acts (Ephesians 2:14-15; Colossians 2:13-17), Hebrews belongs to the period of time covered by the Acts of the Apostles.

The writings of John

John was party to the agreement of Galatians 2:7-9. He also considered his days to be "the last hour" (1 John 2:18). He wrote that "the time is near", and stated, "Do not seal up the words of the prophecy of this book, because the time is near" (Revelation 1:3; 22:10). He expected the imminent return of Christ in his day (Revelation 1:7; 3:20; 22:7,12,20). Indeed what he has to say in his letters, including Revelation, has much in common with the letters written during Acts. Consider, for example, the following:

> "Here I am! I stand at the door and knock." (Revelation 3:20)

> Be patient, then, brothers, until the Lord's coming ... You, too, be patient and stand firm, because the Lord's coming is near ... The Judge is standing at the door! (James 5:7-9)

The great prophetic chapter of 2 Thessalonians 2 has been called a mini-apocalypse. It was written during Acts and is hard, if not impossible, to understand without Revelation.

If all this is the case, why has it become accepted that John did not write during the Acts period? Why have people thought he wrote a considerable time after it, some thirty years later, in the last decade of the first century?

follow that, because the two brothers were commemorated on the same day, they were commemorated as being both martyrs in death who had been slain at the same time. (*New Bible Dictionary*, 602)

James the Lord's brother was stoned to death by a mob in Jerusalem in the year 61-2. His namesake, brother of John, had been beheaded early in 44 by Herod Agrippa 1. Among the "others" who, as Josephus informs us, perished along with James in 61, we may perhaps reckon John, who stands beside him in Paul's list of Pillars. This John, son of Zebedee, brother of the other James, is reckoned a martyr in the same sense as his brother in the earliest gospels. The brothers are assured that they shall drink the same cup of suffering as the Lord, though they may not claim in return pre-eminent seats in glory (Mark 10:39 cf.). John did not suffer with his brother James in 44, because he is present at the conference in 46-7 (Galatians 2:9); but one of the traditions of the Jerusalem elders reported by Papias declared that he was "killed by the Jews" in fulfilment of the Lord's prediction and this early tradition must be accepted in spite of its conflict with one which gradually superseded it after John came to be regarded as author of Revelation and the Fourth Gospel. The statement that he was killed "together with James his brother" may be due merely to the (not infrequent) confusion of the two James. (B.W. Bacon, *The Making of the New Testament*, 104-105).

If this tradition is correct, John was killed not along with his brother James, but along with the Lord's brother James. Certainly, many commentators state that John was the only apostle to die a natural death, basing their views upon the tradition that John died of old age in the last decade of the first century. This view must be seriously questioned in the light of our Lord's words recorded in Mark 10:39, to say nothing of the traditions for his martyrdom in AD 61.

So an early death for John is based upon Christ's words and upon *tradition*, and however weak or strong that tradition may be it must be tested against the internal evidence of Holy Scripture. No doubt the strongest support for the tradition comes from Mark 10:39, where our Lord told both John and his brother James that they would both suffer by drinking the cup of martyrdom. This happened to our Lord on the cross. It happened to James at the hands of Herod in Acts 12:2. But John dying of old age does not fulfil the Scriptures. It breaks them! John being martyred in AD 61 does fulfil the Scriptures and would imply that all John's writings were written before the end of the Acts period. Faced with this argument the *New Bible Dictionary*, on page 602, states:

> Nor again does the reference to the sons of Zebedee as "drinking the cup" and "being baptized with the Baptism of Christ" necessarily imply that both are destined to come to a violent end.

With that statement we cannot agree! The plain reading of Mark 10:39 is that our Lord stated that *both* James and John were to suffer martyrdom.

Earlier we looked at references, in the Gospel and Revelation, to Jerusalem and the Temple which indicated that these books must have been written when the city and the temple were still standing. Thus there is a certain amount of non-doctrinal evidence to support the early date of John's writing, but what of the doctrinal evidence?

John's Epistles

These have references to their time of writing being "the last hour" (1 John 2:18) and state that there are many "antichrists". This imminent end of the age, with Christ returning, is a feature of the Acts period (Acts 3:19-21; 1 Peter 4:7; Hebrews 10:35-37; Romans 13:12; 1 Thessalonians 1:10; 4:15-17; 1 Corinthians 1:7-8; 7:26-29; 10:11; James 5:7-9).

The Acts period gift of knowledge (1 Corinthians 12:8; Romans 15:14), due to the anointing of the Holy Spirit, is seen in 1 John 2:27.

The sin unto death, the judgement of the Acts period (Acts 5:1- 10; 12:21-23; 1 Corinthians 11:27-30) is seen in 1 John 5:16.

John writes of testing the spirits in 1 John 4:1-3 and 2 John 7, another feature of the Acts period (1 Corinthians 12:10).

Thus John's Epistles fit well into the Acts period and the doctrinal content has far more in common with Paul's earlier letters than his later ones. He also had the Jew first, as Paul did during Acts (cf. 1 John 2:2 and Romans 1:16; Acts 13:46).

The Revelation

Had the Jews repented in accordance with Acts 3:19-26, Christ would have returned, but before that there would have been the great and terrible day of the Lord: the subject of Revelation (1:10). John also says these things must shortly come to pass (Revelation 1:1), a phrase very similar to that used in many Acts period epistles, but never seen after Acts 28:28. The Revelation concludes with "Even so, come, Lord Jesus," (22:20 *KJV*), surely the plea and prayer of the Acts period. (Compare Revelation 1:1,3 and 22:6,7,10,12,20 with, for example, 1 Peter 4:7;

Hebrews 10:25,37; Romans 13:12; 1 Thessalonians 1:9-10; 4:15-17; 1 Corinthians 1:7-8; 7:29-31; 10:11.)

The entire content of Revelation, with its symbolic expressions and allusions, has much in common with the Old Testament prophecies and is very Jewish. Also the number of references to Jews, Jerusalem, etc., in Revelation imply that this book was written before the end of the Acts period for the benefit of the Jewish Christians in the seven churches. The Jewish nation is clearly central to the message of Revelation.

Revelation was written to the seven Churches in Asia and from its opening chapters it is clear that the situation in those churches was not healthy. By the time Paul wrote his last letter he stated that "everyone in the province of Asia has deserted me". It would seem that the decline written about by John in the opening chapters of Revelation was complete by the time Paul wrote to Timothy.

The Gospel

The generally held view in Christendom is that the Jews were set aside at the Cross and that the church began at Pentecost. Thus there is the temptation to read the Acts of the Apostles with that in mind, paying special attention to everything which relates to the Gentiles, ignoring everything said of the Jews, and interpreting neutral passages with respect to the Gentiles. In this book we have stressed the need when reading any part of the Bible, including Acts, to pay attention to the place of Israel in that book. True the Gentile had a place in Acts, but the dominant role belonged to Israel.

What has been written above about Acts is also true of John's Gospel. We are tempted to see John as "to the world" and as "being Gentile", to the exclusion of the dominant role of Israel held in God's purposes at the time when Christ was on earth. The world, *kosmos*, occurs 188 times in the New Testament: Matthew 9 times, Mark 3 times, and Luke 3 times, come a long way short of John, 79 times. Thus John is for the "world", but what "world" had John in mind? On certain occasions it is the world of the Jews. For example, consider John 7:1-7 where the word "world" occurs in verses 4 and 7. From the context we see Christ is speaking of "Galilee", "Judea", and "the Jewish Feast of Tabernacles". Again, in John 12:18-19, when the people in Jerusalem went out to meet Christ, the Pharisees said, "Look how the whole *world* has gone after him!" On other occasions John used the word in its wider context, but when doing so, in what way was he writing for the wider "world"?

The word "world" occurs 22 times in John's first epistle, more frequently per chapter than in the Gospel. This epistle, however, was so obviously written when Israel were still part of God's plan, so in what way does John bring in the "world"? Speaking of the Saviour, John wrote:

> He is the atoning sacrifice for our sins, and not only for ours but also for the sins of the whole world. (1 John 2:2).

Here Israel is still seen to be first, as in Romans 1:16 and Acts 13:46. Both John, in his letters, and Paul, in Romans and Acts, are pointing out that Israel may be first, but they are not the only ones. Christ died for the sins of the world and Israel were to take the message of the Messiah and His salvation to the ends of that world, to the uttermost parts of the earth. They were not to keep it to themselves. This is part of what John is saying and we note this in his gospel where Christ is the Lamb of God, who takes away the sin of the *world* (John 1:29); where God so loved the *world* (3:16), and not just Israel, that He gave His only begotten Son so that the *world*, and not just Israel, might be saved through Him (3:17). Christ is described as the Saviour of the *world* (4:42) and the Light of the *world* (8:12). His prayer is that the *world* may believe and that the *world* may know that God sent Him (John 17:21,23). Some have suggested that in John 17 Christ had only Israel in mind. No doubt His desire was that they would believe first, but from the commissions at the end of the other three Gospels it is clear that He wanted them to take the news of Himself to all other nations. With all this in mind, the purpose of John's Gospel seems to be:

(1) to convince the Jews that Jesus was the Messiah;
(2) to convince them that they must take the message of that Messiah to the world.

If this is the case then we should find a number of Jewish passages in the Gospel and we should find the main thrust of any argument aimed at Jewish thought, rather than Gentile thought. Let us test this against Scripture.

The opening words of the Gospel are "in the beginning", the same words as start Genesis. This would have more significance for Jews than Gentiles.

In John 1:31 John records that John the Baptist said "but the reason that I came baptising with water was that he might be revealed to *Israel*". This declaration is not made in any other Gospel.

In John 1:49 he repeats Nathanael's acclamation that Christ is "the King of *Israel*". In Matthew, a very Jewish Gospel, He is termed "the King of the *Jews*" (Matthew 2:2).

In John 1:51 our Lord said to Nathanael, "you shall see heaven open, and the angels of God ascending and descending on the Son of Man". This would have meant little to Gentiles.

Nicodemus was told he had to be "born again", an expression used in the Acts period by Peter (1 Peter 1:3,23). This meant Nicodemus had to be born of "water and the Spirit", (John 3:5), which is similar to Mark 16:16 ("Whoever believes and is baptised will be saved"). This statement of the Lord supports Peter's answer to the question from the Jews, "Brothers, what shall we do?" He told them to "Repent and be baptised" (Acts 2:37-38). Nicodemus was "Israel's teacher" and he should have understood these things (John 3:10) for they were based upon the Old Testament (e.g. Ezekiel 36:25-27). If he did not how were Gentiles at the end of the first century expected to understand them?

Even John 3:16 is based on Moses and the Serpent, a figure unlikely to be understood by most Gentiles of that time (cf. John 3:14-15 and Numbers 21:1-9).

John is also the only writer, apart from Peter and James, to use the technical term *diaspora*, referring to the scattered and dispersed Israelites; (compare John 7:35, James 1:1 and 1 Peter 1:1). Note also the following verse, referring to a statement of the high priest:

> He prophesied that Jesus would die for the Jewish nation, and not only for that nation but also for the scattered children of God, to bring them together and make them one. (John 11:51-52)

All these, and much more, have more to do with the people of Israel than the world at large. The more we look at John's Gospel from this point of view the more we see that John's primary audience was Israel. In fact his writings backed up the ministry of the Apostles during the book of Acts, for John's purpose in writing was that his readers might "believe that Jesus is the Christ (Messiah), the Son of God" (John 20:31). This was the message of the apostles during Acts: e.g. Acts 8:37 (*KJV*); 9:20-22; 18:5,28. At that time they spent much of their efforts trying to convince the *Jews* in the synagogues that Jesus was the Christ, the Son of God. When we read the Gospel we cannot fail to see the primary place of Israel, just as it was in Acts.

It is significant that John does not describe the Lord's mighty works as miracles. Rather he calls them signs and, of course, signs were for the people of Israel. When, in Acts, the Gentiles benefited from mighty works they tended to worship the performer (Acts 14:10-15; 28:3-6). On the other hand the Jews demanded "miraculous signs" and asked, "What does this mean?" when they saw one (1 Corinthians 1:22; Acts 2:12; 3:11). The fact that John based his gospel on eight signs supports the view that he had the people of Israel in the forefront of his mind when he was writing. With respect to these signs:

> Two things stand out most clearly: they all manifest Israel's need, and condition of helplessness and death; and Messiah's glory, and His ability to meet that need and restore Israel's lost condition. (*The Companion Bible*, Appendix 176).

There is no space to go through each sign and state its significance with respect to Israel (see *That you may believe - the eight signs of John's Gospel* by Charles Ozanne). The purpose of John's Gospel was to convince the people to whom he was writing - to convince them with an appeal to signs - that Jesus was the Messiah. The main readership he had in mind was the people of Israel. Israel were the people who required signs (1 Corinthians 1:22). Israel had the oracles of God (Romans 3:1-3), and Israel's Scriptures told them what signs to expect from their Messiah (e.g. Isaiah 35:5-6). Thus, to place John's Gospel in the time covered by the Acts of the Apostles makes a lot of sense. It would back up the ministry of Peter and Paul and others with its appeal to signs and its desire to show that Jesus was the Christ (Messiah), the Son of God. For example:

> "Men of Israel, listen to this: Jesus of Nazareth was a man accredited by God to you by miracles, wonders and signs, which God did among you through him, as you yourselves know ... *God has made this Jesus*, whom you crucified, both Lord and *Christ*." (Acts 2:22,36)

> At once he (Paul) began to preach in the synagogues that *Jesus is the Son of God* ... Yet Saul grew more and more powerful and baffled the Jews living in Damascus by proving that *Jesus is the Christ*. (Acts 9:20,22)

> Paul devoted himself exclusively to preaching, testifying to the Jews that *Jesus was the Christ* ... For he (Apollos) vigorously refuted the Jews in public debate, proving from the Scriptures that *Jesus was the Christ*. (Acts 18:5,28)

John's Gospel was written to convince the Jews that Jesus was the Messiah prophesied by the Old Testament. It also reminded those Jews that the Old Testament stated that all families of the earth were to be blessed through them (Genesis 12:3). They were to take the message of salvation to the world, as stated in the Old Testament and by the Lord at the end of Matthew (28:19), Mark (16:15), Luke (24:47), and at the start of Acts (1:8).

Objections

Naturally there are some objections to the view we have been considering. For instance:

(1) Various Jewish expressions are explained in John's Gospel and this would not be necessary if John was writing for the Jews. Such expressions as "six stone water jars, the kind used by the Jews for ceremonial washing, each holding from twenty to thirty gallons", (John 2:6). The objection states that no Jew would need to be told that. Again, John 6:4 and 11:55 talk of "the Jewish Passover" and 7:2 "the Jewish Feast of Tabernacles". No Jew would need to be told that it was winter at the Feast of Dedication (10:22), and John 9:7 interprets "Siloam", which would not have been needed if John had written exclusively for the Jews.

However, if the Gospel of John was written during the second half of the book of Acts then the explanation of such terms would help the many Gentile Christians who had accumulated by that time. For example, Acts 13:16, 14:1, 17:2-4,12, and 18:4 speak of Gentiles who gathered in the synagogues to hear the Scriptures being read.

Also, during Acts, a number of Hellenised Israelites, and those who had married Gentiles, were being attracted to Christianity and hence had renewed interest in their nation (e.g. Acts 16:1-3). These had almost given up their Jewish identity and would not know much of what went on in Jerusalem and the land of Judea. Many did not identify with their fellow-Jews, some did not circumcise their male children, others made no attempt to keep the Law. Such people would have needed the explanations given by John.

(2) Others state that John must have been written after Acts 28:28 because John 1:11 states that "He came to that which was his own, but his own did not receive him". The argument is that Israel did not finally and completely reject Christ until the end of Acts.

However, we must remember that they rejected Him as a prophet, priest and King in Matthew 12:6,41 and 42. Their complete rejection is in Matthew 27:22-25, when they wanted Him crucified and were prepared to let His blood be not only on them, but also on their children. The cry of the Acts period was for this people to repent of the sin of crucifying Christ (Acts 3:12-19), but they did not repent. The words "*He* came to His own, and His own received Him not" is not a description of the Acts period. Rather it is a description of the Lord's own ministry. The Acts period is the rejection not of Christ's ministry to His own, but of Peter's and Paul's ministry to Israel.

(3) Others state that John must have been written after Acts 28:28 because there is no mention of the Lord's supper. This, they say, clearly shows that the Gospel was written after Acts 28:28, after the people had been set aside, because after that such ordinances had no place (Colossians 2:14-17).

This cannot be right. If it was then we should expect the other ordinance of water baptism to be missing also, yet in John it is given greater place than in the other Gospels. See John 1:25-34 and note also Nicodemus' "water and the Spirit" (John 3:5). Also John is the only Gospel which makes mention of Christ's disciples baptising (4:1,2).

(4) Others state that John must be after Acts 28:28 because the other sheep of John 10:16 cannot refer to Jews, but must refer to Gentiles.

It is more likely that the other sheep John has in mind are those Israelites scattered abroad. He writes that "Jesus would die for the Jewish nation, and not only for that nation but also for the scattered children of God, to bring them together and *make them one*" (John 11:51-52). This is very similar to John 10:16 where we read, "I have other sheep that are not of this sheep pen. I must bring them also. They too will listen to my voice, and there shall be *one flock* and one shepherd."

However, if "the other sheep" does refer to Gentiles, we need to ask which Gentiles? Can we find a group of Gentiles which "shall be one flock" with Israel? The answer is "Yes!".

Romans 11:11-17 describes the Gentiles of the Acts period who were grafted into the Olive Tree of Israel and became *one* with Israel. They partook of the fruit and fat of the olive tree. They shared in the blessings and the promises given to the people of Israel. They spoke in tongues, were healed. They were brought into that flock.

(5) Others cannot see how the message of John's Gospel can be dismissed from the present time as the experience of many shows that John still has a message for today.

The fact is that *all* Scripture is inspired and profitable for today, and much of John is basic with regard to salvation and eternal life. We have been at pains in this book to emphasise that we should attempt to find an application to ourselves of every passage and each subject. Salvation and eternal life are not dispensational issues. What John says on them is still very pertinent today. Similarly, Romans has much truth for today. The just shall live by faith alone; faith is imputed for righteousness; identification with Christ in death and resurrection. All these, and more, are basic truths to be found in Romans, but is the Jew still first (Romans 1:16; 2:9-10)? Has the Jew still an advantage (Romans 3:1-2)? Is Israel still not cast off (Romans 11:1)? Are Gentiles now saved to provoke Israel (Romans 10:19; 11:11,14)? Of course not. Thus we must distinguish between fundamental truth and dispensational truth. John contains both.

(6) Some state that the teaching of the "word" (*logos*) is derived from Greek philosophy, which implies that the very introduction of the Gospel is aimed at the Hellenistic world.

However, the "word" is also used in the Aramaic translation of the (Old Testament) Scriptures which had been around for a considerable time before Christ was born.

One could continue dealing with many other points, but lack of space prevents us from going into greater detail.

Conclusion

By interpreting John's Gospel as being written in the second half of the book of Acts, and as being written primarily for Jews - to convince them that Jesus was their Messiah and that they should take the message of Him to the World - we are making John an Apostle to the Jews. In doing that we are in harmony with Galatians 2:7-9, which states that John was given the gospel to the circumcision, and Matthew 19:28, which has John as one of the twelve judging the twelve tribes of Israel. Dating John's Gospel late and making him a teacher of the Gentiles is going against the testimony of Scripture.

Which tradition is right? The late natural death of John and the late date of his writings or the earlier martyrdom of John and the earlier date of his writings? Which tradition is most Scriptural? It would seem to be the martyrdom of John, with all his writings being completed before AD 61. This is in harmony with the words of our Lord Jesus Christ recorded in Mark 10:39.

Index of Subjects

Index of Quoted Texts

Index of Greek Words

Bibliography of Books Quoted and Referred to

Allen, Stuart, *The Early Centuries and the Truth*, 315
and Welch, Charles H, *Perfection or Perdition?* 310
Andersen, Daniel, *Bible Study - a personal quest*, 191
Anderson, Sir Robert, *The Silence of God*, 201, 202
Augustine, *To Marcellinius*, 189
Bacon, B W, *The Making of the New Testament*, 319
Barnabas, Letters of, 190
Baxter, J Sidlow, *The Strategic Grasp of the Bible*, 210-211
Bishop, A E, *Armour of Light*, 209
Tongues, Signs and Visions - Not God's Order for Today, 209
Bruce, F F, *The Apostle of the Free Spirit*, 310
Bullinger, E W, *A Critical Lexicon and Concordance*, 145-146, 149, 267-268
How to Enjoy the Bible, 231, 268
The Companion Bible, 163, 167, 176, 212, 245, 310, 324
The Foundations of Dispensational Truth, 212
Things to Come, 211
Clement of Alexandria, *The Stromatia or Miscellanies*, 188
Conneybeare, W J, and Howson, J S, *The Life and Epistles of St. Paul*, 310
Coverdale, Miles, *Coverdale Bible*, 27, 305
Coxe, A Cleveland, *The Ante-Nicene Fathers*, 188, 194-195, 199
Cromwell's Bible (The Great Bible), 27, 192, 215, 306
Darby, John Nelson, *Collected Writings*, 195
Synopsis of the Books of the Bible, 200
Douglas, George, *Moody Bible Institute Monthly*, 205
Edwards, John, *A Compleat History or Survey of all the Dispensations*, 193
Ehlert, Arnold H, *A Bibliography of Dispensationalism, Biblitheca Sacra*, 216
Englishman's Greek New Testament, 54
Enoch, The Book of, 48, 312
Eusebius, 315-316
Farrar, F W, *The Life and Works of St. Paul*, 310
Fuller, Daniel P, *The Hermeneutics of Dispensationalism*, 217
Gaebelein, Arno C, *Gospel of Matthew*, 203, 207
Our Hope, 207
Geneva Bible, 307
Great Bible, The (Cromwell's Bible), 27, 192, 215, 306
Hadden, Robert A, *Christian Fundamentals Magazine*, 206
Holden, Richard, *The Mystery: The Special Mission of the Apostle Paul, The Key to the Present Dispensation*, 209-212, 302-303
Howson, J S, and Conneybeare, W J, *The Life and Epistles of St. Paul*, 310
Irenaus, *Against Heresies*, 187

Ironside, H A, *In the Heavenlies*, 218
Jarvis, Samuel Farmer, *Church of the Redeemed*, 194, 199
Josephus, Flavius, *The Antiquities of the Jews*, 168
The Wars of the Jews, 318
Justin Martyr, *Dialogue with Trypho*, 187
Kessler, John H, *Forgotten Truths Reafirmed*, 213
Larson, Martin A, *The Religion of the Occident*, 191
Mackintosh, C H, *The Life and Times of Elijah the Tishbite, The Mackintosh Treasury*, 200-201, 206, 212-213
Marsh, F E, *Will the Church or any part of it go through the Great Tribulation?* 208
McLain, Clifford E, *Elijah's Coming and other Unfulfilled Prophecies*, 263
Metropolitan Anthony, *Jesus, Then and Now*, 176
Mills, J Eustace, *Before Acts 28:28 and After*, 213
Morrish, George, *New and Concise Bible Dictionary*, 138, 318
Morton, H V, *In the Steps of St. Paul*, 310
Moses, The Assumption of, 48, 312
New Bible Dictionary, 165, 313, 318-320
Newton, Benjamin Willis, *The Christian Witness*, 196
Orwell, George, *1984*, 179
Osgood, David, *Grace and Truth*, 305
Ozanne, Charles, *That you May Believe - the eight signs of John's Gospel*, 324
Penny, Michael, *The Miracles of the Apostles*, 150
Poiret, Pierre, *The Divine Oeconomy of An Universal System of the Works and Purposes of God Towards Man Demonstrated*, 193, 216
Robinson, J A T, *A Redating of the New Testament*, 82, 167, 313
The Priority of John, 82, 167, 313
Ryrie, Charles C, *Dispensationalism Today*, 197, 218, 222, 233, 253, 261
Scofield, C I, *The Scofield Reference Bible*, 197, 203, 217, 254, 317
Scroggie, W Graham, *Know your Bible*, 204, 206, 310
Ruling Lines of Progressive Revelation, 218, 269
The Acts of the Apostles, 204
Smale, Joseph, *Christian Fundamentals Magazine*, 204
The Greatest Truth I know after twenty-five years' ministry, 203
Streets, Ernest, *Another Look at the Gospel of John*, 313
Thompson, Frabnk Charles, *A New Chain Reference Bible*, 254
Tucker, Leon, *His Son, or Studies in the Epistle to the Hebrews*, 205
VIne, W E, *Expository Dictionary of New Testament Words*, 260
Watts, Issac, *Watts' Works*, 194, 216
Welch, Charles H, *An Alphebetical Analysis*, 200-221
An Autobiography, 211
Dispensational Truth, 212
That Blessed Hope, 261
The Berean Expositor, 212
and Allen, Stuart, *Perfection or Perdition?* 310

Manual on the Gospel of John

by Michael Penny

The ideal book for
youth groups and house groups
personal study and small Bible study groups.

"This book was written primarily for teenagers. As such it is wholly admirable and should be eagerly sought after. The treatment consists very largely of questions and answers. It is the first time we have seen the Gospel of John presented in this way. This means it will be equally welcome to those who no longer claim to be teenagers. This is an ideal present for any boy or girl."
Marcus Beverely, *The Christian Herald*

"When I received a copy of Michael Penny's excellent work, I was at a loss as to how to comment on it. But I have been able to experience it by using it with house groups. The manual was produced with the aid of a number of young people, and is designed for young people. However, as I found in my own group, it is really ideal for any age range from teenagers upwards. If you are stuck for ideas with your Youth Fellowship try the Manual."
Eric Thorn, *The Prophetic Witness*

"It is a very workable manual produced with teenagers for teenagers. The wealth of material is clearly presented. It's ideal for the person wanting to come to grips with the gospel in depth."
Bob Moffat, *Buzz*

"This work takes the student through the Gospel of John with questions and answers as well as comments by the author. A useful way of getting to know the book."
Dr F Tatford, *The Prophetic Witness*

Manual on the Gospel of John

ISBN 0 947778 13 6

£4.50 **$9.00**

THE OPEN BIBLE TRUST
36 St Laurence Ave, Brundall
Norwich, Norfolk, NR13 5QH, GB

GRACE PUBLICATIONS INC
4800 South Calhoun Road
New Berlin, WI 53151, USA

The Miracles of the Apostles

by Michael Penny

The book which deals with every type of miracle performed by the apostles.

The book which explains the reasons behind each type of miracle.

The book which leaves miracles in their biblical context.

"We have here a meticulous discussion of the miraculous gifts which formed so prominent a feature of the Acts period. Each one is treated with characteristic care and attention, its nature defined and its purpose explained."

Charles Ozanne, *Search*

The Miracles of the Apostles

ISBN 0 947778 34 9

£6.00 **$12.00**

THE OPEN BIBLE TRUST
36 St Laurence Ave, Brundall
Norwich, Norfolk, NR13 5QH, GB

GRACE PUBLICATIONS INC
4800 South Calhoun Road
New Berlin, WI 53151, USA

The Bible - Myth or Message?

by Michael Penny

Amazing facts about the book Christians call God's Word.

What is the Bible?
Where did it come from?

Is it a collection of ancient myths and stories?
Or a mixture of fact and fiction?

Does it contain a message for mankind?
If so - from whom? Man or God?

Is it unique?
Is it reliable?
Is it inspired?

In answering these questions, Michael Penny, an enthusiastic student of the Bible, communicates his enthusiasm through the liveliness of his writings. He quotes evidence of the Bible itself as well as the findings of respected bible scholars - and he has assembles a fascinating array of facts and figures to demonstrate that the Bible is a unique books which ought to be read; that it is a reliable books which should be studied; and that it is a divinely inspired message to mankind, which must be believed.

"If you want to reinforce your trust in the uniqueness of the Bible - or need ammunition to use with friends who claim the Bible is merely a book - try Michael Penny's *The Bible - Myth or Message?*"
David Hall, *Family*

The Bible - Myth or Message?

£1.95 **$3.90**

THE OPEN BIBLE TRUST
36 St Laurence Ave, Brundall
Norwich, Norfolk, NR13 5QH, GB

GRACE PUBLICATIONS INC
4800 South Calhoun Road
New Berlin, WI 53151, USA

The use and abuse of Joel's Prophecy

by Michael Penny

"This is a verse by verse exposition of the book of Joel, followed by a study of its application in Acts chapter 2. In his usual racy style, the author rejects the interpretation commonly held by Pentecostalists and charismatics, arguing that a correct understanding can only be gained by carefully considering the original text. Helpful maps, diagrams and indexes make this book excellent value for money."

The Methodist Recorder

The use and abuse of Joel's Prophecy

£2.00 **$4.00**

THE OPEN BIBLE TRUST
36 St Laurence Ave, Brundall
Norwich, Norfolk, NR13 5QH, GB

GRACE PUBLICATIONS INC
4800 South Calhoun Road
New Berlin, WI 53151, USA

Order form

Please send me the following books by Michael Penny:

___ copies of *Approaching the Bible* (£7.50; $15.00)
___ copies of *The Bible: Myth or Message?* (£1.95; $3.90)
___ copies of *The Manual on the Gospel of John* (£4.50; $9.00)
___ copies of *The Miracles of the Apostles* (£6.00; $12.00)
___ copies of *The Use and Abuse of Joel's Prophecy* (£2.00; $4.00)

___ Please send me a free sample copy of *Search* magazine, edited by Michael Penny.

Name ____

Address ____

____

____

Please send your orders to:

THE OPEN BIBLE TRUST
36 St Laurence Ave, Brundall
Norwich, Norfolk, NR13 5QH, GB

Please make cheques payable to:
"The Open Bible Trust".

GRACE PUBLICATIONS INC
4800 South Calhoun Road
New Berlin, WI 53151, USA

Please make checks payable to:
"Grace Publications Inc."

Search

Magazine of the Open Bible Trust

Woman to Woman

Young Searchers

Feed Back - your letters

Search the Scriptures

Problem Passages

Powerful Passages

Poetry Corner

Prophecy

Reviews ... and more.

Search is published six times a year.

Write today for a free sample copy to:

Britain:	The Open Bible Trust, 36 St. Laurence Avenue, Brundall, Norwich, Norfolk, NR 13 5QH.
Australia:	Ruth Andrew, 4 Schnapper Close, Emerald Beach, NSW, 2450.
Canada:	The Canadian Bible Fellowship, 8 Duke Street, Bowmanville, Ontario, L1C 2T8.
Netherlands:	Nico Baalbergen, Hogestraat 21, 7122 BN Aalten.
New Zealand:	A Daniel Doubleday, 61 Mailer Street, Mornington, Dunedin.
South Africa:	South African Berean Bible Study Trust, 1 Bethel Road, Clovelly 7975.
Spain:	A2Z Pubilcations, Appartado de Correos 252, 03730 Java, Alicante.
U.S.A.:	Grace Publications Inc., 4800 South Calhoun Road, New Berlin, WI 53151.